NEW FRONTIERS IN HISTORY

series editors

Mark Greengrass
Department of History, Sheffield University

John Stevenson
Worcester College, Oxford

This important series reflects the substantial expansion that has occurred in the scope of history syllabuses. As new subject areas have emerged and syllabuses have come to focus more upon methods of historical enquiry and knowledge of source materials, a growing need has arisen for correspondingly broad-ranging textbooks.

New Frontiers in History provides up-to-date overviews of key topics in British, European and world history, together with accompanying source material and appendices. Authors focus on subjects where revisionist work is being undertaken, providing a fresh viewpoint, welcomed by students and sixth-formers. The series also explores established topics which have attracted much conflicting analysis and require a synthesis of the state of debate.

MANCHESTER
UNIVERSITY PRESS

Published titles

David Andress French society in revolution, 1789–1799

Jeremy Black The politics of Britain

Paul Bookbinder Weimar Germany

Michael Braddick The nerves of state: taxation and the financing of the English state, 1558–1714

Michael Broers Europe after Napoleon

David Brooks The age of upheaval: Edwardian politics, 1899–1914

Carl Chinn Poverty amidst prosperity

Conan Fischer The rise of the Nazis

T. A. Jenkins Parliament, party and politics in Victorian Britain

Neville Kirk Change, continuity and class: Labour in British society, 1850–1920

Keith Laybourn The General Strike of 1926

Frank McDonough Neville Chamberlain, appeasement and the British road to war

Evan Mawdsley The Stalin years, 1929–1953

Alan O'Day Irish Home Rule, 1867–1921

Panikos Panayi Immigration, racism and ethnicity, 1815–1945

Daniel Szechi The Jacobites

David Taylor The New Police

Michael Turner British politics in the age of reform

John Whittam Fascist Italy

Forthcoming titles

Ciaran Brady The unplanned conquest: social changes and political conflict in sixteenth-century Ireland

John Childs The army, state and society, 1500–1800

Barry Coward The Cromwellian protectorate

Simon Ditchfield The Jesuits in early modern Europe

Bruce Gordon The Swiss Reformation

Susan-Mary Grant The American Civil War and Reconstruction

Tony Kushner The Holocaust and its aftermath

Keith Mason Slavery and emancipation

Alexandra Walsham Persecution and toleration in England, 1530–1660

The age of faction

Court politics, 1660–1702

Alan Marshall

Manchester University Press

Manchester and New York

Distributed exclusively in the USA by St. Martin's Press

Copyright © Alan Marshall 1999

The right of Alan Marshall to be identified as the author of this work has been asserted by him in accordance with the Copyright, Designs and Patents Act 1988.

Published by Manchester University Press
Oxford Road, Manchester M13 9NR, UK
and Room 400, 175 Fifth Avenue, New York, NY 10010, USA
http://www.man.ac.uk/mup

Distributed exclusively in the USA by
St. Martin's Press, Inc., 175 Fifth Avenue, New York,
NY 10010, USA

Distributed exclusively in Canada by
UBC Press, University of British Columbia, 6344 Memorial Road,
Vancouver, BC, Canada V6T 1Z2

British Library Cataloguing-in-Publication Data
A catalogue record for this book is available from the British Library

Library of Congress Cataloging-in-Publication Data applied for

ISBN   0 7190 4974 1 *hardback*
        0 7190 4975 X *paperback*

First published 1999

06 05 04 03 02 01 00 99   10 9 8 7 6 5 4 3 2 1

Printed in Great Britain
by Bell & Bain Ltd, Glasgow

Contents

v

Acknowledgements

As with any academic book, this volume has been given much help, advice, information and timely assistance from a number of people. I wish to thank Janet Clare, Stuart Handley, Mark Knights, Erica Fudge, Tracey Hill, John Stevenson and Bobby Anderson, amongst others. Special thanks must also go to Louise Edwards at Manchester University Press for her help, and to Jane Raistrick for her work on the manuscript. I am also greatly indebted to the staffs of the following libraries and copyright holders for their permission to quote from the documents in their care: the Royal Historical Society for the extracts from *The Memoirs of Sir John Reresby*, A. P. Watt Ltd on behalf of the Trustees of Major Peter Evelyn and Oxford University Press for the extracts taken from *The Diary of John Evelyn*, the British Library, the Bodleian Library, the Institute of Historical Research, the Public Record Office in London, Downside Abbey Library, Bath Spa University College Library, the University of Bristol Library, the University of London Library at the Senate House, and the Royal Commission on Historical Manuscripts.

The dedication for this book goes to Claire Tylee with affection, for it was originally her idea.

Introduction

Monarchical government in the seventeenth century was a political fact of life. The power structures of the early modern state were centred on monarchy. Society's writs ran in the monarch's name. The tastes and aspirations of monarch and courtier dominated high culture, and together they set the trend for the fashionable leisure pursuits of the day. In Britain, as elsewhere in Europe, the crown stood at the head of religious life, and the state Church was now firmly, if sometimes reluctantly, under monarchical control. Indeed the most common European political and religious ideology became a form of divine right, which emphasised the monarch as central to its doctrines in a direct relationship with God.[1] It was in such a milieu that the royal court became the stage upon which the drama of high politics was played out.

Historical work on the European royal courts is variously located in a burgeoning field of academic monographs, research papers, theses and articles in specialised historical journals.[2] The subject of this book is the court of the later Stuart kings in the period 1660–1702. Its purpose is to provide a general introduction to some of the emergent themes of court politics, court culture and court society in this era. While others have taken up the baton for Queen Anne and the Georgian age, and the reigns of the early Stuarts have been, and no doubt always will be, extensively debated, the courts of the last three Stuart kings are a comparatively neglected era, particularly after 1690.[3] Yet in a number of ways this age of the court's history remains one of the most notable periods of the history of the British state. For the later Stuart court stood in a period of political transition. It represented both the old system of government, which had been in existence in the country since at least the Renaissance, and a new world of parliamentary authority and party politics. The period also saw one of

1

those periodic shifts in the growth and development of that most flexible of beasts, the British monarchy. A monarchy that had almost been destroyed in 1649 was revived in 1660, only to be threatened once more in 1688. It was to re-emerge in a new partnership with Parliament in the 1690s as 'court government' developed, albeit gradually, into 'constitutional monarchy'.

As the last flourishing of a court society with which the political nation could engage before the coming of the modern age, it is clear that the court of the later Stuarts represents a political system somewhat different from our own. The processes of power in seventeenth-century England were still able to operate in a limited and intimate environment made up from personalities, institutions and ideas. Indeed the later seventeenth century was an age in which a mixture of formal and informal structures routinely governed events on a day-to-day basis. As we shall see, the royal court presented the ideal framework for such politics. Life there was governed as much by personal visions of state, culture and society as ideology. In an intimate political system such as this, the cult of personality loomed large and particular economic, social, cultural, institutional or political changes invariably led to tensions in the system in the form of infighting, factions, tactical alliances, groupings, and eventually the formation of political parties.

Of course we must first define what exactly contemporaries meant by the idea of the royal court in which many of these actions took place. Naturally there are various definitions of the 'court' at the time and they can vary with place and circumstance.[4] Contemporaries tended to use the phrase 'the court' to cover a multitude of meanings. This ranged from wherever the monarch happened to be, to actually paying one's court to the monarch in one of the crown's many palaces, houses and departments, to a particular political grouping which became beholden to the monarch's favour. However, it is possible to put forward a functional and fourfold definition of what we mean by the royal court and to take this as the starting point for debate. First, it is clear that the court was as much a cultural idea as a political fact of life. In fact this idea was recognised by contemporaries in the environment surrounding the monarch, particularly in the ritual, literary and artistic worlds. A variety of cultures permeated the court and emanated from it. Together they produced not only artefacts, but also ritual and literary devices, which help to explain the court's processes. Secondly, the court was a presence; that is to say it took place in particular physical structures (palaces and other buildings) which had their own shape and regulation. Thirdly, the court was made up of individuals and groups of people in a relationship with other individuals and above all with the central figure of the monarch. It was a stratified hierarchical structure and it possessed offices and functions which related to and sometimes clashed with each other. Lastly, the court was a political concept, which drew its roots from a number of sources: factional and party politics, the courts of other monarchs, and the ideas of men such as Castiglione, Machiavelli, Hobbes and Locke and a number of other philosophical authors both ancient and modern.

In the first half of this book we will explore some of the structures and ideas of the later Stuart court. Concentration upon the court's processes of power, style and component parts will hopefully illuminate many of the court's structures and the mechanics of government. The second half of the book will attempt to place these structures, style and processes in some specific historical and narrative context. By so doing we may see court politics in the age of faction in operation and decline as it moves into the age of party in the long eighteenth century.

Notes

1   J. N. Figgis, *The Theory of the Divine Right of Kings* (Cambridge, 1896). G. Burgess, *The Politics of the Ancient Constitution: An Introduction to English Political Thought, 1603–1642* (London, 1992). D. Wootton (ed.), *Divine Right and Democracy: An Anthology of Political Writing in Stuart England* (Harmondsworth, 1988).

2   See, for example, V. J. Scattergood and J. W. Sherborne (eds), *English Court Culture in the Late Middle Ages* (London, 1983). W. M. Khun, *Democratic Royalism: The Transformation of the British Monarchy 1861–1914* (London, 1996). R. M. Smuts (ed.), *Court Culture and the Origins of Royalist Tradition in Early Stuart England* (Philadelphia, 1987). D. Starkey (ed.), *The English Court from the Wars of the Roses to the Civil War* (London, 1987). J. Guy (ed.), *The Tudor Monarchy* (London, 1997). J. C. Sainty and R. O. Bucholz, *Officials of the Royal Household, 1660–1837. Part I: Department of the Lord Chamberlain and Associated Offices* (London, 1997). R. O. Bucholz, *The Augustan Court: Queen Anne and the Decline of Court Culture* (Stanford CA, 1993). J. M. Beattie, *The English Court in the Reign of George I* (Cambridge, 1967). K. Sharpe, *The Personal Rule of Charles I* (New Haven, 1992). R. G. Asch and A. M. Birke (eds), *Princes, Patronage and Nobility: The Court at the Beginning of the Modern Age c.1450–1650* (Oxford, 1991). R. Sherwood, *The Court of Oliver Cromwell* (Cambridge, 1977). A. Barclay, 'The impact of James II upon the departments of the royal household' (Ph.D. dissertation, University of Cambridge, 1993). L. L. Peck, *Court Patronage and Corruption in Early Stuart England* (London, 1990).

3   H. Horwitz, 'The 1690s revisited: recent work on politics and political ideas in the reign of William III', *Parliamentary History*, XV (1996), 361–77.

4   See Halifax, 'Political, moral and miscellaneous thoughts and

reflections', in H. C. Foxcroft, *The Life and Letters of Sir George Savile, Bart., First Marquis of Halifax* (2 vols, London, 1898), II, p. 507. L. Mair, *Primitive Government* (Harmondsworth, 1972), pp. 138, 192, 214. A. G. Dickens (ed.), *The Courts of Europe: Politics, Patronage and Royalty, 1400–1800* (London, 1977), p. 7.

Part I

The court structure and the mechanics of government

1

The themes of monarchical government

The emergence of the court into the wider historical consciousness of early modern British history has been a relatively recent development. For much of the period prior to the 1970s the royal court was something of a fallow field in historical terms. The main interests of political historians of the era were largely focused upon the institution of Parliament, upon radical thought, and upon the causes and consequences of the civil wars. An increasing realisation that the court and its activities were also significant to contemporaries was the result of a revisionist approach to the period. In this approach Parliament now became seen as more of a periodic body, not always opposed to the court, and certainly not to monarchy as such, but frequently prorogued and dissolved as the monarch willed. The court on the other hand remained in permanent being around the crown and thus represented a major focus for the political life of the nation.

The beginnings of the court as an idea and a physical presence in early modern Europe are often difficult to unravel. Werner Sombart, writing in 1913, claimed that the early modern court's origins were to be found in princely structures such as that which congregated around the papacy in Rome. He argued that this court was significant for it was never the mere abode of martial warrior nobility, but a centre for a learned elite. The individuals there became conspicuous as consumers of culture as much as for their religious beliefs.[1] The courts of the Italian Renaissance princes as a whole can claim to have produced a tradition of courtly icons for others to follow. Their lifestyle was influenced by ideas of 'courtly love', by nobility, and by concepts of honour. The role of women played an important part in this lifestyle, for their presence appears to have brought with it obligatory forms of peaceful conduct to an otherwise violent martial nobility. As this Renaissance style of courtly life refined itself, its beliefs spread throughout princely and monarchical Europe, and it adapted as it went to circumstance and nationality. It developed its own literature and promulgated acceptable codes of behaviour for potential courtiers and princes alike.[2]

In the modern historical world the publication of Norbert Elias's book *Die höfische Gesellschaft* (The Court Society) arguably marked a change in historical attitudes to the European court as a historical concept. Elias's work began to push forward the boundaries of discourse upon the nature and activities of courts in European history. By using an anthropological and sociological perspective, he sought to consider the whole concept of 'court society', not just the functions of the court, and to define the patterns of behaviour which existed between individuals in such a social formation. Elias's specific case study became located in the court of Louis XIV of France, mainly because of the evidence he used, although comparisons were also made in his work with the court of Charles I of England and those of the German princely states. However, Elias's views on the court also had a broader perspective. They formed part of his ideas on the 'civilising process' outlined elsewhere in his work. In brief, Elias saw an actual civilising process as an ongoing phenomenon in the period. A previously 'uncivilised' warrior class in a feudal relationship with monarchy was to be contained, tamed and moulded by channelling its energies into new areas of social and political life. Thus was created a 'court nobility', a new elite society, pacified, socialised and in debt to monarchy.[3]

The pacification of the warrior class, 'courtisation' or *Verhöflickung*, was also meant to fit into the view of early modern monarchy as absolutist, and the process whereby the French aristocracy in particular was reconstructed to fit into this new form of courtly life was a significant one. Undermined by inflation, by a demanding lifestyle, and by increasing centralisation in government, it was argued that the ideal of French aristocratic lives became residence at court. They were placed in structures which restricted access to the 'face of the monarch', who became the fount of all honour. They were also under pressure to perform in a restrained and civilised manner, and the creation of the court society with social life as its main occupation, the axis of honour as its guiding rule, and conspicuous consumption as the norm, came to its full flower under King Louis XIV.[4]

Since their publication, Elias's views have naturally been subjected to some stringent criticism as to their general applicability. Inevitably the historical world moves on and French historians such as Emmanuel Le Roy Ladurie have led a critique of his work. Ladurie's recent analysis of the court of Louis XIV and Louis XV, using the memoirs of the duc de Saint-Simon, thus pointed the study of the

French court in particular in new directions.[5] Ladurie has added yet more layers to the already complex image of the French court, by rejecting the linear sequence of 'courtoisie médiévale – courtisanerie classique ou "curialité" – courtoisie moderne et contemporaine' and the view of the court as part of a production of present-day bourgeois conventions. Most of all Ladurie noted the significance to contemporaries of all the ramifications of social status in the court's private and public manifestations, the importance of the cabals at Louis XIV's court, and the separation of the sacred and profane as contemporaries saw it. The latter was an unofficial but important distinction that contemporaries made between the pure and impure: the 'illegitimate, the pox-ridden, homosexuals, in short the "dirty", by contrast with the "unpolluted" of legitimate birth, healthy in body and heterosexual'.[6]

While the European arguments have proved significant for the interpretation of the court, what value are they in a British context? There is little doubt that some of these broader European elements are to be found in the royal courts of the British monarchy. But it is arguable that the English court, while it might sometimes have aped European models, manners and etiquette, had its own distinctive evolution. A number of factors may go some way to explain this distinctiveness. Centralisation in government began that much earlier in England than it did in many European monarchies, and the English aristocracy at its height was unlike its European counterpart in a number of ways. There was no *noblesse d'épée*, while outlets for aristocratic martial activity were restricted, tax and legal privileges were almost non-existent, and the younger sons of aristocrats had to make their own way in the world, with no hereditary position to fall back upon. On the contrary the fluid and permeable English political nation meant that the aristocracy and gentry had some things in common: their wealth was land-based, they shared a particular style of life, and they could compete in, and had potential access to, the institutions of power.[7] Moreover, even at its height the English court never reached the size, ideals, control and restraint imposed upon the French.

In a British context it was Geoffrey Elton who set the tone for court studies by outlining the position of the royal court as a major 'point of contact' for the political nation with its monarch.[8] The idea of the court as an area of debate where the political nation could meet with the monarchy has been further elaborated since the publication of Elton's address to the Royal Historical Society in 1975. In fact the study of the British royal court has undergone something of a renaissance, particularly for the Tudor period. A seminal collection of essays, edited by David Starkey, who had already completed some notable work upon the subject, has been joined by further work on various aspects of the English court under the Tudors and early Stuarts.[9] John Guy's recent collection of essays and work on the Tudor monarchy has gone further and outlined an agenda for a 'new political history' which deserves consideration. For this is an agenda into which court studies and the study of early modern politics seems to be now expanding.[10]

There are further themes in the English context to consider. In dealing with the English crown of the period, we are also exploring an institution which has successfully practised what John Cannon has called a 'study in adaptation'.[11] In 1982 Cannon put forward a pragmatic pattern of evolution for the British monarchy which provides some of the background to its development in our era. In this pattern the first phase of the monarchy (a governing monarchy) had the court firmly at the centre of the decision-making process. The monarch remained a powerful figure with his or her prerogative powers in place. The personalities of the political nation were also ordered around the monarch as the 'well head' of government. And it seems to have been such a system, with some variations, which was re-established in 1660. By 1688 it is argued that both Charles II and James II had gone some way to making the crown so effective and bolstering royal power sufficiently enough for it to be resented by the political nation. As a result, the Revolution of 1688 eventually remade the government into a 'balanced monarchy'. Under this new system monarchy remained as the mainspring of government, but its activities now took place in the context of permanent parliamentary pressure. This, it was argued, was the result of two crucial revolutions in the years from 1688 to 1689. The first revolution saw the removal of the Roman Catholic King James II. The second revolution, however, became focused upon a need for regular supply to fund the European war in which the nation became involved in the 1690s. This continental war required finance that could only be obtained from Parliament. While William III won the first of these revolutions (crushing the popish monarchy and replacing it with himself in the process), it has been argued that he lost the second revolution and soon found his crown subject to the tides and eddies of the House of Commons in particular.

It was thus that Parliament emerged as an ever more important part of the constitution. The transition to a 'mixed monarchy' (the next phase of monarchical government) thus took place. This transition was to last at least until 1832, or even until 1917, when George V finally changed his family name from Saxe-Coburg Gotha to Windsor after popular demand. Certainly the third phase of monarchical evolution saw the institution of the crown develop its more popular appeal as many of its formal powers either fell away or were seized by the prime ministerial office and cabinet system. Cannon concludes his system with this 'popular monarchy' in 1982, but naturally enough the process has continued. At the time of writing, the present-day British monarchy once more appears to be undergoing another of those periodic sea-changes, or even another revolution, as the end result of popular or 'populist' politics.

How far can these explanations help us understand monarchical government in an age of change? There seems little doubt that in the course of the fifteenth century there was acceleration in both the purpose and the influence of the English crown. The old feudal trappings of government were gradually exposed and discarded in favour of a more modern, Renaissance idea of what monarchy should be. An expanded 'point of contact' between the monarchy and the political nation was created and this point of contact was the royal court. The court was to provide a suitable social, political and cultural arena for the nation's debates until at least 1642, and the political nation, or at least that portion of it which had survived the civil wars of the late fifteenth century, gradually became subsumed into this new structure. The personal resources and ambitions of its members began to focus upon the court and the goal of the monarch's favour. Under the Tudor dynasty, the great and the good became 'courtiers', and periodically placed themselves within or near the royal household by taking office there, or eagerly entering into the cultural, social and physical environment that monarchy now provided for them. Monarchy now played a central role in this brave new world and sought, consciously or unconsciously, to monopolise high politics, society and culture. As an author of 1633 eloquently put it: 'The Sovereign is the Sun of the Court, from whose glory all courtiers as stars borrow their attracting splendours'.[12]

By the beginning of the seventeenth century the royal court and its leader had become the focus of political, social and cultural power within the Three Kingdoms. The private and public sides of the monarchy jostled alongside each other and the court contained the hub of executive government, with all of its ramshackle administration. Indeed the administrative arm of early modern government was originally an outgrowth of the royal household, and in a maze-like manner stretched from the Privy Council to the royal secretariat, to the various boards and offices of state, both high and low. Thus was created a system of government, in its various guises, which the Stuart dynasty lost in the 1640s. It collapsed because of the effects of the civil wars and regicide. Indeed in 1649 with the execution of Charles I the court structure appeared to have been destroyed for good. However, the short-lived replacement forms of government in the 1650s, a republican culture under the Rump Parliament and the ersatz monarchy of Oliver Cromwell, were soon ended in their turn by the Restoration of the Stuart dynasty in 1660. With this triumphant return to royal power, another court system was established and it was to survive in one form or another until the reign of Queen Anne.[13] Arguably this system had few real rivals in the state until 1690, and in reconstructing a form of government which we can, for want of a better term, label 'court government', the crown sought to re-establish many of the old points of reference for the nation. Put simply, in a period of social, political and religious upheaval the later Stuart court became what Ladurie has defined as 'the physical environment surrounding the exercise of power as embodied in the process of the king and his ministers'.[14] Yet it was also more than just this. Equipped with splendid and stylish buildings, the court's interior life complimented the process of power in cultural terms.

Extravagant, rich and replete with iconographic images that preached the divine and well-established nature of monarchy, a direct contrast to the reality of the 1650s, monarchical culture in the later seventeenth century sought to influence all who came within its grasp in more subtle ways. It used display, cultural artefacts, day-to-day ceremonies and etiquette to construct, as well as structure, a world view. Indeed by curbing the access of courtiers to the physical presence of the monarch through a filter system of rooms, ceremonial and etiquette, monarchy itself could accentuate its differences from the norm and elevate its mystique. Consequently the court was a machine of government, as well as a social milieu with its own specific culture, which became a whole way of life.

Yet the later Stuart court also existed in an era of transition and transformation. Changes had occurred and continued to occur in society, and this meant that even as the old forms were being taken out and dusted off in May 1660, they were proving themselves to be too brittle to suit the new nation being born around them. Resurgent forms of political power, in the shape of Parliament and the judiciary, bolstered by the needs of external war and domestic conflict, were soon to take a more formidable place in the scheme of things, and cause waves of conflict in the processes of government. After 1660 and particularly after 1688, the crown thus faced renewed political challenges to its position, as well as social and cultural changes within the country itself.

The search for the nature of this change, which eventually saw a move from court government to constitutional monarchy as we have seen, has occupied the minds of many a historian. Although there remains some dispute over how long the system of court government and personal monarchy actually lasted in the English, and later

British, political system, it is clear that by 1714, if not before, there had been a substantial decline in the royal court's fortunes. The court of the Georgian monarchy was not that which had been re-created under Charles II.[15] What were the substantive reasons behind this change? They almost certainly included the increased development of the political nation through the broader social changes taking place throughout the century. Changes in agriculture, industry and urban life led to growth in the nation's population. The result was linked to the problems of a wider franchise. In addition, the rise of the professions and moneyed interests and the emergence of a vocal London-based, then national, press, as well as a new form of political discourse in the shape of political party, meant that a broadening of the political life of the nation took place. In this the court was merely a part of the whole system. According to some historians, the impact of war also created extraordinary pressures which resulted in the creation of a fiscal-military state in which finance became a dominant force. In this 'brave new world' the old court techniques and system, which had served the crown so well for so long, thus began to lose their way. They were already declining due to the changes of dynasty in 1688 and 1714 and no longer could the court reach the broad mass of the population. Very soon even the smaller group of the political nation began to be less preoccupied by the wiles and temptations of the court.[16]

A further element of change lay in those immense religious schisms and questions that to all intents and purposes had dogged English history from the sixteenth century. They were most problematic in the seventeenth century mainly because the Stuart dynasty, for good or ill, was decidedly untrustworthy upon matters of religion. The dilemmas of dissent from the established Church, and the matter of Roman Catholicism, or 'popery' as contemporaries labelled it, were complicated by the fact that at least two of the heads of the state Church, Charles II and James II, were inclined towards Roman Catholicism, the latter openly. The difficulty was that Roman Catholicism in the English mind was always linked to 'foreign ideas', to arbitrary government, and to violence and destruction. It was therefore seen as a threat to English liberties. The courts of the two Stuart brothers seemed to reflect an unnatural leniency to Catholicism, and this was seen as evidence of corruption and decay at the heart of government. Conversely Parliament became seen as both staunchly Protestant and a part of a natural system of English liberties.[17] On another level the theological schisms which existed within the English Church itself also proved significant. So that which way people went to their God remained a vexed question in the erastian state that the Stuarts were attempting to rule. There was certainly

13

little room for ideas of dissent, toleration, or seeking other, less official, ways to God.

Rising above all of this there was also the question of the tendency of the Stuart monarchy to move towards a form of 'absolutism' like its European cousins. Heated arguments have flowed, and still flow, from this basic historical question: were the Stuarts bent upon becoming absolutist monarchs? It is possible to argue that since 1603, consciously or unconsciously, the Stuart dynasty had appeared to conceive of its main task as extending the boundaries of royal power. This was true of all European monarchies at the time and the Stuarts were in this respect at least little different from their European cousins. The expansion of royal power can be found in the dynasty's political propaganda, its iconography and ideological expression. But whether such measures could have been put into practical policies by creating a 'absolutist' state along the lines of their European neighbours is the point of issue. In fact the varying degrees of centralisation, growing bureaucracy, viable fiscal system, freedom from parliamentary interference, a standing army, interference in local and regional government, and attempts to resolve the religious problem by the crown at various times, met with stubborn resistance and most of this programme, if it can be so dignified, was brought to a halt in 1688.[18] So monarchical absolutism in the British context proved in the end a mere chimera.

In spite of this the monarchy, shaken as it was by revolutions in 1649 and 1688, was still at the heart of government, and the personality of the individual monarch was still of some importance in setting the trends of political life until at least 1832.[19] For monarchs in the early modern era ruled as well as reigned. The functions of early modern government were few and basic: to govern, to maintain order, to conduct war and sustain a foreign policy. It is true that the revolutions of 1649 and 1688 reset some of the boundaries as to how much individual monarchs could actually do, and how far they could go, but personal monarchy still held sway in many areas of English political life. Within this context the rise of a form of ministerial government, with power delegated by the monarch to certain individuals, was yet another element to contend with. Power became shared between the monarch and his or her advisers. An executive style of government emerged, in which monarchical authority could only work by being shared throughout the system in a number of key offices. The inhabitants of these posts, while they still remained the monarch's servants, were naturally eager for power and endlessly sought and struggled for it on a number of levels. Given the increasing complexity of government, there was a proliferation of offices within this system. The emergence of this swelling administration, although still relatively primitive by modern standards, has been variously dated.[20] Bureaucratic and administrative growth continued throughout the Restoration. The enterprising individual fed it here and there, until in the 1690s a major continental war forced the system into what some historians have labelled an 'administrative revolution'.[21]

At the same time Parliament, whose life-spans and impact in the early seventeenth century had been somewhat intermittent, gradually became a partner in the government of the state. After 1660, while the monarchy still held the cards of dissolution in its hands, Parliament's power had wavered, but as Parliament became more and more vital as the basis of supply, particularly in the 1690s, it could no longer be ignored. The court government, faced with this phenomenon, sought the answer in management: the use of offices, titles, cash bribes, or patronage to create a bloc of members of Parliament who would vote for its needs. A direct consequence of this was the arrival of party conflict as those who refused to be managed, or to be bought off, or were still ignored by the government, sought to oppose it. Party and all of its ramifications have been the subject of intense debate amongst historians over the years. As a result, a kaleidoscopic image of the subject has emerged in the literature, in which the very term has been doubted.[22] These arguments need not be rehearsed again here, but will be touched upon below. Needless to say, party complicated the process of court government still further and further added to the dissipation of royal power. Thus the court politics described in the first part of this book hold true at least for the reigns of Charles II and James II. In the reign of William III, as we shall see, new structures and a new world of party politics and parliamentary management were to join and adjust the system as its nature, grounded in the Revolution of 1688–89 and fostered by the pressures of war, finance and social expansion, underwent a seachange.

Modern interpretations of the seventeenth century, still apparently the most significant and formative period of British history whichever way one looks at it, are thus now located in an intricate landscape – a landscape indeed whose contours, let alone dark valleys, are often difficult to discover. Nevertheless, the court and its politics have now been firmly placed at the centre of the political system of the day. It now has a place of significance in the new narratives, for they are so often centred on short-term struggles for power. Again in such narratives the 'motor of change' in society is now more than occasionally located within the court's precincts. This new political history has illuminated a world of 'place and patronage' where there was apparently little room for ideologues and much room for cynical personalities engaged in factional day-to-day activities. But in order to understand the later-seventeenth-century court and its activities and their place in the political life of the era, it is clear that we need not merely the prurient rendition of the facts of day-to-day life there, a shortcoming of many popular histories, but the re-creation of the court's mentality. This includes its relationships, personal as well as physical, its spatial politics, institutions, art, literature, language, ceremony, concepts of honour and blood, grace and favour, entertainment and leisure, as well as those natural outgrowths of high birth, personal influence and competition, and the capture of access to the monarch's person – in short a recreation of court culture, and this includes politics, in its broadest sense.

Notes

1 W. Sombart quoted in R. G. Asch and A. M. Birke (eds), *Princes, Patronage and Nobility: The Court at the Beginning of the Modern Age c.1450–1650* (Oxford, 1991), p. 3. See also N. Elias, *The Court Society* (Oxford, 1983), p. 39.

2 S. Angelo, 'The courtier, renaissance and changing ideas', in A. G. Dickens (ed.), *The Courts of Europe: Politics, Patronage and Royalty, 1400–1800* (London, 1977), pp. 31–5.

3 Elias, *Court Society*, pp. 146–213.

4 Ibid., pp. 215–16. Also N. Elias, *The Civilising Process* (2 vols, Oxford, 1982), pp. 258–70.

5 E. Le Roy Ladurie, *Saint Simon ou le système de la Cour* (Paris, 1997). E. Le Roy Ladurie, *The Ancien Régime: A History of France, 1610–1774* (Oxford, 1996). J. Rogister, 'A well-stocked zoo of courtly animals', *Times Literary Supplement*, XVII (1998), 36. J. Diundam, *Myths of Power: Norbert Elias and the Early Modern European Court* (Amsterdam, 1995). Pierre Verlet, *Le Château de Versailles* (Paris, 1985).

6 Ladurie, *Saint Simon*, p. 516. Ladurie, *Ancien Régime*, p. 226.

7 L. Stone and J. C. Fawtier Stone, *An Open Elite: England, 1540–1880* (Oxford, 1984), pp. 256–8.

8 G. R. Elton, 'Tudor government: the points of contact: III the court', *Transactions of the Royal Historical Society*, 5th series, XXVI (1976), 211–28.

9 D. Starkey (ed.), *The English Court from the Wars of the Roses to the Civil War* (London, 1987). J. Guy (ed.), *The Tudor Monarchy* (London, 1997). J. C. Sainty and R. O. Bucholz, *Officials of the Royal Household, 1660–1837. Part I: Department of the Lord Chamberlain and Associated Offices* (London, 1997). R. O. Bucholz, *The Augustan Court: Queen Anne and the Decline of Court Culture* (Stanford CA, 1993). J. M. Beattie, *The English Court in the Reign of George I* (Cambridge, 1967). K. Sharpe, *The Personal Rule of Charles I* (New Haven, 1992). R. Sherwood, *The Court of Oliver Cromwell* (Cambridge, 1977).

10 Guy (ed.), *Tudor Monarchy*, where it is argued (pp. 7–8) that the new political history is now to be a genuine political investigation and should examine both the cultural and institutional aspects of the topic. It should also realise the interrelationships between politics, ideas and contemporary imaginative literature, not only basing itself on traditional archive research, but upon an understanding of the classical and Renaissance underpinning of the political culture of the day. It should also be aware of the issues of language and the relationship of policy to personality. Above all perhaps, the new political history should focus upon the 'interrelationships of, and interactions between, people, institutions, men and ideas'. It should place them in context by 'envisioning politics as … the active expression of a social organism'.

11 J. Cannon, *The Modern British Monarchy: A Study in Adaptation*, The Stenton Lecture 1986 (Reading, 1987). Also J. Cannon, 'The survival of the British monarchy', *Transactions of the Royal Historical Society*, 5th series, XXXVI (1986), 143

12 British Library (hereafter BL), Harleian MS 3364, 'A discourse on court and courtiers 1633', fo. 5.

13 See S. Kelsey, *Inventing a Republic: The Political Culture of the English Commonwealth, 1649–1653* (Manchester, 1997). R. Sherwood, *Oliver Cromwell, King in All but Name, 1653–1658* (Stroud, 1997). Beattie, *English Court*, pp. 1–6.

14 E. Le Roy Ladurie, 'Versailles: the court of Louis XIV in 1709', in E. Le Roy Ladurie, *The Mind and Method of the Historian* (Brighton, 1981), p. 149.

15 Beattie, *English Court*. H. T. Dickinson, *Walpole and the Whig Supremacy* (London, 1973), T. Harris, 'From rage of party to the age of oligarchy? Re-thinking the late Stuart and early Hanoverian period', *Journal of Modern History*, LXIV (1992), 700–20.

16 T. Claydon, *William III and the Godly Revolution* (Cambridge, 1996), pp. 64–89.

17 J. Scott, *Algernon Sidney and the Restoration Crisis* (Cambridge, 1991), pp. 32–8.

18 N. Henshall, *The Myth of Absolutism: Change and Continuity in Early Modern Monarchy* (London, 1992). M. Whinney and O. Millar, *English Art, 1625–1714* (Oxford, 1957), pp. 7, 245, 299. Also see J. Miller (ed.), *Absolutism in Seventeenth-Century Europe* (London, 1990) and J. Miller, 'The potential for absolutism in later Stuart England', *History*, LXIX (1984), 187–207.

19 Beattie, *English Court*. See also C. Hibbert, *George IV* (Harmondsworth, 1976) and J. H. Plumb, *The First Four Georges* (London, 1956), pp. 9–10.

20 G. Holmes, *The Making of a Great Power: Late Stuart and Early Georgian Britain, 1660–1722* (London, 1993), pp. 257–65. L. Stone, *An Imperial State at War: Britain from 1689–1815* (London, 1994). G. E. Aylmer, 'From office holding to civil service: the genesis of modern bureaucracy', *Transactions of the Royal Historical Society*, 5th series, XXX (1980), 91–108.

21 Holmes, *Making of a Great Power*, pp. 257–65.

22   G. Holmes, *British Politics in the Age of Anne* (revised edn, London, 1987). T. Harris, *Politics under the Later Stuarts: Party Conflict in a Divided Society, 1660–1715* (London, 1993). J. C. D. Clark, 'A general theory of party, opposition and government, 1688–1832', *Historical Journal*, XXIII (1980), 295–325. A. Browning, 'Parties and party organisation in the reign of Charles II', *Transactions of the Royal Historical Society*, 4th series, XXX (1946), 21–36.

2

Machines of government, office and ceremony

Axis of honour: the royal palace

If the early modern royal court was a 'machine of government', then it was also a place of ritual and a political theatre. In this theatre the monarch as the principal actor paraded before a large number of audiences: courtiers, the political nation at large, the domestic population and foreign states.[1] These actions took place in the buildings that also provided the monarch's home. As such they reflected their owner's personality. It comes as no surprise to find conflict in the royal palace of the later seventeenth century, for it was a conflict between emergent ideas of privacy and political theatre which merged and blended alongside historical conventions, rules and regulations. A key theme of court politics in the period, and one to which we will return, lay in access to the 'face of monarchy'. With so much invested in royal authority, access to the monarch's person meant access to power, favour, land, title and government.

As buildings, royal palaces remained apparently open to all, but the physical layout of the court naturally dictated what happened there, and the design and development of any early modern palace was a reflection of the spatial distance between ruler and subject.[2] By the latter half of the seventeenth century the English royal court, with its offices, buildings, rituals and customs, was a fairly well defined instrument. Indeed shrewd courtiers could often calculate to a fine degree their success or failure in the game of the court, and where they happened to stand on the social or political scale, by their relative position in the rooms of the palace. The further one could penetrate into the multitude of 'privy', or private rooms, the more status one had. Such a scale, labelled the 'axis of honour' by subsequent historians, was an outcome of the spatial politics of court life and it beholds us to examine closely the buildings in which it took place.[3]

In itself the English court of the later seventeenth century had grown into a more sedentary organisation than many of its earlier predecessors. In theory the 'court' was a mobile entity which surrounded the monarch wherever he or she may be, but the later Stuart court was not really the widely travelled institution of its medieval, Tudor or early Stuart predecessors. Medieval monarchy had always been something of a roving circus, rarely staying long in one place, and the medieval court remained very much a 'court of occasion' rather than a permanent structure, only settling down in the Renaissance. Nor was the later Stuart court as peripatetic as that of the Tudors in its use of the royal progress.[4] In fact the later Stuart monarchy's base of operations in the south-east of England was centred around seven main establishments: Whitehall Palace, Hampton Court, Windsor Castle, St James's Palace, Somerset House, Greenwich and Kensington Palace; with occasional forays to the races at Newmarket, the spas at Bath or Tunbridge Wells, and the cities of Oxford, Portsmouth or Winchester. In his later years Charles II had planned a new palace at Winchester to rival Versailles, but as with many of the King's schemes it soon faltered and much of the building lay uncompleted at his death, to be subsequently abandoned in his brother's reign.[5] None of the later Stuarts were in fact able to produce an English Versailles. Financial restraints and inclination therefore led them to improve Whitehall Palace as the centre of the English monarchy and the royal court for much of the later seventeenth century.

Despite various architectural improvements, the palace of Whitehall, situated along the banks of the Thames, remained a huge jumble of buildings and styles. Henry VIII had originally removed it and a number of other palaces from the hands of Cardinal Wolsey. And it had been used by his successors for generations. Faced with this large and rather old-fashioned set of buildings, for a number of years after his Restoration Charles II, as his father had before him, flirted with the idea of rebuilding Whitehall completely.[6] The scheme proved financially impossible, although despite its discomforts Whitehall still had some attributes worthy of monarchy. The Stuarts tended, as had the Tudors, to prefer its centrality in the midst of London's streets. The palace also had a lavish interior decoration and this was frequently redesigned for particular occupants. Change only really came for Whitehall after the Revolution of 1688, when the new King, William III, could not overcome his dislike of it. Thereafter William tried to avoid the palace as much as possible, preferring to nurture his health by escaping from London's smog to Hampton Court and

Kensington Palace. Circumstances then dictated the further decline of Whitehall as a royal residence. It became impossible to live there after a fire in 1698, and the final removal from Whitehall to Kensington set the trend for the smaller and more homely English court of the eighteenth century. The palace's grandeur and the atmosphere of 'good King Charles's golden days' thus passed into history.[7]

Of the other royal residences little more needs to be said here. St James's Palace became the traditional residence of the heir to the throne, and was occupied by James when he was duke of York in the 1660s and 1670s. Various ministers and royal servants were also given lodgings there, as indeed they were at Whitehall. Somerset House was given to Queen Catherine of Braganza and remained for many years her home. Windsor Castle, as will be seen, was Charles II's most favoured palace after Whitehall, and, foiled at Whitehall, Charles had plans made to have the interior reconstructed in an attempt to make it the headquarters of the Stuart dynasty.[8] A number of old Tudor and early Stuart residences that had once been occupied by the royal family in various guises had either fallen into decay during the course of the Civil War or had been sold off by the penurious English Republic.[9]

We can find the roots of the early modern English palace in the Middle Ages. By the later seventeenth century it had been subjected to the heavy influence of a French style in terms of decoration, furniture and organisation. Inevitably the state apartments, the block of rooms which made up the monarch's suite, had borne the brunt of this reconstruction and this had led to increasing sophistication, as well as complexity, in the daily routine of these rooms. As the fount of all honour, the personal monarch's life was naturally central to that of his or her courtiers. It was a practical necessity for them to attend the monarch in order to discover what he or she wished to do, and, if possible, to undertake it on the monarch's behalf. Thereby they could win favour. Automatically the monarch's household became a place of some significance and was crowded with courtiers. Naturally it was neither practical, nor desirable, for everyone to have access to the monarch on an intimate basis. The old medieval great hall and great chamber thus soon disappeared, to be subsumed by more specialised rooms designed to filter the crowds, restrict access, increase the distance between monarch and subject, as well as to give some privacy to the royal person. The original division into a chamber for state business and eating, and a rather large bedsitting room for living and sleeping, had soon divided and sub-divided again. By the time the Tudor monarchy arrived upon the scene a regular threefold division of household, chamber and privy chamber had become the norm.[10]

Samuel Pegge, an eighteenth-century commentator, noted that the disposition of the rooms above stairs in the palace of Whitehall by the time of the Stuarts had taken on the following system:

Guard or Great Chamber
|
Presence Chamber—Privy Chamber—Privy Gallery/Privy Garden
|
Withdrawing room
|
Bedchamber
|
Private Closet[11]

As the outer rooms became ever more public, the inner or privy chambers became more private and select – literally privy to the monarch's person. In the early years of the Restoration the etiquette of these rooms was certainly more relaxed than it had been prior to 1642, but some formality was incorporated into the new court. Privy Councillors, for example, were to be allowed into a lobby near the bedchamber, a lord's son into an antechamber, but others, even 'persons of quality', were to remain in the presence chamber or gallery.[12] Given the personality of Charles II, such formality soon slipped and the King's bedchamber seems to have been rather too accessible on occasion, as well as somewhat crowded, dirty and squalid.[13] New household ordinances, which strictly ordered the activities of the court and which are our main source for such matters, were promulgated in 1683, mainly as a result of increased security stemming from the recent discovery of the Rye House Plot, and some reform began. In fact these ordinances provided the basis for the governing of the household until at least the end of the century with one or two minor alterations.[14] Access to the bedchamber and to the King's person began to be more limited. In 1683 only James, duke of York, the King's ministers, Secretaries of State and those specifically invited could enter. The door to the bedchamber was also to be kept locked and guarded. Access to the King's private closet beyond the bedchamber became very restricted indeed.[15] This room, or closet, was invariably richly decorated, and it remained very much a holy of holies, an inner sanctum which, with the exception of the Groom of the Stole and William Chiffinch, the Page of the Backstairs, only those specifically invited by the King could enter. They processed either through the bedchamber or via the more secretive route of the backstairs escorted by the ever-faithful William Chiffinch. In this suite of rooms the King could be private and see only those he wished to see.[16]

Despite the growing desire for privacy amongst British monarchs, it still proved necessary for the monarch to see the court. More significantly perhaps, it was necessary for monarchy to be seen. As we shall see, given the character of William III the restrictive nature of the ordinances by which he governed his court naturally increased. It caused the poet Fleetwood Sheppard to comment sarcastically that most days:

[William] Benting uplocks
His King in a box
And you see him no more till supper[17]

While a slight exaggeration, access to William III always remained difficult for any courtier. One growing innovation to overcome William's reluctance to make an appearance at all was the continued emergence of the levee. This meeting of monarch and subject was set at various times during the day, but it usually took place in the morning and it allowed those at court into a withdrawing room, to greet and perhaps, if fortunate enough, to talk to the monarch. James II held his levee after rising. After Mary's death, when he was at home and not on campaign, William III took to seeing 'company on Sunday morning … [or for] an hour before dinner and the like before supper'. His successor Queen Anne chose to hold her drawing room levees in the early afternoon, and they began to set the trend for the dull affair the meetings became.[18]

What was it was actually like to be in the court in Whitehall Palace on any given day in the reigns of these men and women? There are in fact a number of sources available which enable us to provide a brief pen portrait.[19] There is little doubt that with the monarch in residence one of the royal palaces resembled nothing so much as a major tourist attraction of today during the summer, full of noise, chatter and bustle with the rumble of coaches before the gates. As the outer court of Whitehall was located in the midst of Westminster it was hardly immune from the clamour of the surrounding streets at the best of times. At the gates of Whitehall, the entrance to the court during the day, there was 'a continual throng, either of gallants standing to ravish themselves with the sight of ladies' handsome legs and insteps as they took coach; or of the tribe of guarded liveries, by whom you could scarce pass without a jeer or saucy answer to your question'. Once through this mob, and into the actual courtyard of Whitehall, the social vista became slightly more select. This area remained a 'School of complement, where the young courtiers used to shew their new brought over French cringes, and the whole body wriggled into a gesture of salutation'.[20] Various diversions awaited prospective courtiers thereafter. For the most part they would parade up the grand staircase into the guard chamber, trailed, if important, by a number of followers, supplicants or servants. Here most of them would remain, awaiting the daily appearance, or not, of the royal personage, a patron, or friends, and taking stock of the more important courtiers as they went in and out of the doors at either end of the room. The courtier stuck here had little enough to do but chat and try not to get too bored. One could admire the ladies who were sure to comment on 'your form, your carriage, your garb, language, and whole deportment'. For those of more significance, entrance to the actual apartments of the monarch awaited. In the inner rooms there was usually more waiting about for the courtier. Here business was transacted in 'whispering consultations', ministers chattered about government, fancies were attended to, understandings were made, schemes were hatched, and much went on to keep the courtier occupied and in touch with events. The select few might then proceed further into the monarch's actual domain of the bedchamber, with its rich and costly hangings and furniture, but for the majority it was the antechambers, terraces and public areas that were their lot. There they awaited the monarch's passing or, at selected times, his dining in public or some other ceremonial event when the ambitious courtier could attract attention.

An alternative to this life did exist on a lesser scale, albeit the need to see the monarch could never be neglected. A courtier could always partake of a visit to a great man at the lodgings which some of them kept in the palace. This would enable him to keep up his connections and there be overwhelmed by the 'smell and odour of the perfumes and tinctures of a morning's curling and dressing'. Attendance at a great courtier's morning toilette was a privilege and a chance to catch his eye and ask for some favour: possible employment perhaps, or what scraps he could throw in the courtier's way. We do know from the diaries of John Evelyn and Samuel Pepys that to be one of the select crowd who followed Charles II into his mistress's rooms when Charles went to make his morning visit was a significant coup.[21] Of course once out of his inner sanctum the monarch would invariably be followed around by a trail of helpful, or not so helpful, courtiers intent on catching his eye. Indeed it was this demanding crowd which Charles II, with his lengthy stride, often sought to walk away from as fast as possible, but never entirely succeeded.

The organisation of the household

The organisation and administration of the late Stuart court rested upon four pillars. These departments and their senior officers were the Lord Chamberlain, who governed the royal household above stairs; the Lord Steward, who ran the royal household below stairs, as well organising the supply for the whole household; the Master of the Horse, who ran the smallest of the departments of the household, dealing with transportation and supervision of the horses, stables and carriages of the monarch; and the Groom of the Stole, who had control of the bedchamber. The office of Groom of the Stole, while a relatively late development, was in the closest proximity to the monarch's person. As such it could prove important and with its intimate nature was symbolically redolent of all the offices of the royal household.

The household below stairs throughout our period was a vast catering and service establishment created to feed, supply and house the court. Considerably enlarged by Charles II at the Restoration, it suffered frequent bouts of retrenchment, beginning in 1667 as the financial problems of the regime emerged.[22] In comparison with some of its neighbours the later Stuart court was still a contained unit.[23] Although in general there were around 1,100 court posts under Charles II, retrenchment cut this back in 1685 by nearly a third and indeed may have been another reason why the new King James rapidly became unpopular. That said, while the number of court posts had risen by 1700 to 1,300, it was still relatively small in comparison with the vast army which serviced Louis XIV's Versailles.[24]

In the later Stuart court, as elsewhere in Europe, the Lord Chamberlain's department centred its work upon the ceremonial and policing of the King's rooms above stairs. The Lord Chamberlain remained a post of great honour at court, with his triple keys giving him access to a number of important rooms. He oversaw the officers of the King's chamber and nearly all those above stairs. It was an office that usually fell to a high-ranking politician, who naturally left the day-to-day business to his Vice-Chamberlain.[25] The Lord Steward and Master of the Horse were as much honorific titles as practical ones. Both offices oversaw their staffs who catered for the domestic and field requirements of the monarch. These offices were of course desirable as they entitled the holders to both rank and privilege and, of course, to daily access to the monarch's person.

The more significant office developments at the court actually took place in the bedchamber. From having been originally an offshoot of the Lord Chamberlain's department, by the 1660s the bedchamber had become divorced from it. And within the bedchamber the position of Groom of the Stole had emerged as a controlling officer of the King's private chambers, with various numbers of gentlemen and grooms of the bedchamber to help him.[26] Given their proximity to the monarch, the bedchamber posts were much coveted by courtier and politician alike and their disposition was inevitably politically significant. While the posts remained in theory those of body servants, who assisted in dressing the King, waited upon him, and took watch, by rota, over his person at night, they also tended to be his companions in leisure. They also acted to separate the 'private parts of monarchy', as Pepys called them, from the rest of the court.

The Groom of the Stole (or Stool) was one of the most important offices of all at the court and provides a good example of what a court office was actually about, not merely functional, but symbolic and highly politicised. It was originally an office whose functions were implicit in its title; as the bedchamber ordinances of William III make clear, the Groom was the only person to have the unique privilege of attending the monarch when he was at his close-stool. Otherwise the Groom's duties ranged from this attendance at the King's bodily functions, to performing 'all other offices and services of honour about our person'. He also acted as an administrative officer and organiser of the bedchamber, as well as confidential messenger and regulator of access to the King's private rooms. The post had its own badge of office: 'a Gold key in a blew ribbon'.[27] This icon of status of course was highly significant, for the key not only gave authority, appointment to the office was symbolised by handing it over to the occupant; it signalled to others by its presence on the wearer's costume that this individual held an intimate post in relation to the monarch. It was personally returned to the monarch when the individual was dismissed or resigned. Moreover, the key was symbolic in other ways. It reflected both intimacy and access, both to the most private rooms of the palace and to the privy body of the monarch. Given the potential power that went with the post, in many ways it represented the ultimate office in the axis of honour for any courtier.

As an example of the office in operation, we may take the Groom of the Stole under William III. Following a trend common in early modern courts, William III gave the office of Groom of the Stole, as well as £5,000 a year in salary, to his long-time Dutch favourite William Bentinck, earl of Portland.[28] This move, while it was understandable, naturally came to be resented by the English courtiers for in this office Portland increasingly acted as an intermediary for his sullen master. As William Bentinck, Portland had been the friend, confidant and servant of the Prince of Orange for some twenty-three years before the Revolution of 1688. He had been close to William in sickness and in health, and on the latter's accession he was given a most privileged position next to his new King. According to Hoffman, the Imperial ambassador, Portland stood 'first in the confidence of their King'. Naturally Portland's progress was resented not only as he was a foreigner, but because William also used the Groom to reject petitions and disappoint aspirants for offices and favour. Relations between the Groom of the Stole and the other courtiers were thus soon strained, especially as Portland regarded the English with some hostility, if not contempt, and native English xenophobia was in any case rife at William's court. Indeed Sir John Knight, member of Parliament for Bristol, noted on his visit to the court that he was 'offended by the sound of foreign accents in the palace of the King ... [and] there is no entering the court ... for the great noise and croaking of the frog-landers [that is the Dutch]'.[29] Portland was also in the frontline because of his alleged greed, haughtiness of manner and because the Jacobites proclaimed with monotonous regularity in their propaganda that he had homosexual relations with William. The view was taken that Portland was a minister above ministers, a sort of 'spin doctor' of his day, although in practice despite the use he made of Portland it was clear that William was very much his own first minister. However, as a result of this belief, Portland was not only actively disliked, but subject to some satiric comment alongside his King. The cry was that 'Lord Portland takes all things', but the whole regime was not immune to this, as Henry Hall in an ironic hymn of praise on William's return from yet another interminable campaign in Flanders commented:

> Rejoice you sots, your idols come again
> To pick your pockets and kidnap your men
> Give him your money, and his Dutch your lands
> Ring not your bells ye fools, but wring your hands.[30]

As this brief example has hopefully illustrated, the monarch's bedchamber remained a battleground for those who served there and those who wanted to serve there. It would always prove the best place to catch the monarch at ease, sometimes literally, and to request favours. It was here that access to the monarchical body was most possible and although the hours could be long and somewhat tedious on occasion, they could be profitable and the formalities between monarch and subject sometimes relaxed. Sir John Reresby in the early 1680s noted of a typical night under Charles II's regime that 'There was but four present; and his Majesty being in good humour ... was that night two hours putting off his clothes, and it was half an hour past one before he went to bed'. A presence in the bedchamber therefore meant opportunities to talk privately and ask for favours from the monarch in more intimate surroundings.[31]

Ceremony and ritual

One cannot underestimate the importance of display and ritual in the early modern court. The later writer Thomas Paine, in a scathing attack upon monarchy as a whole, was to point out that all monarchy was really 'the most prosperous invention the devil ever set on foot for the promotion of idolatry', indeed a 'popery of government' which was kept up to amuse the ignorant.[32] In this sense rulers of the House of Stuart, as with other royal dynasties, were not unaware of the uncertainties of their position, a position which was held together as much by the trappings of state as by their personalities. The fear that the opinion could lay hold upon the minds of their subjects that monarchs were like ordinary humans meant that the ritual and symbolism attending monarchy still proved significant.[33] The fact that the symbolic rhetoric of monarchy was frequently brought into conflict with the reality of the occupants of the throne in the period was also significant. The classic resolution to this problem was to favour the idea of the monarch's two bodies, the profane natural body of the person divorced from the more sacred and ceremonial body of the monarchy. But given the material with which it had to work after the Restoration, the adoption of this philosophical idea never proved entirely successful.[34]

If externally the English monarchy's residences were unprepossessing, internally, beyond the physical restrictions of the walls, a considerable degree of ritual, organisation and custom governed these structures. It is essential to view the later Stuart court in theatrical terms. The ritualisation of the daily life of monarchy was a continuous celebration of royal sovereignty. Such rituals allowed a series of mini-dramatic performances to unfold before a selected audience in a form of politics by other means. From the monarch's rising (lever), their levee (an early morning reception), to the main meals of the day, to their retirement for the night (coucher), most of early modern monarchy's actions still retained their symbolic, quasi-religious function. These related not only to the semi-divine nature of the occupants and their surroundings, but also to the creation of a cultural framework within which monarchy could define itself, advance its claims as a form of political theology, and exclude unbelievers. The courtiers were themselves a significant part of this drama, providing on the one hand an audience and on the other the actors in the drama. In fact this series of dramas, both individual and interactive, sought to structure the day-to-day life of the royal court. The central performer of the drama, however, was clear to all: the monarch.[35]

Attitudes to this fact of life varied. While some monarchs accepted their role reluctantly, others relished the performance. William III appears to have endured the ritual of his court, as much else, with scant respect. This was mainly due to his character, rather than his Dutch background.[36] He even condemned the coronation as a 'comedy' and 'silly old Popish ceremony', and the many restrictions of day-to-day court life weighed upon him. William claimed he felt like 'a king in a play', which of course in one sense he was. Constantly struggling against the restrictions of court life, William frequently hid himself away in his closet. Yet in reacting to the ritual of the court in this way he undoubtedly alienated many of his subjects, particularly his courtiers, and his aloof, silent and unapproachable manners when he did emerge only made things worse. While Queen Mary, until her death, tried to compensate for her husband's peevishness, she never wholly succeeded in doing so, and as Burnet pointed out, the 'face of the court, and the rendezvous usual in the public rooms, was ... quite broke'.[37] This had not only a cultural impact but a social one. William's reluctance to take part in the ritual of court life was seen as a dereliction of his duties as King and did nothing to increase his waning popularity. Unlike Captain Manly in Wycherley's play *The Plain Dealer*, most monarchs and courtiers were only too willing to go along with the 'decorums, supercilious forms and slavish ceremonies ... [the] little tricks which ... the spaniels of the world, do daily over and over, for and to one another'.[38]

To his detriment William was also measured by the stance taken by his predecessors in the job. Charles II, while he never relished the ritual side of monarchy, 'the arts and rules, the prudent of the world walk by', nevertheless saw how useful it could be as a tool in re-establishing the monarchy.[39] In 1638 the earl of Newcastle had pointed out to the young Charles Stuart that 'what is a king, more than a subject, but for ceremony & order, when that fails him, he's ruined ... therefore your Majesty will be pleased to keep it up strictly ... show yourself gloriously, to your people: like a god'. Charles was certainly a master at his role, although even he would have balked at godhead, but his personal aversion to formality and his unwillingness to be restricted to the daily round made an impact. Ceremony did take place at the Caroline court, and for the most part its boundaries were usually respected. In the 1660s Charles might well have gone through the ritual of retiring to his bedchamber at night, only to slip out through the backstairs to frolic with Lady Castlemaine, but he went through the ritual all the same. His successor, James II, was much more diligent and for the most part tended to stand on his dignity, intent not only upon raising the profile of his monarchy through increased ceremonial and ritual, but also keeping a dignified distance between monarch and courtiers. Such truancy as his brother had practised certainly had no place at James's court and indeed may have been a reaction to it.[40]

The culture of monarchy, its symbolic and ceremonial nature, was mainly designed, consciously or unconsciously, to create a moral universe in which the boundaries were stated. Monarchy was good;

chaos, also known as republicanism and which monarchy held in check, was bad. Ceremonial within the context of court government was usually either grand or minor. The grand ceremonies of royal iconography – coronations, marriage, the opening of Parliament, and to some extent funerals – extolled mytho-historical themes both to the observers and, through the printed word, to the nation at large. They emphasised, as they still do, the privilege of the principal actors and observers, who were also, it was presumed, conscious of the sense of awe such spectacles were meant to convey. They sought to make the observer a worshipper at the semi-divine shrine of monarchy. Such ceremonies also had another purpose. They created a much-needed link with the past. In ceremony the past could be depicted as a golden age of stability, place and purpose, for which the nation should again strive. The present was, as ever, a much more uncertain interval and the future remained something to be won through majestic imagery.[41]

Minor royal ceremonies took place in the context of the day-to-day business of the court at strategic points of the day, such as the morning levee or evening coucher, meal times, banquets, balls and masquerades. Most served to dramatise the differences and accentuate the social distance between the ruler and his or her subjects. In between such strategic points there lay the minutiae of etiquette, in which the passing monarch recognised, or neglected, one courtier or another with a smile, a nod, a word of thanks or praise, or a frown. This minutiae was followed in all of its ramifications by courtiers. It resulted in an endless reading of the royal face, by which fate and future could be decided. Hence the popularity of the 'science' of reading faces, and thus character, at court. In addition there were also times when monarchy was able to come down from its high places and perform, however disingenuously, as a normal human being. Sir John Reresby saw this in action from the master of such performances at Newmarket in March 1682 when Charles II 'let himself down from majesty to the very degree of a country gentleman. He mixed himself amongst the crowd, allowed every man to speak with him that pleased, went a hawking in mornings, to cock matches in the afternoons … and to plays in the evenings, acted in a barn and by very ordinary Bartholomew-fair comedians.'[42] This was the apparent magic of monarchy, the common touch, at which Charles was always rather better than his successors, but which is with us still in the royal visit to the public building or the factory floor.

The ceremony seen at court therefore was part of the politics of performance, which not only celebrated the idea of monarchy, but in the case of the subjects their own submission to the monarchy as an idea. In this ritual drama both courtiers and monarch took part in elaborate systems of gesture and visual display while participating in the events at court. Thereby they could deliberately show off their taste, political authority, social influence and power. In a structured system such as the court, changes in status were also recognised by ceremonies that were meant to display and acknowledge them.[43] So ceremony, as with all of the ritual at court, was neither purposeless nor meaningless, but part of a presentation of the self, which answered ideological, social or even spiritual imperatives.

What the continual round of royal pageantry at court attempted to convey to all concerned, even after the Revolution of 1688, was the timeless moral order to royal life: this is how it was, it is and ever shall be in the public life of the realm. The necessity of this to the newly restored monarchy of 1660 was obvious. For only as recently as eleven years beforehand the royal pantomime had been laid open and a king had died not in glory, but on the block executed by his own people, in a symbolic as well as literal severing of the royal head of government.

Notes

1   D. Cannadine and S. Price (eds), *Rituals of Royalty: Power and Ceremonial in Traditional Society* (Cambridge, 1987), p. 1. P. Burke, *The Fabrication of Louis XIV* (New Haven, 1992), pp. 5–19.

2   See document 2 and H. M. Ballie, 'Etiquette and the planning of the state apartment in baroque palaces', *Archaeologia*, CI (1967), 182–4. See also N. Elias, *The Court Society* (Oxford, 1983), pp. 41–65. R. W. Berger, *A Royal Passion: Louis XIV as a Patron of Architecture* (Cambridge, 1994), p. 2. J. Brown and J. H. Elliott, *A Palace Fit for a King: The Buen Retiro and the Court of Philip IV* (New Haven, 1980).

3   See document 2. Also M. Girouard, *Life in the English Country House: A Social and Architectural History* (New Haven, 1978), pp. 134–5, 144–6. D. Howarth, *Images of Rule: Art and Politics in the English Renaissance 1485–1649* (London, 1997), pp. 11–49.

4   Historical Manuscripts Commission (hereafter HMC), 6th Report (1877), p. 336. HMC 7th Report (1879), p. 469. Originally the idea of the progress had been partly propagandist, to celebrate the idea of monarchy, to show the monarch to his or her people, and to help to spread the cost of the court. Circumstances changed after 1660. While in his youth Charles II had been something of an involuntary traveller, from May 1660 he soon settled into the southern half of the country. And it was there that the monarchy largely remained for the rest of the century. James II, an old-fashioned monarch in a number of ways, was briefly to revive the royal progress in the course of his reign, mainly in an effort to win support, and both he and William III took the road to war, but royal progresses as such became relatively uncommon.

5   H. M. Colvin, *The History of the King's Works* (7 vols, London,

1976), V, 1660–1782, pp. 22–3, 305. J. Milner, *The History and Antiquities of Winchester* (2 vols, 3rd edn, London, 1863), II, pp. 32–4.

6 C. Whitaker-Wilson, *Whitehall Palace* (London, 1934), pp. 125–42. See also S. Thurley, *The Whitehall Palace Plan of 1670* (London, 1998), pp. 1–4. I am indebted to Dr John Stevenson for this reference.

7 N. Robb, *William of Orange: A Personal Portrait* (2 vols, London, 1966), I, p. 286. G. S. Dugdale, *Whitehall Through the Centuries* (London, 1950). Colvin, *History of the King's Works*, V, 1660–1782, pp. 23, 153, 264, 286, 289, 290–3. Thurley, *Whitehall Palace Plan*, pp. 1–16.

8 Colvin, *History of the King's Works*, V, 1660–1782, pp. 236, 313–14, 324, 330.

9 R. Sherwood, *The Court of Oliver Cromwell* (Cambridge, 1977), pp. 15–31. S. Kelsey, *Inventing a Republic: The Political Culture of the English Commonwealth, 1649–1653* (Manchester, 1997), pp. 25–52.

10 D. Starkey (ed.), *The English Court from the Wars of the Roses to the Civil War* (London, 1987), p. 6

11 S. Pegge, *Curialia* (2 vols, London, 1791–1806), I, p. 68

12 See R. Crawford, *The Last Days of Charles II* (Oxford, 1909), pp. 22–49.

13 M. E. Grew, *William Bentinck and William III: The Life of Bentinck, Earl of Portland, from the Welbeck Correspondence* (London, 1924), p. 148. J. Miller, *Bourbon and Stuart: Kings and Kingship in France and England in the Seventeenth Century* (London, 1987), pp. 181–3, 230–1, 234–5. Pegge, *Curialia*, p. 68.

14 British Library (hereafter BL), Stowe MS 563, 'Bedchamber ordinances of William III' (1689), fos 2–38. J. Beattie, *The English Court in the Reign of George I* (Cambridge, 1967), p. 11.

15 Beattie, *English Court*.

16 See documents 2 and 9. Also D. Allen, 'The political function of Charles II's Chiffinch', *Huntingdon Library Quarterly*, XXXIX (1975–76), 277–90. In fact in his post as Page of the Backstairs and Keeper of the Cabinet Closet, William Chiffinch proved to be a discreet and, as far as we can tell, a significant figure in the history of the reigns of the royal brothers. He became one of the means by which Charles in particular could make his views known to the court and also a confidential go-between in all sorts of backstairs intrigue whether political, religious or sexual. Unfortunately for all historians, unlike today's royal confidants he left no memoirs.

17 F. Sheppard, 'A description of Hampton Court life', in W. J. Cameron (ed.), *Poems on Affairs of State: Augustan Satirical Verse, 1660–1714* (7 vols, New Haven, 1963–75), V, 1688–1697, p. 56.

18 H. Manners Sutton (ed.), *The Lexington Papers* (London, 1851), pp. 52, 60. Girouard, *Life in the English Country House*, p. 150. E. Gregg, *Queen Anne* (London, 1984), pp. 135–8.

19 Of value here is *A deep sigh breathed through the lodgings at Whitehall deploring the absence of the court and the miseries of the palace* (1642). Crawford, *Last Days of Charles II*. See also R. Latham and W. Matthews (eds), *The Diary of Samuel Pepys* (11 vols, London, 1970–83), X, pp. 477–84.

An answer to Timothy Touchstone at John the brewer's lodging at the sign of the naked truth at Tyburn (1679), p. 2.

20   *A deep sigh*, p. 2.

21   Ibid., p. 3. E. S. de Beer (ed.), *The Diary of John Evelyn* (6 vols, Oxford, 1955), IV, pp. 343–4.

22   See document 1. Also Pegge, *Curialia*, I, p. 62. J. C. Sainty and R. O. Bucholz, *Officials of the Royal Household, 1660–1837. Part I: Department of the Lord Chamberlain and Associated Offices* (London, 1997), pp. lii–lxvi.

23   J. H. Plumb, *The Growth of Political Stability in England, 1675–1725* (London, 1991), pp. 100–2. Also C. Roberts, 'The growth of political stability reconsidered', *Albion*, XXV (1993), 237–55.

24   Sainty and Bucholz, *Officials of the Royal Household*, pp. lii–lxvi.

25   See document 1.

26   D. Starkey 'Representation through intimacy: a study of symbolism of monarchy and court office in early modern England', in I. Lewis (ed.), *Symbols and Sentiment: Cross-cultural Studies in Symbolism* (London, 1977), pp. 187–224, gives a useful introduction to the post of the Groom of the Stole.

27   BL, Stowe MS 563, 'Bedchamber ordinances of William III', fos 2–3, 7–12. Starkey 'Representation through intimacy', pp. 187–224

28   Grew, *William Bentinck and William III*, p. 153. Also N. Japikse (ed.), *Correspondentie van Willem III en van Hans Willem Bentinck, eersten graf van Portland, eerste gedeelte het archief van Welbeck Abbey* (2 vols, The Hague, 1927–28), I, pp. xxv–xli.

29   Hoffman quoted in Grew, *William Bentinck and William III*, p. 154. Sir John Knights quoted in F. A. Ellis (ed.), *Poems on Affairs of State: Augustan Satirical Verse 1660–1714* (7 vols, New Haven, 1963–75), VI, 1697–1704, p. 224.

30   H. Hall, 'Upon the King's return from Flanders (1695)', in Cameron (ed.), *Poems on Affairs of State*, p. 455

31   M. K. Geiter and W. A. Speck (eds), *Memoirs of Sir John Reresby* (2nd edn, London, 1991), p. 208. Also see Crawford, *Last Days of Charles II*, pp. 22–49.

32   T. Paine, *Commonsense* (Harmondsworth, 1981), pp. 72, 76.

33   H. D. Molesworth, *The Princes* (London, 1969), pp. 43, 53, 57, 61. J. Hayden, *Symbol and Privilege: The Ritual Context of British Monarchy* (Tuscon, 1987). D. Cannadine, 'The context, performance and meaning of ritual: the British monarchy and the invention of tradition, c.1820–1977', in E. Hobsbawn and T. Ranger (eds), *The Invention of Tradition* (Cambridge, 1983), pp. 101–64. C. Geertz, 'Kings and charisma: reflections on the symbolics of power', in J. Ben-David and T. N. Clark, *Culture and its Creators: Essays in Honour of Edward Shils* (Chicago, 1977), pp. 150–71.

34   E. H. Kantorowicz, *The King's Two Bodies: A Study of Medieval British Theology* (Princeton, 1957). P. Hammond, 'The King's two bodies: representations of Charles II', in J. Black and J. Gregory (eds), *Culture, Politics and Society in Britain, 1660–1800* (Manchester, 1991), pp. 13–48.

35   Burke, *Fabrication of Louis XIV*, p. 87.

36 J. R. Jones, 'The building works and court style of William and Mary', *Journal of Garden History*, VIII (1988), 1–13. R. P. Maccubbin and M. Hamilton-Philip (eds), *The Age of William III and Mary II: Power, Politics and Patronage* (Williamsburg VA, 1989), pp. 8–10.

37 Halifax, 'The Spencer House journals', in H. C. Foxcroft, *The Life and Letters of Sir George Savile, Bart., First Marquis of Halifax* (2 vols, London, 1898), II, p. 204. G. Burnet, *A History of My Own Times* (6 vols, Oxford, 1833), IV, p. 3.

38 W. Wycherley, *The Plain Dealer*, in W. Wycherley, *The Country Wife and Other Plays* (Oxford, 1996), I, i, lines 1–4, 8, p. 292.

39 Ibid., I, i, line 8, p. 292.

40 William Cavendish, earl of Newcastle, in T. P. Slaughter (ed.), *Ideology and Politics on the Eve of the Restoration: Newcastle's Advice to Charles II* (Philadelphia, 1984), pp. 44–5. Latham and Matthews (eds), *Diary of Samuel Pepys*, IV, p. 1. The Venetian resident in December 1673 complained about the lack of ceremony at the Caroline court. See A. B. Hinds (ed.), *Calendar of State Papers Venetian*, 1673–75 (London, 1947), p. 86.

41 M. Bloch, *The Royal Touch: Sacred Monarchy and Scrofula in England and France* (London, 1973), pp. 211–12. P. Hammond, 'Mystical politics: the imagery of Charles II's coronation', in P. J. Korshin (ed.), *Studies in Change and Revolution: Aspects of English Intellectual History 1640–1800* (Menston, 1972), pp. 19–42. C. A. Edie, 'The public face of royal ritual: sermons, medals and civil ceremony in late Stuart coronations', *Huntingdon Library Quarterly*, LIII (1990), 311–36. Howarth, *Images of Rule*. E. Muir, *Ritual in Early Modern Europe* (Cambridge, 1997).

42 Geiter and Speck (eds), *Memoirs of Sir John Reresby*, p. 259. The Venetian ambassador observed another problem with some court etiquette in December 1673. There was so much resentment over the newly installed Mary of Modena's grant of a 'tabouret opposite the Queen' that many of the native born English ladies stayed away from a ballet and it had to be cancelled. See Hinds (ed.), *Calendar of State Papers Venetian*, 1673–75, p. 188.

43 See C. H. Josten (ed.), *Elias Ashmole 1617–1692: Autobiographical and Historical Notes, His Correspondence and Other Contemporary Sources Relating to his Life and Work* (5 vols, Oxford, 1967), III, 1661–72, pp. 879–80, 912–22. C. Mukerji, *Territorial Ambitions and the Gardens of Versailles* (Cambridge, 1997), pp. 198–203, 223–39.

3

Power, government and faction

Processes of power

For a political historian the processes of power, the means by which it is captured and used, are invariably important factors in any political system. The golden key to success in the intimate political world of the later Stuart court was to gain access to the ear and the person of the monarch. By such access a courtier could sway the monarch's opinions, advance his or her interests at court and formulate policy. Regular access enabled men and women to argue for their own policies, for their friends, for their family, for their 'party', or for their clients. It allowed them to become brokers for the distribution of the crown's favour and patronage in the form of land, title, honour, wealth and office. In other words it allowed them to govern. In physical terms, as we have seen, access was deliberately restricted by the design of the court system, the nature of the household and its officers, and subject to other pressures from official and unofficial rules and regulations, custom, guards and forms of conduct. For the majority of courtiers, those who sought power but had little access to the monarch, the choice was inevitable: they gravitated towards those who possessed such access and who could offer gratuities, service or support in exchange for their clientage. In effect they sought access to those who had access to the monarch. The earl of Chesterfield once likened this system to a great chain. This connected monarchy through various gradations to the lowest levels of the court and government, and because courtiers were always seeking to climb this chain there came into being, particularly under the later Stuart monarchy, a web of client–patron relationships at court.[1]

The aim of any client–patron web was proximity to the monarch and the first necessity for any enterprising courtier was to get as close to the monarch as possible. There were a number of ways in which this could be achieved. If the courtier failed to attract the monarch's attention through his or her personal charm, or via the brokerage of some other person, then one further approach for a male courtier was by gaining and holding an office at court or in the government. The actual usefulness of an individual in a post of significance could easily assist a courtier along the axis of honour towards power. The more useful an individual became, the more chance of his promotion. Of course there were a number of means by which office could be attained. Gerald Aylmer has classically delineated the three basic forms in his works on the Stuart and Republican civil service. Here we find patrimony, or inheriting office; purchase, actually buying office (with the monarch's permission); and perhaps the most significant of the three, acquiring office through patronage, that is being given office by another more significant individual, who in turn held their office as a result of someone's patronage higher up the chain, which led ultimately to the fount of all office: the monarch.[2]

Client–patron relations often proved to be the most significant fluid of court politics in the widest sense. As the demand for honours and office outstripped supply at court, conflict and competition became inevitable. The result was a factional form of politics, in which various groups or individuals banded together in a client–patron relationship and competed with others in a similar relationship for the axis of honour. The actual mechanics of faction lay in groups of individuals, invariably centring around a great patron at court, a minister, or friend to the monarch. These groups bonded together in alliances, sometimes temporarily, to attack others and to seize control, wherever possible and where the monarch permitted, of the levers of power.

For the most part the aim of the great courtiers and ministers at court was to gain and then to retain power. Most sought to use their influence at court and their persuasive techniques with the monarch to ensure their lines of policy were followed. They sought to exploit their direct access to the King to ensure that their 'creatures' gained office, thus surrounding the monarch with their clients. They also used court intrigue to restrict their opponents' access and, if possible, force dangerous rivals out of court government. As leaders, the patrons inevitably sought to use their resources effectively in order to build up as large a following as possible. The more power and access a patron had, the more rewards and credit he could give out to his supporters. A successful patron could even go on to control the government temporarily. On a personal level such activities undoubtedly brought with them a sense of power, and pandered to the personal vanity of the great man, elements that should never be underestimated. At the same time, of course, other great men at court were using similar practices to bolster their own position.

In general the client–patron structures within the later Stuart court should not be seen as simple pyramids, but rather as a series of overlapping circles whose focus lay upon the great man at the centre: their patron, and whose focus in turn was upon his monarch. The standard client–patron relationship was thus never a straightforward one, nor was it simply bi-polar; it contained a number of connections and sub-groups, the limits of which depended upon where an individual stood in the scheme. Factional groupings did not just include the great man and his followers, who were tied to each other by bonds of subordination and favour (or hoped-for favour). They could also include the patron's friends, who gave their aid and assistance; servants, who held positions of trust in the great man's household and whose position could bring access; and lastly there were always the patron's relatives, eagerly using their blood ties to gain office, power or favour and who, at least, had a claim upon the great man to further his own family interests.[3]

All clients or followers were potential social and political animals, intent upon climbing the slippery pole of status and thereby gaining favour. As such their loyalty was rarely unconditional and tended to last only so long as their needs were met. Although such needs would naturally run parallel with those of their patron for some of the time, following a failing patron was never a profitable business for any client and moreover it could be dangerous, as it could lead to the abyss of social and political death, loss of honour and removal from office, all of which naturally lay in wait for any courtier whose schemes or reputation collapsed.[4] Fear of failure appears to have been a major preoccupation of most clients most of the time and the client-courtier's life was inevitably a tense one, full of passion, envy of others, hyper-sensitivity to personal slights, whether real or imagined, and even paranoia. The fact that much of the courtier's life, like that of the soldier in war, was spent waiting about with other courtiers invariably meant boredom, and courtiers who frequently had a lot of time on their hands were often left to worry, engage in gossip and quarrel with each other.[5]

In such a hothouse community there was a continual engagement in both positive and negative tactics by courtiers. In positive terms the greatest talent a client could have when seeking favour or a place was to be useful to the patron. It could, depending upon the circumstances, involve much flattery and sycophancy. The marquis of Halifax ironically noted that anyone with 'too much pride to be a creature ... had better stay at home [for a] man who will rise at court must begin by creeping upon all four[s]; a place at court, like a place in heaven, is to be got by being much upon one's knees'.[6] A good-looking person, who was fluent in wit and conversation and able to amuse, would often go far. Still personal charm was not everything, although Roger Ascham had noted that one needed the ability 'To laugh, to lie, to flatter, to face Four ways in court to win men's grace'.[7] Some technical skills, an ability actually to do something, might also prove useful. A good secretary's position was not to be frowned upon, for it usually brought with it day-to-day contact with the patron himself, and knowledge of his business life, which was usually a valuable commodity. John Evelyn noted of Sir Joseph Williamson's rise in Lord Arlington's favour that the earl 'loving his ease more than his business … remitted all to his man Williamson, & in a short time let him so into the secret of affairs, that (as his lordship himself told me) there was a kind of necessity to advance him'.[8]

For an outside observer there often appears to have been little objectivity in who rose or who fell in a patron's favour. Much depended upon the patron's moods, which one tried to anticipate, and his whims, which one couldn't. Moreover, as demand was inevitably high and the resources of patronage were invariably limited, clients could usually only gain by vaulting over their rivals, especially when they stumbled through illness or misfortune. The negative side to the client's life therefore was to seize upon every opportunity which fell one's way to cast aspersions on rivals and adversaries, abuse them, either subtly or blatantly, to the patron when it was safe to do so, and engineer quarrels either directly or as a third party. By so doing one could gain advantage for oneself. In the great game of client life much could be lost or won by the possession of such skills.

Brokerage in court life remained slightly different from patronage in that it may be properly defined as 'influence peddling'. Unlike the patron, the broker was a middleman, putting individuals in touch with each other either through direct introductions or acting on a customer's behalf. Again in contrast to the client–patron relationship, it did not resemble the semi-permanent relationship of such affairs. Most of those at court acted as brokers or negotiators between those who were seeking a place, or office, and those who had such a commodity to give away at some time in their lives. In doing so, brokers tended to trade upon their own credit, their status or contacts with persons of influence and their willingness to use their position for personal gain. While the broker's commission could be financial, it could also revolve around concepts such as personal status, prestige and even being seen as having the ability to affect opinion at court, which in itself gave a certain kind of kudos. Brokers did not necessarily hold major office, although they could be more influential if they did, for proximity to the monarch, or those close to the monarch, was usually the most important factor in a broker's life.[9]

The career of Sir Stephen Fox illustrates how part of this system operated at one level within the court.[10] Aside from being a royal financier in the 1660s and 1670s, Fox held the post of Clerk of the Green Cloth from 1661 to 1689 in the household below stairs. Primarily an office that made a useful contribution to his income, it was also a post from which he could exercise some individual patronage, and act as a broker for those who wished to sell offices which they held as a gift, of right or through reversion. While Fox's own office was a relatively minor one in the world of the court, it naturally gave some access to a number of lesser positions and to his superiors who had other connections. Fox, by occupying it, could thus offer his advice to them as to how vacant offices could be filled. Through his good offices Fox was able to insert many a relative and friend into posts in the household below stairs. His brother John, for example, gained the office of Clerk of the Spicery, and then in turn passed it on to his own son; three of Sir Stephen's nephews entered the household in minor posts in 1682, alongside the husband of his niece and the latter's son-in-law. Fox's servants were also given positions. These offices were not very lucrative, but each could be a step to preferment, or a safe old age, and they fulfilled Sir Stephen's responsibility to both his relatives and immediate servants.

Another example of a broker in operation is the career of Daniel O'Neill, who was a Groom of the Bedchamber in the early 1660s and was thus in day-to-day contact with the King. The Irishman O'Neill frequently acted as a broker between ministers, courtiers and even for the King himself. His credit for doing so led to an increased status for himself at court. In 1663, for example, when the command in a troop of horse in Ireland became available due to the death of Lord Falkland, O'Neill used his skills to engineer a new appointment. Although the duke of Ormonde had already asked the King to give the place to another, Charles passed the word to O'Neill to inform the duke that it would be better for all concerned if the place went to Arlington's brother and moreover that Ormonde should be seen to offer it himself to Arlington rather than the King 'will him to do it'. In doing so it would 'give your grace an opportunity of obliging Mr Secretary', who, he said, 'believed your Grace was not kind to him'. O'Neill reported that the King commanded 'me to say nothing of it to Mr Secretary'.[11] O'Neill therefore acted as a middleman for the King in this ingenious but not uncommon scheme.

Faction

While the aims of factions at court were often particular or peculiar to the circumstances in which they had been born and in which they found themselves, in general all factions had some common core aims. Naturally individual aggrandisement in terms of wealth, power and status, the classic Weberian triumvirate, was most significant for both client and patron.[12] In general the political 'lone wolf' was a very rare commodity, for a campaign of aggrandisement inevitably meant that one acquired followers who in turn gained something from the relationship. To paraphrase John Donne, at court 'No man [was] an island, entire of itself'. In other cases there might be a particular political, ideological or religious cause that united individuals. Clearly all factions were united in some way by an eagerness to gain power and, as much as was possible, to seize a monopoly of office and position.

Interaction between factions at court was commonplace. Day-to-day contact and rivalry at court inevitably caused friction, for such factions were, of course, competing for many of the same things. In itself this provides an interesting parallel to Thomas Hobbes's views in *Leviathan* (1651) of both the state of nature and mankind's 'perpetual and restless desire of power after power that ceaseth only in death', a motive which Hobbes, an *habitué* of the court himself, thought primary to the human condition.[13] Occasionally such activities could cause friction within factions, especially if the great man found his fortunes at court crumbling, something which could occur quite rapidly on occasion. While some factions provided a relatively stable period of mutual advancement, drawn together by ideological objectives, more commonly the factions at the later Stuart court were unstable, a fluid association of sometimes temporary and particularlist alliances which could wither and die once goals were achieved. Indeed the very fluid situation that prevailed in court politics in the latter half of the seventeenth century enabled clients to shop around for new patrons in what was effectively a free market. Only in the 1690s with the construction of some ideological boundaries into Whig and Tory did this market become more restricted. Between such factions there was a wide range of relations, from co-operation to some collective end, to life and death struggles which would inevitably cause a political crisis. On a day-to-day basis, as we shall see, much depended on the personnel of the groups involved, their personal rivalries, political and religious issues at hand, or the struggle for offices to be filled. When these factions began to emerge as parties in the 1680s, the struggle became yet more bitter.[14]

To some extent all factions were products of the monarch's favour. They could be created, encouraged, outmanoeuvred or destroyed by the monarch. They existed on sufferance and the extent of this activity depended upon the monarch, who would have relations, favourites, friends and mistresses to consider. In general it became a truism that a wise monarch would not let any one faction dominate for very long. If he or she did so then they might well fall into the power of that group and allow them to win the game. The losers in such cases might then turn to alternative sources of power, or even violent means, to regain control. It was significant that generally the later Stuart monarchs, with the exception of James II (and it was arguably one of the factors which was to cost him his throne), sought to balance factions or play one off against another. Charles II became a master at the complex dance of court politics, sometimes bamboozling himself into the bargain. William III, on the other hand, was proud of being a 'trimmer' and strove for balance in the 1690s, although in the end he failed to achieve it.[15]

Ultimately individual monarchs set the tone for these struggles at court. Those who chose to be 'distant' monarchs tried to remain aloof from the game of factional politics. Those who sought to be 'participatory' monarchs engaged as players in the game. The task of personal monarchs in early modern England was to rule, so inevitably their style of management was crucial. Some English monarchs, of whom James VI and I was a notable example, had in the past chosen to rule through a favourite, a choice which often gave them greater freedom because the favourite took the blame and the monarch the credit. Others tried to rule by themselves and allowed no freedom of manoeuvre. Some of course were too weak as personalities and let the court rule them. All of them, however, sought to increase their *gloire*, the very quintessence of princeliness. In the end, all who engaged in faction were servants of their monarch and could be hired or fired as he or she chose, so that all power finally depended upon the monarch's whims.[16]

The Buckingham faction, 1667–1674

The faction led in the mid to late 1660s and early 1670s by George Villiers, second duke of Buckingham, provides one example of such an organisation in operation. Although this faction operated on a variety of levels both regional as well as national, in Buckingham's years of influence there is little doubt that some of its origins lay in Yorkshire politics. Through his wife the duke was related to the Yorkshire magnate and former parliamentary general Thomas Fairfax, and he also possessed land in the county. This move also gave him entrée into the world of the Yorkshire gentry. By the early 1660s Buckingham's appointment as Lord Lieutenant of the county also confirmed his status there as a local magnate with court connections. The result was that he was automatically someone to be cultivated by the local gentry and as such soon gathered around him a series of clients. These included Sir Thomas Gower, Sir Henry Belasye, Sir William Lowther and Sir Thomas Osborne, the future earl of Danby.[17] Of these men Osborne in particular stood out, for with Buckingham's assistance the enterprising Yorkshireman soon rose through the ranks of West Yorkshire politics into national prominence.

Certainly even in his early days as a Buckingham client it was Osborne who stood out in a number of ways from the crowds who flocked to join the duke's cause. But some of these men are worth noting by way of contrast. They included Sir Richard Temple, 'a nimble tongued fellow', who had shifted his cause to the duke after the demise of the earl of Bristol's political career and who would again move out of Buckingham's orbit in the 1670s to join Arlington. Edward Seymour, another of the duke's men, took the lead against Clarendon and Ormonde in 1667–68. He was pro-toleration, even citing Thomas Hobbes to sustain his arguments, but this did not prevent him becoming Speaker of the House in 1673; by this stage he was also friendly to the court and Danby, as well as disillusioned by Buckingham's antics. William Garway, another tolerationist who remained a 'bold speaker' in the House, also joined the Buckingham group. Lastly there was Sir Robert Howard. He was openly anti-French and anti-Catholic, but he remained something of a bridge-builder in politics, and a man who swapped sides with apparent ease.[18] Self-interest and the needs of the moment, as with most of their kind, largely motivated these men. While some favoured a form of toleration, most, like Osborne, were frustrated by the hold that Clarendon had upon power in London circles. They joined the duke because he too hated Clarendon and hoped to control the government after the Chancellor's fall, and in doing so they might achieve the much-coveted offices in government.

Below these men were a number of lightweight courtiers and 'bully boys' whom the duke could also use and associate with from time to time. Always a gatherer of the strange and wilful, Buckingham's pack also included some lesser luminaries whose odd careers interacted at times with Buckingham's own activities. John Heydon, an astrologer, Thomas Braithwaite, a former Cromwellian, and Thomas Blood, a professional adventurer, were all part of his entourage at various times.[19] Sir Charles Wolsely was a former Cromwellian courtier who advocated liberty of conscience, while Martin Clifford, the duke's secretary, was both a scholar and a wit. Thomas Sprat, Buckingham's chaplain, and John Wilkins, a well-established churchman, were both advocates of scientific enquiry and reasonable Christianity. The most notorious follower of Buckingham was perhaps John Wildman, a former Leveller and political opponent of Cromwell in the 1650s. He also held true to republican ideals and came into Buckingham's orbit as the duke sought connections with the remnants of the previous era, as well as non-conformists. Wildman was also notable for his business acumen and he was originally hired to resolve the problems of the duke's notoriously bad finances.[20] Lastly there was Edward Christian, a highly strung former royalist, who had begun life as the duke's rent-collector on his estates but was soon promoted to become his chamberlain and the chief financial figure in his affairs. In the end this proved the duke's undoing, for Christian was corrupt above the normal sense of the word in the period and managed to embezzle large sums of money from Buckingham's estates before his dismissal in 1673. By 1676 he had approached Danby and been taken into the earl's service.[21]

In 1667 the ball of government seemed to most observers to lie in the hands of the anti-Clarendonians, as the duke of Buckingham, his friends, clients and followers were soon labelled.[22] With Buckingham's fortunes in the ascendant, for he took credit for Clarendon's fall, it was thought by many that he would now 'govern all' and lead this group of new men in a ministry able to achieve Charles II's desires. Unfortunately Buckingham ultimately proved himself to be a political gambler par excellence and such aims as he possessed were not only a reflection of his privileged background, but harked back to the old-style noble politician of some bygone era. Even his somewhat pragmatic commitment to toleration and his fashionable creed for 'reasonable' Christianity was a fad, and, as with other fads of the duke, merely a useful vehicle for his own *gloire*. It was the latter characteristic that remained the main motivation in all of his affairs. Buckingham was a witty, over-privileged and politically unstable man, who expected honour and power rather than striving for them. A dilettante in the world of politics, the duke was uncomfortable with rigid political doctrines and believed that the normal rules of politics simply did not apply to him. In any case politics was only one of his many interests and it seems clear that to be seen to be in power was to him often more significant than to do anything with such power. His poor judgement was eventually to bring him dismissal and ridicule and in the end his was a career of much sound, fury and frustration with little by way of actual achievement. Apparently in office as parliamentary manager in the wake of Clarendon's fall, Buckingham soon squandered his chances. As Sir John Reresby noted:

> The King consulted him chiefly in all matters of moment, the foreign ministers applied themselves to him before they were admitted to have a audience of the king ... but he was soe unfitt for this ... by reason of his giving himself up to his pleasures, that (turning the night into day and the day into night) he neglected both his

attendance upon the King, the receiving of ministers and other persons that waited to speak to him, and indeed all sort of business, so that he lasted not long.[23]

As Buckingham's standing rose at court, however, it was Osborne who most seized his opportunities. While he acted as Buckingham's spokesman in the House of Commons and defended him there, he also took minor government office, which he received in turn as a favour from his patron. Osborne was thus able to play his part in the struggle against the Clarendonians, the removal of Ormonde and the disgrace of Coventry. As a client Osborne appears to have taken a philosophical line on his patron's activities.[24] It is doubtful whether he ever really shared the duke's aims, such as they were, and in fact once in power Osborne's politics more than once resembled a robust form of Clarendonianism and were to appeal to many a country gentleman, at least for a time. By that stage, however, Osborne had realised just how much a handicap Buckingham really was in the formation of constructive policies for the state, and having gained some notice at court he used his industry and energy to bring himself still further into the charmed circle of government. As ever, this delicate political dance soon brought him the possibility of becoming a rival to his patron. Indeed with Clarendon removed from office, the duke's performances at court, in Parliament and in his personal life quickly brought him into disrepute. He had policies of a sort to follow, he was pro-toleration and in terms of foreign affairs quick to perceive the 'undoubted interest of England is trade ... [and] without a powerful navy we should be prey to our neighbours ... From hence it does follow that we ought not to suffer any other nations to be our equals at sea.'[25] But most of all he longed for glory and command of armies, which naturally enough the shrewd Charles, well aware of Buckingham's shortcomings, never gave him.

From 1669 to 1674 Buckingham's limited role kept him away from real power and he became an early ministerial casualty in the Dutch war. Additionally the laboriously created faction which Buckingham led was to prove as unstable as the man himself, being largely held together by the duke's own needs, energy and passions, and when these faltered in the 1670s, alongside his championship of the disaffected, then so did his faction. For despite his continued prominence at court, Buckingham never gained any major political office, other than the token Master of the Horse, and was in continual trouble with the King due to his antics. From 1674 to 1679 he realigned himself in conjunction with the country element in Parliament and with Shaftesbury, who became a rival for its affections. While Buckingham pretended to dictate to this group of country politicians where he thought they should be going, Shaftesbury seems to have guided them where they actually wanted to go. Buckingham made a number of unsuccessful attempts to undermine his former client, but with Danby's fall and his own disgrace in 1680, mainly over accusations of sodomy, Buckingham's career came to a halt. Even before this, Buckingham had little to offer his clients. Unable himself to progress any further along the axis of honour, he was a man quickly forced to resort to futile spoiling tactics against other ministers. So it was that Osborne quietly drifted away from his former patron towards the real source of power at court – the King – and in 1673 Osborne was available to be promoted by Charles to be Lord Treasurer and earl of Danby.[26]

Government, office and Parliament

One aim of courtiers and politicians alike, as we have seen, was the capture of office, whether in the royal household or in the administration, although as the two were linked certain offices became more privileged than others. At the heart of government lay the central executive of monarch and ministers who dealt with the day-to-day running of the state, its finances, administration, domestic, religious and foreign polices, and military and naval affairs. Throughout the seventeenth century these posts were undergoing a transition from mere outgrowths of the royal household to modern-day bureaucracy and ministerial government. It occurred on a wide variety of fronts, with some crucial innovations taking place in the English Republic, continuing though the Restoration and culminating in the 'administrative revolution' of the 1690s. In effect English bureaucracy, while still somewhat primitive by modern standards, became increasingly complex, needing mechanics to service it as well as overseers (in the form of ministerial office) to supervise its processes.[27]

Ministerial and administrative developments were thus a part of the process of court government for they allowed access points for individuals to rise within the society. The idea of a chief minister in later Stuart monarchy, rather than a prime minister in the modern sense, emerged mainly as a result of the capture of an office which brought with it the chance to become a chief adviser to the monarch. In the later Stuart period these forays into ministerial government were generally the result of the intrusion of a forceful personality into government rather than the significance of the actual office itself, although some offices were ultimately to prove more desirable than others. In many senses all of the later Stuart monarchs were more likely to become their own first minister with no 'prime' minster as such, and although some historians find this strange, contemporaries did not. An active and enterprising king was usually desired by all concerned. A weak king meant control by an individual or group and thus instability. Only with the emergence of party as a force did the desire for a 'prime' minister who could control a majority in the House of Commons become more important. However, even an active king had to take advice from the ambitious and forceful personalities who often surrounded him, and as monarchs were unable, or occasionally unwilling, to do everything themselves, they were forced to have chief advisers. Such personalities could be located either in the court or ministerial office, although later in the period some hold upon an actual departmental office did become essential.

Of the offices of state that began to flower under the later Stuarts, some were still firmly located in the court structure, such as the already described post of Groom of the Stole. Others, however, had begun that climb towards departmental authority and separation from the court that was to culminate in the major arrival of the independent offices of government in the nineteenth and twentieth centuries. One perceptible trend was the desire by various monarchs to place particular posts in commission. Here groups of politicians could be promoted to sit at a board and collectively perform the relevant tasks of the office. This promotion of collective responsibility came about mainly because of the fear that a major office held by one man could make that one man much too powerful. But this trend also allowed the placement of experts on particular boards. Going into commission, therefore, was a fate that particularly befell the Treasury and the Admiralty, as both were places where the 'expert' could prove to be a significant addition to its work.

There is no doubt that from the 1670s it was the Treasury that began to hold the key to government and the offices there became the ones most desired by energetic politicians and courtiers. As such offices literally held the financial purse strings over the rest of the regime and with financial considerations becoming ever more paramount, so the office of Lord Treasurer was usually the goal of the most aspiring politicians. After the failures of Southampton in the early 1660s, Charles II placed the office in commission until it came to Clifford in 1672 and Danby in 1673. After the fall of the latter, however, the office again lapsed into commission. James II, who looked equally askance at ambitious politicians or rivals in government after Rochester's fall, sought to keep the Lord Treasurership in commission during his reign. William III, following his uncle's views, again placed it in commission after 1688, from whence it did not return as a major office under his reign.[28]

At the Restoration the office of Secretary of State, previously held by John Thurloe alone under the Cromwellian regime, reverted to its old pre-war division. During the period that followed the two secretaries theoretically split the business of the office between them. In practice, however, one or the other invariably came to dominate the scene. The Secretary of State posts were thus made into major offices by the presence of such forceful personalities as Arlington and Sunderland, but could lapse into more functional roles under lesser lights or a strong-minded monarch. The offices' role in domestic and foreign policy, however, made them particularly desirable places and the part played by the secretariat in administration was a significant one.[29] Only later did the work of the twin secretariat become so complex that it divided into three and then a multitude of departmental posts. The Lord Chancellorship, used by Clarendon from 1660 to 1667 as a power base, was located in the legal world and included the role of Speaker of the House of Lords, but it never became really powerful again after Clarendon's tenure. Other offices of state were of lesser importance, but still significant enough to be fought over.[30]

Increasingly what the monarch came to look for in a chief adviser was the ability to manage Parliament. As a burgeoning new force in the political world, the members of this august body looked askance at attempts to govern them. And it was the role of the political manager post-1660 which became a crucial development in the government of the state. This 'third force' in government, as Geoffrey Holmes has described it, was to prove a significant development in the reigns of both William and Anne, but the idea of a political manager can perhaps be traced back to the career of Danby, if not before to the career of Arlington and even that of Buckingham.[31] It became the norm that those who wished something from the government had to go through these courtiers, middlemen, or managers, particularly after the reconstruction of the Williamite ministry in 1692 and especially after the return of the earl of Sunderland to power.

It was the born-again Sunderland in fact who set the tone for the role of the new court managers under William with his aptly expressed philosophy of 'What matter who serves his Majesty, so long as his Majesty is served'.[32] Acting as a broker in politics and refusing office until he became Lord Chamberlain in 1697, Sunderland's counsels 'behind the curtain' were able to negotiate the final arrival of the Whig Junto in the state's political life, while at the same time remaining free of official responsibility. In their position as managers, men such as Sunderland, Shrewsbury, Godolphin and Marlborough combined the roles of courtier and political officer to form a new breed called 'undertakers'. They were men who sought to put their loyalty to the monarchy above any allegiance to party, and even, to some extent, their own interests. It was to prove a dangerous but indispensable position in the era of the first political parties.

If the political managers sought to promote stability in government so that its business could be carried through, then this business mainly lay in financing the Stuart monarchy's penchant for war in Europe. Achieving a degree of co-operation between the Parliament and the court in such matters was the aim. The court had some advantages over Parliament through its power of dissolution and electoral interference, but getting a good, that is 'packed', Parliament was only the beginning of the affair; the court then had to keep these men in line. Within the Commons itself the government could expect to control only a small group of MPs who made up a loyal party, or as it came to be seen a 'court party'. They were close friends or personal dependants of the managers and non-party groups of placemen or 'civil servants', being the normal cannon fodder in such affairs. In other respects the court's relationship with Parliament was one of negotiation, secret deals and in some cases outright corruption.

The development of some form of cabinet and parliamentary government under the later Stuarts seems in retrospect an inevitable one, although most of the Stuart monarchs disliked the potential of cabinets. Certainly the cabinets which had existed prior to 1690 had generally garnered a bad reputation as a whole. They were coupled with the much more pejorative ideas of a 'cabal', secrecy and covert designs, and, more significantly for Parliament, an inability to pin down bad ministerial advice, but they had proved necessary for business. After 1660 the Privy Council, which Clarendon had tried to revive as the centre of Restoration government, had shown itself to be something of a spent force. This traditional and therefore much-lauded body proved to be so unwieldy and so prone to leaks that both Charles II and James II had increasingly bypassed its discussions and maintained it only for formal decisions. They began to seek advice from more manageable and smaller groups of ministers who could keep business to themselves. Under Charles and James such groups had a variety of titles – Committee of Foreign Affairs, Cabal or cabinet – and although usually short-lived affairs and dominated by the monarch, they established a new trend of confidential consultation and joint decision-making in English government. The trends in William's reign continued the development. The creation of the Lords Justices from 1690 to give Mary advice when William was absent on campaign in Europe was one example. Though arguments have been intense amongst historians of the period over the exact meaning of such groupings, there seems little doubt that the Lords Justices themselves were a foretaste of the cabinet government to come in the eighteenth century.

It must be said that William remained a reluctant convert to this type of government, and the idea of forming a ministry from one party or the other was still alien to him. Also the intense rivalry amongst the ministers of the government, based in equal proportions on personal dislike and party rivalry, as well as the competition to be included at any cost on a committee close to the King, meant that any hope for unity in such a body was too ambitious a project, but the form was a tenacious survivor. William also followed his preferred style of government by using a form of closeting, with the consultation of ministers on a one-to-one basis. This had been a long-standing arrangement for the Stuart monarchs, but William's decision to be his own master meant that it grew in significance. Even so, by 1694 meetings of the chief counsellors themselves were regular enough to be noted and even William agreed 'the necessity of a Cabinet council' to monitor affairs in his absence.[33] Of course conflicts still took place over who was to be included and which of the helpful supporters of the regime, if any, could safely be left out. Nor were William's cabinets ever fully taken into the King's confidences or allowed that much independence. As a rule, when in the country the King followed his predecessors: consulting where he saw fit and making the final decisions himself. William was also reluctant to share his power with any 'prime' or first minister, although, as we have seen, he did come round to employing political managers, such as Sunderland, who often appear to have performed a similar function. Indeed only Sunderland and William Bentinck, earl of Portland, came close to the position of first minister under William. Given the Dutchman's background, though, he was wise to decline any such station. Whatever their situation in a ministry, all of the chief advisers to monarchy remained in a somewhat shaky position due to the continual backstairs intrigues which went on at court and the increasing dangers of Parliament.

Female politicians

As the historiography of the later seventeenth century has begun to move away from its more traditional channels, there has also been a shift from defining politics only through its formal structures and institutions. A more intimate and informal world based upon personal relationships, patronage and kinship has often been revealed in high politics as a result. In the 'politics of intimacy' which made up the later Stuart court, the role of women has often been neglected. We have, as Karl von den Steinen so pithily put it, usually to choose between books on 'politics without women or [books on] women without politics'.[34] The reason behind this absence has been that information on women's political activities is all too often filtered through the opinions of men, in which rumour, gossip and outright misogyny often contend with the truth.[35] Having said this, it is true that the reality of women's political influence must to some extent always be measured at one remove: through the failures or successes of the activities of the men with whom they associated. Moreover, given the reluctance of men of the period to admit any such influence, it is often difficult to trace. There was certainly a prejudice against the idea of the female politician, ranging from the Restoration satire, which as we will see often concentrated on the traditional beliefs in women's rampant sexuality, to the Victorian historians who trivialised the female role so much that the ladies of the court were often restricted to mere walk-on parts in a masculine world.

That the early modern scene, even in the court, was very much still a male-dominated society there is no doubt. The woman's role was restricted in terms of its structural possibilities: lack of voting rights, or rights to hold office, early marriage and frequent pregnancies. Nor were educated women encouraged at the Restoration court. The move against the 'learned lady' at court had indeed begun as early as the reign of James I.[36] Yet quite often the very informal nature of court politics, especially in the reign of Charles II, did allow opportunities for the female politician. In the top rank were those royal princesses and mistresses who could arguably influence the politics of the day; underneath were the plethora of other aristocratic women who had their way to make in the world and were out to win the prizes which were on offer there: land, title, cash, or husbands who possessed all three. Moreover, as Lord Chesterfield was to note, 'women [were] very apt to be mingled in court intrigue'.[37] In a number of ways, therefore, the world of the court provided a platform for a certain group of elite women to advance themselves beyond the norm of Restoration society. While it clearly lacked many of the restrictions that were placed upon women elsewhere in society at this time, one must be circumspect in drawing too many conclusions from this atypical liberality. Women were still seen as dangerous elements in the body politic, damaging not only to the monarchy but the state itself. Governed by 'unnatural lusts', they were the wild card in politics. Naturally women also entered the court on masculine terms and were ultimately restricted by the patriarchal male society as to how far they could penetrate its heartland of rank and privilege. In addition the familiar double standards still operated. Their sexual conduct, for example, was regarded with suspicion, and was therefore more prone to condemnation than that of their male counterparts.

As courtiers women were constrained in other ways. Mme de Motteville was to note that the houses of monarchs were 'like a large market place where it is necessary to trade for the maintenance of the life and for the interests of those to whom we are bound'.[38] The women of the court were rarely able to act as lone wolves making decisions for themselves; they were bound into, and entangled by, a network of family relationships. Their movement along the axis of honour towards the goal of the monarch would, or so it was often hoped, also drag alongside them members of their family. Indeed many of the women of the court were deliberately used as family vehicles to produce this effect.

While a number of the women of the court fell by the wayside or settled for being the wives or mistresses of the lesser mortals who inhabited the court, a few made it to the top of the pile and became mistresses to the King himself. Sarah Churchill, the duchess of Marlborough, and no mean politician herself, was to note that 'Women signify nothing unless they are the mistress of a first minister'.[39] There was little moral condemnation of a man who kept a mistress, although not vice versa, as witness the many references to 'rakes', who were given a largely positive treatment in the literature, as opposed to 'whores', who were linked with negative attributes. It was unusual for men not to possess a mistress, and the King tended to indulge this passion more than most. While there was no semi-official position of *maîtresse-en-titre*, as had developed in France, in the English court there were many rivals for the place of 'prime mistress' so to speak. In some respects it was a role similar to that of a royal favourite, likely to involve intrigue, influence and patronage, and it was thought that women's passionate, imaginative, sentimental and intuitive natures suited them to this aspect of the role.

In the role of mistress the functions of sexual partner, confidante and mediator often apparently contended with one another for dominance. It was widely believed that a woman such as Portsmouth or Cleveland could have an influence upon Charles II, and that her associates could seek to manipulate this. In any case competition to catch Charles II's eye was intense at the best of times, and a pretty face and some skill, sexual or otherwise, in addition to some intelligence, were necessary attributes. In fact the courtier Sir John Reresby noted that many of the women Charles was involved with often 'seemed to be the aggressors'. Ever generous with his favours, Charles tended to accept that as monarch women would fling themselves in his general direction, although he was still relatively restrained in catching them.[40] This was not true of his brother, who was later guilt-ridden as a consequence; his nephew William III's relations with women remained obscure enough for (unfounded) rumours of homosexuality to be current during his reign.

In general the tendency of historians, mostly men it has to be added, has been to dismiss the mistresses of Charles II as sexual toys which the King played with and then discarded.[41] This will clearly not suffice. Charles of course spent a large part of his life with many of these women and whether we like it or not they do at times appear to have played more than a purely sexual role in his unscrupulous calculations. Often they were used merely to ward off too close an interest in his activities in the manner of a favourite. Alternatively they could be used as a route for intelligence on the activities of the court itself, or for secret messages from a minister. When a careful court navigator such as Sir Henry Bennet, earl of Arlington, chose to cultivate a friendship with both Cleveland and Portsmouth, some influence must have been evident. As Halifax noted, 'A mistress either dextrous in herself or well instructed by those that are so, may be very useful to her friends'.[42]

Some of Charles's mistresses, most notably the notorious Elinor Gwyn or Moll Davis, do on the whole appear to have had little, if any, influence upon the King. These 'lewd and bouncing orange girls and actresses', as Arlington called them, merely remained willing, albeit greedy, bed partners. Others, however, especially Barbara Villiers, duchess of Cleveland, and Louise de Keroualle, duchess of Portsmouth, gave the appearance of being as close to power and royal decision-making as any minister and they are therefore more significant.[43] All the evidence suggests that Charles formed a genuine attachment, whether of lust or love, with those he took up with. They in turn proved demanding, greedy for wealth and status, and tried to use their position as best they could to achieve much the same as other courtiers of the time: land, title or straight cash, outmanoeuvring their rivals and finding favour in the King's eyes. In addition, as Antonia Fraser has pointed out, Charles II was often surprisingly wracked with guilt over his women and more often than not appears to have been somewhat embarrassed by the scenes they could make.[44]

Cleveland's position as *maîtresse-en-titre* in the early years of the reign unquestionably gave her some authority at court. Her power and influence, however, were often a dubious commodity. It is clear that the King's interest in Barbara tended to decrease as her temper and greed increased. Barbara remained an amusing, highly sexed companion and the couple consequently had five illegitimate children as a result. But she was always her own woman and not only took other lovers, but argued and quarrelled with Charles, so that her influence remained fitful to say the least. Some thought that she was 'very wary in her attempts to lessen the credit of those ministers whom she hated most', but her rooms did provide some focus for those plotting the downfall of Clarendon in 1667, or so the exiled Chancellor himself thought.[45] In the middle years of the reign Barbara lost out to the more fun-loving and less tempestuous Nell

Gwyn, who remained a regular companion for Charles II thereafter but was more of an amusement for the King than a female politician. For the last half of the reign, however, the 'prime mistress', so to speak, was Louise de Keroualle. Louis XIV believed the Catholic Frenchwoman, amongst others, to have a great influence on Charles, and as Nancy Klein Maguire has ably pointed out there is undoubtedly some truth in this.[46] Historians have neglected Portsmouth's role as both mediator and broker, but as the epitome of the political mistress her rooms became the focal point for the use of informal power at court. In her rooms one could gain domestic access to the King and access meant power.[47] Portsmouth's tears, hysteria and playing upon Charles's guilt for giving her the pox in the initial stages of their relationship were possibly as legitimate a technique as any other courtier's cogging and fawning, but have merely been ignored by historians as 'women's wiles'. Her eventual rejection was kept in check by the air of domesticity she gave Charles II in his later years.[48] During this latter period she was, in all but name, Charles II's proxy queen and it was her influence which undoubtedly rehabilitated Sunderland's career in the 1680s.[49]

When we turn to the royal partners and queens of the Stuart kings we find a different tale to tell. Catherine of Braganza, the queen of Charles II, was a political nonentity for the most part. Charles himself swiftly crushed her only real attempt at rebellion against her husband, over the presence of Barbara Villiers in her domestic entourage, in the first months of their marriage.[50] Thereafter Catherine more or less disappears from view as a force at the court, only reappearing in social situations and in times of religious stress such as that which occurred during the Popish Plot crisis.[51] In the case of James II there are some grounds for believing that his second wife, Mary of Modena, had some influence over him. Certainly he was forced to put away his mistress, and Mary's Roman Catholicism sustained his plans. Mary also acted as a force at his court during the course of his reign.[52]

Women provided little diversion to William III. While his wife Mary seems to have loved him deeply and at some level he apparently reciprocated these feelings, she proved to have little influence on his actions. In general Mary accepted her 'womanly weakness' as a deterrent to the active political life. Her views were simple enough.[53] The fact that Mary shared the crown was not an insignificant point in itself. Until her death in 1694 it was Mary who to some extent legitimised William's rule and while her obvious subservience to him prevented any rivalry at court between their respective followers, it is difficult to rule out any political ambition in Mary. She was after all a Stuart, and while she provided the sympathetic front of the regime she could also cause difficulties. She was a champion of the causes of her religion, and a staunch supporter of the state Church, albeit with an odd penchant for suffering and, if her personal diary is to be believed, a wish to die of consumption in order to prove her faithfulness.[54] Aside from this peculiarity, Mary's political views were fairly conventional for the era. Her guilt over the deposition of her father was only matched by a faith in providential events. Politically she saw 'idleness', a broadly defined pastime of courts, as the great corrupter of human nature. For her the 'chief end of power ought to be the doing of good'. Being by nature timorous, her view that women should not meddle in the world of politics, or if they did they should take their husband's lead, naturally suited William. The major difficulty that Mary created for William was in her relationship with her sister Princess Anne.[55]

Both William and Mary were suspicious of Anne's role in the politics of the era. William may well have resented the Princess's better claim to the throne, but her support for her favourites the Marlboroughs also produced petty jealousies and resentments which were to lead to a cold war between the two sides. Personal differences between the two sisters, however, arose out of a number of factors, not the least Anne's constant ability to bring forth offspring, though unfortunately they were short-lived. Stemming from a series of rows over lodgings and money, the trouble between the two sisters was undoubtedly kept going by the ambitions of aspiring and current favourites. Mary's demand that Sarah Churchill be removed after Marlborough's disgrace in 1692 only revealed Anne's stubbornness. Only with Mary's death in 1694 was a superficial form of reconciliation obtained between Anne and William.[56]

William is believed to have had one mistress at least: Elizabeth Villiers, who was kept very much in the background and whose political role was minimal. William's most intimate companions were the Dutchmen William Bentinck, earl of Portland, and Arnold Joost van Keppel, earl of Albermarle. Both were incidentally linked to William in Jacobite propaganda as his lovers, although outside the fetid imagination of Jacobites this was unlikely. William cared for few diversions and sex never appears to have been very high on his list of entertainment.[57]

Of course ultimately the significance of women at court depends upon whether one believes that the personal influence between a man and a women can override other factors and influences or at least affect them so much as to change opinions, but whether one does or not, in the case of the later Stuart court such personal relations were a legitimate part of the nexus of court politics.

Notes

1   C. Strachey (ed.), *The Letters of the Earl of Chesterfield to his Son* (2 vols, 2nd edn, London, 1924), I, p. 355.

2   G. E. Aylmer, *The King's Servants: The Civil Service of Charles I, 1625–1642* (London, 1961), pp. 61–96. See also G. E. Aylmer, *The State's Servants: The Civil Service under the English Republic, 1649–1660* (London, 1973), pp. 58–82. J. Boissevain, *Friends of Friends: Networks, Manipulators and Coalition* (Oxford, 1974). R. Kleinman, 'Social dynamics at the French court: the household of Anne of Austria', *French Historical Studies*, XVI (1990), 517–35. An important article that deals with faction is R. Shepherd, 'Court factions in early modern England', *Journal of Modern History*, LXIV (1992), 721–45.

3   See documents 6, 7 and 24.

4   See, for example, the fall of Clifford in 1673. At the time Sir Robert Southwell noted that 'My Lord Clifford gave up his staff on Wednesday morning, and … Till Tuesday night there was, for many days before, whole throngs of people of all qualities attending at all hours; the next day all was as silent as in a convent'. W. D. Christie (ed.), *Letters Addressed from London to Sir Joseph Williamson while Plenipotentiary at the Congress of Cologne in the Years 1673 and 1674* (2 vols, London, 1874), I, p. 56.

5   J. Levron, 'Louis XIV's courtiers', in R. Hatton (ed.), *Louis XIV and Absolutism* (London, 1976), pp. 130–53. Also J. Wildeblood, *The Polite World: A Guide to English Manners and Deportment from the Thirteenth to the Nineteenth Century* (Oxford, 1965), pp. 13, 26, 34, 197.

6   Halifax, 'Political, moral and miscellaneous thoughts and reflections', in H. C. Foxcroft, *The Life and Letters of Sir George Savile, Bart., First Marquis of Halifax* (2 vols, London, 1898), II, p. 507.

7   Roger Ascham quoted in S. Anglo, 'The courtier, the Renaissance and changing ideas', in A. G. Dickens (ed.), *The Courts of Europe: Politics, Patronage and Royalty, 1400–1800* (London, 1977), p. 44.

8   See document 5.

9   S. Kettering, *Patrons, Brokers and Clients in Seventeenth-Century France* (Oxford, 1986). S. Kettering, 'Brokerage at the court of Louis XIV', *Historical Journal*, CCCLXI (1993), 69–87.

10   C. Clay, *Public Finance and Private Wealth: The Career of Sir Stephen Fox, 1627–1716* (Oxford, 1978), pp. 114–18.

11   Bodleian Library, Carte MS 32, fos 346–7. D. F. Cregan, 'An Irish cavalier: Daniel O'Neill in exile and restoration 1651–1664', *Studia Hibernica*, LI (1965), 42–76. Historical Manuscripts Commission, Sutherland, III, p. 157.

12   W. G. Runciman and E. Matthews, *Max Weber: Selections in Translation* (Cambridge, 1978), pp. 212–25. Shepherd, 'Court factions in early modern England', 721–45.

13   See T. Hobbes, *Leviathan* (1651) (Harmondsworth, 1985), p. 186.

14   See chapters 5–7.

15   Halifax, 'The Spencer House journals', in Foxcroft (ed.), *Life and Letters of Sir George* Savile, II, p. 206.

16   H. D. Molesworth, *The Princes* (London, 1969), p. 13.

17   See J. H. O'Neill, *George Villiers, Second Duke of Buckingham* (Boston, 1984). A. Browning, *Thomas Osborne, Earl of Danby and Duke of Leeds, 1632–1712* (3 vols, Glasgow, 1951), pp. 30–50. M. K. Geiter and W. A. Speck (eds), *Memoirs of Sir John Reresby* (2nd edn, London, 1991), p. 88. G. D. Gilbert (ed.), *Marie Catherine d'Aulnoy, Memoirs of the Court of England in 1675* (London, 1913), pp. 17–18. M. Lee, *The Cabal* (Urbana, 1965), pp. 161–201. B. Yardley, 'George Villiers, second duke of Buckingham and the politics of toleration', *Huntingdon Library Quarterly*, LV (1992), 317–37. C. Phipps (ed.), *Buckingham, Public and Private Man: The Prose, Poems and Commonplace Book of George Villiers, Second Duke of Buckingham (1628–1687)* (New York, 1985).

18   B. D. Henning (ed.), *The History of Parliament: The Commons, 1660–1690* (3 vols, London, 1983), II, pp. 373–80, 595–603; III, pp. 537–8. C. Roberts, 'The impeachment of the earl of Clarendon', *Historical Journal*, XIII (1957), 117–18.

19   A. Marshall, *Intelligence and Espionage in the Reign of Charles II, 1660–1685* (Cambridge, 1994), pp. 113–15, 164–6, 192.

20   Ibid., pp. 239–40.

21   Ibid., pp. 217–18, 221–2.

22   Roberts, 'The impeachment of the earl of Clarendon', 17–18.

23   Geiter and Speck (eds), *Memoirs of Sir John Reresby*, pp. 71–2. Also J. Ralph, *The History of England during the Reigns of King William and Queen Anne and King George I with an Introductory Review of the Reigns of the Royal Brothers Charles and James* (2 vols, London, 1744–46), I, pp. 147, 162, 173. R. North, *Examen* (1740), p. 453.

24   Browning, *Thomas Osborne*, II, pp. 62–3.

25   Buckingham, 'A letter to sir Thomas Osborne, one of his majesties privy council upon the reading of a book called the protestant interest of England stated (1672)', in Phipps (ed.), *Buckingham, Public and Private Man*, p. 94.

26   See chapter 5 below.

27   G. Holmes, *The Making of a Great Power: Late Stuart and Early Georgian Britain, 1660–1722* (London, 1993), pp. 257–65. J. H. Plumb, *The Growth of Political Stability in England, 1675–1725* (London, 1991), pp. 98–128. J. Brewer, *The Sinews of Power: War, Money and the English State, 1688–1783* (London, 1989), pp. 64–87.

28   Holmes, *Making of a Great Power*, p. 415.

29   A. Marshall, 'Sir Joseph Williamson and the conduct of administration in Restoration England', *Historical Research*, LXIX (1996), 18–43.

30   There is currently no general survey of the administration of the later Stuart monarchs.

31   G. Holmes, *British Politics in the Age of Anne* (revised edn, London, 1987), pp. 188–9.

32   Ibid., p. 189.

33   J. Carter, 'Cabinet records for the reign of William III', *English Historical Review*, LXXVIII (1963), 97. See also J. H. Plumb, 'The organization of the cabinet in the reign of Queen Anne', *Transactions of the Royal His-*

torical Society 5th series, VII (1957), 137–57.

34 K. von den Steinen, 'The discovery of women in eighteenth century political life', in B. Kanner (ed.), *The Women of England from the Anglo-Saxon Times to the Present: Interpretative Bibliographical Essays* (London, 1980), p. 247.

35 Ibid., pp. 229–30.

36 See B. Anderson and P. Zinsser, *A History of their Own: Women in Europe from Pre-history to the Present* (2 vols, Harmondsworth, 1990), II, pp. 3–25.

37 Strachey (ed.), *Letters of the Earl of Chesterfield to his Son*, I, p. 355.

38 Mme de Motteville quoted in Anderson and Zinsser, *A History of their Own*, II, p. 13.

39 Sarah Churchill quoted in von den Steinen, 'The discovery of women in eighteenth century political life', p. 247.

40 Geiter and Speck (eds), *Memoirs of Sir John Reresby*, pp. 35–6.

41 J. P. Kenyon, *The Stuarts: A Study in English Kingship* (London, 1979), p. 114. But as a counter to this see Kanner (ed.), *Women of England*. P. J. Jupp, 'The roles of royal and aristocratic women in British politics c.1782–1832', in M. O'Dowd and S. Wickett, 'Chattle, servant or citizen: women's status in Church, State and Society', *Historical Studies*, XIX (1995), 103–13. Also B. J. Harris, 'Women in politics in early Tudor England', *Historical Journal*, XXXIII (1990), 259–81, and L. G. Schwoerer, 'Women and the Glorious Revolution', *Albion*, XVIII (1986), 175–218. A. Fraser, *The Weaker Vessel: Women's Lot in Seventeenth-Century England* (London, 1987), pp. 444–64.

42 Halifax, 'A character of Charles II', in Foxcroft (ed.), *Life and Letters of Sir George Savile*, II, p. 349.

43 N. K. Maguire, 'The duchess of Portsmouth: English royal consort and French politician, 1670–85', in R. Smuts (ed.), *The Stuart Court and Europe: Essays in Politics and Political Culture* (Cambridge, 1996), p. 247. See also document 8.

44 A. Fraser, *King Charles II* (London, 1980), pp. 312–14, 411.

45 C. MacCormick (ed.), *The Secret History of the Court and Reign of Charles the Second by a Member of his Privy Council* (2 vols, London, 1792), II, pp. 215–16. Fraser, *King Charles II*, p. 253.

46 Maguire, 'The duchess of Portsmouth', p. 247.

47 Ibid., pp. 256–7.

48 Fraser, *King Charles II*, p. 411.

49 Maguire, 'The duchess of Portsmouth', pp. 267, 273.

50 R. Hutton, *The Restoration: A Political and Religious History of England and Wales, 1658–1667* (Oxford, 1985), pp. 189–90.

51 J. P. Kenyon, *The Popish Plot* (Harmondsworth, 1974), pp. 125–8.

52 J. Miller, *James II: A Study in Kingship* (London, 1989), pp. 122–3.

53 Document 29 and H. W. Chapman, *Mary II, Queen of England* (London, 1953), pp. 181–2.

54 Document 29.

55 Chapman, *Mary II*, pp. 177–81. E. Gregg, *Queen Anne* (London, 1984), pp. 74–104.

56   Gregg, *Queen Anne*, pp. 105–29.
57   See below chapters 4 and 7.

4

Social and cultural life

In the popular historical imagination the court of Charles II still retains its salacious reputation for being licentious and witty, while that of James II is condemned as dull, Catholic and worthy. Upon the court of William and Mary popular historical imagination expresses little opinion, for it is largely unknown territory.[1] Certainly in terms of reputation the idea of the later Stuart court as a place of vice, immorality, greed and general viciousness precedes any study of it. It was believed to be a court with few equals for its depravities since the time of Caesar. The early historians of the period took great care to condemn the 'prevailing licentiousness [of] the most corrupt part of a corrupt society', to use Lord Macaulay's words. In doing so they set a trend for any study of Restoration court culture by seeking to disguise the especially lurid details, particularly the sexual activities of the courtiers, under the romance of the 'merry monarch', a romance which to some extent is still with us.[2] Popular history has usually tended to follow these old-established trends. Clearly the social, literary and cultural history of the later Stuart court deserves a fresh examination, because it can reveal much about the nature of the court environment and government in the latter half of the seventeenth century.

Literature and satire

The first port of call for any understanding of the court culture of the later Stuarts lies in the literary outpourings of the court and its courtiers. In their own way they can reveal images of a cultural world which is otherwise now lost to us. An established and well-defined cultural ambience existed for some fifty years or so after the Restoration and this only began to change with the reign of Queen Anne, when as one contemporary put it 'an Old Age is out, / And time to begin a New'.[3] In this Restoration age many scholars have argued that the court literature of the day contains traces of a far older tradition.[4] Anti-court commentary was in fact as old as the institution of courts themselves, for the royal court had always contained within its nature two possibilities: to be a place of culture, learning and statesmanship, or to be a place of idleness, pleasure, and consequently depravity. From the time of Aristotle the myth of the virtuous leader and his equally virtuous elite had struggled valiantly with the realities of court life. While the ideal court was meant to be replete with manners and the personal qualities which made up 'courtliness' and to which all were to aspire, the reality was much more human and thus much more flawed. It was this make-believe world of the court that was most frequently honoured by the critics. An additional element of rancour was also clear in such writings. Because the privileged tended to move in a world of more than conspicuous consumption, and rarely stinted themselves on their pleasures, they were always commented upon, and were largely found wanting, mainly by those less successful at working the system than themselves. Thus once the resources of the printing press were available, the disappointed, as well as the disillusioned, tended to turn their thought to creating satires to focus their criticisms.

'The end of Satire', as Daniel Defoe once pointed out, 'is reformation', and the satirical charges made against the court in the Restoration era were not only moral, but social and economic. The social and economic strictures against the court almost inevitably revolved around the court's alleged parasitic nature as a way of life which was far too attractive, or so it was said, to members of the old landed gentry. Court life, it was claimed, stole them away from their natural home in the regions, and damaged the local economy as a result. The envy of a London-based consumer society is also to be found in such satire. This can also be seen as the outcome of the venality and excess of which courts were always accused. Ambition and power, two of the things for which courts were also notorious, were also condemned, for they not only bent emotional ties and divorced members of the court from honesty and hard work, but encouraged the other court vices of deception and flattery.

A tradition of the corrective thus existed in such work and had been established by Castiglione and other Renaissance authors in the books of civility of their time. In this genre authors could claim that by establishing the correct standards for the *habitués* of the court good conduct would naturally follow. The sister to the corrective literature, a polite literature of manners, was actually very popular after the Restoration, especially it seems amongst parvenus who sought some guidance about what actually went on there. Thereafter it still retained some popularity as an actual process of a reformation of manners, backed first by James II and then by William and Mary amongst others, took hold.[5] Yet other literature sought to show how men and women lived at court and how one could actually join this elite. The interesting angle of these allegedly practical survival guides was that while they purported to be exercises in realism, for their presumably middle-class readership, they only occasionally matched the reality of life at court. For that one must arguably turn to the satires.

It is with the classic genre of the period, verse satire, that we begin to establish the problems of using literary sources for studying the culture of the court, that social, artistic, physical, architectural and moral nexus. If we read the variety of literary sources available to us on the court's culture then we swiftly tend to assume that neither the court of Charles II nor that of his brother James were places of monastic virtue and contemplation. Many of the most intimate portraits of the court were in fact literary ones whose interpretation is a more problematic area than one might suppose. Some literary theorists have argued that texts, plays or poems, although they belong to a particular era, can only be appraised from our current and limited perspective. If true, this is naturally rather unhelpful for our purposes as the 'past' in such documents can never be recovered. However, other opinions have stressed a more reflective practice, that is how such texts can help to provide an imaginative representation of specific historical moments or periods, although allowance must be made for the fact that such texts are actually caught up in a contemporary mode of discourse, as well as rhetoric. From a historian's perspective it is possible to argue that literary texts can be revealing in a number of ways and assist in an exploration of aspects of the court's culture, if used with caution and respect for the view that the 'reality' they depict tends to be rather more indistinct than at first appears.[6]

In fact, much of the satirical commentary on the court that emerged in the later Stuart period was somewhat formulaic in structure. It expressed the ideas of entropy, social evil, hedonism and sexual tension. The Restoration satirical commentaries, whether play or poem, often drew upon the classical satiric models of Juvenal. They were invariably both bitter and somewhat obscene in nature. This obscenity, one of the most striking elements to the modern reader, had a purpose. It was daring and bawdy and it provided amusement by its use of sexual language in association with contemporary notions of the constant battle between rampant sexuality (women) and reason (man). Obscene language was in any case common parlance at the court itself, if we are to believe Pepys, but in this case the shock of the printed page may have been more creative than that of the ephemeral verbal swear word.[7]

One mode of discourse was for the authors of such verse satires to adopt the familiar guise of the outraged moralist, or naive shepherd, a persona of the visiting innocent as observer in a wicked world. As outsiders, such characters were thus able to dissect the institution of the court and find a variety of wickedness flourishing in its crowded rooms. The satirists were keen to note that the overt sumptuousness of the court so obviously failed to disguise the actual squalor of the life there. Of course, whether these satiric poems can be taken solely as historical documents is a moot point, as has already been noted above. They are as much literary constructs, pieces of art, as genuine portraits; indeed Alvin Kernan has called them a 'construct of symbols'. It is true that in such verse the court was always disorderly or squalid, and crowded with faces who bore the marks of their own depravity, stupidity, greed and sexual excess. Just occasionally there may have been a glimpse of some unsullied purity which still existed amidst the squalor, but such glimpses were often for literary effect and as such were always shown as endlessly on the edge of ruin, with men and women usually portrayed at their basest and most extreme. Restoration court poets were in any case aggressive in their impulses. Concerned with 'sin' on a multitude of levels, they took great care to trace the internal rottenness that they believed lay at the heart of the court and mankind itself.[8]

The satires, which circulated in manuscript at Whitehall, were initially written for a select audience, who would be only too well aware of the personalities and scandals of the court they targeted. When they were products of an impulse of real indignation, rather than merely literary effect, we may also assume that some of them were reasonably well informed. By using a scattergun technique the authors were also able to hit as many targets as possible. The corrective qualities of the verse are only matched by the contempt and scorn which percolates throughout them. In such verse, of course, the innocent suffered alongside the guilty. But whether historical or literary, the satirists did try to reveal a genuine corruption that they felt lay at the heart of court life and attempted thereby to diminish their subjects by ridicule.[9]

Such poetry also tended to be written by misogynists, or those who took on that mask. Reputations were lost in court satires, never to be regained, as they were continually kept fresh by repetition. For such works were also disposed to regurgitate their own mythology. This is true, for example, of the attitude towards women at court. The court satires were invariably concerned with women's sexuality, which was linked to a general fear of women as uncontrolled, passionate creatures who represented disorder, chaos and rebellion against the normal early modern patriarchal structures of reason, order and honour. Women therefore acted as a metaphor for all that was offensive in such a society. In addition, women were drawn as inclining towards that apparently great occupation of court life: sexual deviance. While the satirist claimed to see sexual deviance everywhere as an expression of the sin and corrupt nature of life at court, it was invariably women who created such sexual need in reasonable men and overwhelmed their rational facilities. In itself this might be merely an interesting literary question, but the distinctive nature of Restoration court satire was that its sexual elements were inextricably mixed up with affairs of state, with the body politic itself. Often the focus was upon an actual representation of the body politic: the easily swayed, or 'swived', monarch. In 'A Satire on the Court Ladies' (1680), for example, the poet noted how Portsmouth's lust not only 'Destroys our prince's honour, [but his] health and soul' and through this debilitation Charles II, as the state, would become weak and lustful, damaging not only himself in the process but the society he represented. To the court satirists, therefore, the royal bed and council were often different sides of the same problem.[10]

Those who had actually experienced life at court, and had thereby undoubtedly become disillusioned with its activities, frequently based their views on a vision of the court where whatever the good intentions one entered with, one found oneself in a Dantesque dark wood of crooked turnings. The view that courts were, and always had been, places of sin and corruption, the habitation of 'politicians' (then, as now, a dirty word), and full of flattering sycophants, the dissolute and 'infamous' persons, whose morals could never be changed, rigidly set the boundaries of discourse. Naturally the bitter self-contempt of the most famous court satirist of the day, John Wilmot, earl of Rochester, invariably went far beyond this. In fact although the aggressive sexuality of Rochester's language was redolent of a generally projected fear from the *habitués* of court, his was a particular fear of the women at court, who seem to have left him both impotent and powerless, and thus needed to be corrected. Aside from his defiant braggadocio in naming names in the court's alleged sexual gymnastics, common with others at the time, Rochester, for all of his obscenity, expresses a certain naiveté in the number of ways he hoped to change things with his verse.[11] Others, who were perhaps more cynical than he, often merely portrayed the court as no worse, or at least no better, than the world outside. It remained a world in miniature with all of its foibles, frailties and stereotypical characters.

Thus in the literature of the period the Restoration court came to be regarded as a place of sin, squalor and corruption. In the life of the

Restoration court this view began as early as 1660 when the blind John Milton feverishly proclaimed, to those who would listen, of the approaching horrors of the return of a 'dissolute and haughty' court; it would lead, he thought, to 'vast expense and luxury, masks and revels, to the debauching of our prime gentry both male and female ... by the loose employments of court service'.[12] Nor was Milton alone. Others frequently compared the newly established court to Hell as a place of little real love and still less faith. In such a Hobbesian state of nature, and it is worth noting that Hobbes had seen for himself the world of the court, the atmosphere there did appear to be one of 'continual feare ... And the life of man, solitary, poore, nasty, brutish and short.'[13]

Yet away from the negative aspects of court life some historians have argued that the court was not merely a brutish place for brutish people, but played a decisive role in civilising and domesticating those who went there. As we have seen above, the work of Norbert Elias in particular put forward the case for the court as an instrument by which the dangerous elements of the aristocracy could be domesticated, neutralised and the central absolutist state consolidated.[14] There is indeed some evidence of a new climate of manners, which was created to assist in this process. Certainly in social terms the court always established its own value systems, which occasionally filtered down to the world outside. In effect the court, for a time, became a cultural arbiter of the nation. One consequence of this was that courts and courtiers always tended to stand apart from the rest of society in terms of their conspicuous consumption, dress, ceremony and even speech patterns. In England it was this almost separate society, heavily influenced by French styles and dress, which largely exemplified the court–country division, which became so prominent in the seventeenth century and provided the ammunition for the many critiques of court life.

Court style

From 1660 to 1702 the cultural language of the court represented a world of extravagance, a baroque splendour with absolutist overtones.[15] This cultural environment was a living one in which all the day-to-day activities of the court took place and were given public expression. All societies, particularly elite ones, require a framework of reference within which to operate. This framework, or culture, enables them to define themselves and their aims, to justify their existence or order their actions. It is a form of 'political theology'. In this theology, cultural artefacts and modes of expression have a functional use: they become part of the means of social control created to inspire, amaze, instruct, entertain or suppress both the elite who view them and the outsiders to whom they are projected.

For the most part the style of the later Stuart court, whether in architecture, the decorative arts, painting or music, was that of the baroque. In its essence style is always something that results from an array of contacts and practices among craftsmen, 'professionals' and patrons. Undoubtedly the epicentre of the cultural world, Louis XIV's France heavily influenced the Stuart court style in the seventeenth century. French ideas, fashions and sensibility became the norm amongst the elite who inhabited both the court and the upper echelons of English society. While it was often given an English gloss, the roots of such influences could not be disguised. Under Louis XIV French style proved itself to be neo-classical, hierarchical, conservative and nationalistic, in so much as it emphasised Louis's own *gloire*.[16] It reached back towards classical Greece and Rome to pull out concepts of authority and decorum and it comes as no surprise to find the newly re-established Stuarts imitating Louis in this as in other matters.

Royal edifices, ceremony and artefacts were always intended to 'speak' to a wide audience. They were part of a conscious system of power projection – expressions of the monarch's political power, material wealth and artistic taste. However, as with other elements of the later seventeenth century, elite culture, as expressed at court, was not simply artistic expression for art's sake. Indeed, the duke of Newcastle, Charles II's old tutor, had informed his pupil that 'such divertissements will amuse the people's thoughts and keep them in harmless actions, which will free your Majesty from faction and rebellion'. In other words, like many another political system the arts must be studied for the political use that could be made of them.[17] As such, all of the later Stuarts encouraged artistic and cultural endeavours, to a greater or a lesser degree, not merely to give prestige to their courts but as modes of expression to create an atmosphere of splendour in an attempt to rival that of their foreign competitors and to increase their *gloire*, the essence of princeliness and the very heart of early modern sovereignty.

While Charles II and James II took some pleasure in art, they had acquired somewhat cosmopolitan tastes during exile, although of a French style. Indeed when James became king he even ordered those who visited Versailles to observe closely the trappings of state there so that he could copy them at his own court.[18] In other respects, however, the royal brothers were fairly typical patrons of the arts of their period, being dilettantes and amateurs, as well as irregular in paying the bills. While Charles II was not a bad purchaser of old masters, and encouraged contemporary Roman Catholic French artists, as well as

Dutchmen such as Kneller, his real diversion lay in the dramatic arts. Without doubt, and even if one discounts the popular mythology, Charles II raised the prestige of drama, actors and actresses, not merely by his attendance at the theatre, but by his patronage of certain dramatists. Indeed he has some claim to have changed the dramatic history of the era, for, as John Dryden noted, Restoration comedy, as well as its lesser known but more typical partner, heroic tragedy, were very much 'courtiers' drama'. As such they were patronised by distinguished courtiers and in some way reflected their lives. Heroic drama in particular projected many of the ideals which courtiers and kings wished to find at their court, being full of lavish costume, extravagant action, hyperbole and rhetoric. In this sense they were a heightened version of the realities of court life, which was itself somewhat unreal.[19] Unfortunately for English drama, Charles II's successors were less keen upon the theatre. As usual William III took a minimal interest in such matters, while his wife Mary did attend performances but, unlike her uncle, felt guilty about it afterwards. Following her death in 1694 court interest in the dramatic arts, while never completely dissolving, was somewhat dissipated.[20]

In the case of the decorative arts and architecture we can gain some clues as to the tastes of Charles II and James II by their patronage of the work which they began at Windsor and Whitehall. Architecture fell into the area of Stuart public iconography that was always contentious. Towards the end of Charles's reign, Windsor became the palace where he felt most at home and consequently he spent as lavishly as possible upon it in an effort to keep up with the splendours of Versailles. Charles commissioned two splendidly decorated royal suites over the period 1675–80 and gave his patronage to a collaboration between Hugh May and Antonio Verrio to produce a 'golden glow of triumphalism'.[21] The employment of the Italian decorative painter Antonio Verrio to create his baroque illusions on the ceilings and walls of the King's chambers was also revealing. As patron of such arts Charles was able to indulge, in relative seclusion, the ideals of absolutism which such baroque paintings projected, even if he was unable to express them outside the palace walls. Verrio illustrated the Gods assembling in the Queen's drawing room, sexual motifs such as Leda and the Swan in the King's bedroom and Jupiter and Danae in his dressing room, while Charles, enthroned in glory, was depicted overcoming rebellion and faction in St George's Hall. In his bedchamber the four continents, including, without a sense of irony, France, were pictured bringing him gifts; while in the ballroom Charles disguised as Perseus rescued Europe disguised as Andromeda.[22] Verrio also found employment under James II on the major Roman Catholic work of the era, the new Chapel Royal at Whitehall.[23] With architecture by Wren, walls and ceilings by Verrio, altarpieces by Gernani and carvings by Grinling Gibbons, the Roman Catholic chapel was a place to delight the eye, glorify God and shock the average Protestant. James II's commitment to the Roman faith, divine right and his own prestige were all bound up in this creation.

There was no dramatic change in artistic taste in 1688, although a number of pictures at Whitehall may have disappeared from its walls into various courtiers' collections in the confusion of the Revolution. In fact William and Mary had inherited not only a lavish collection of artwork, they were expected to continue in the role of patron. To some extent this did take place. While William was apparently a sober individual, he was well aware of the propaganda value of art to an unsteady regime. In the event William, frequently portrayed as Hercules in a triumphant manner, did not hesitate to copy the French style in art and architecture in the 1690s.[24] Dutch taste was very heavily influenced by French style in any case and as Stadholder in the Netherlands William had demanded the same splendour at his court as his great rival Louis XIV had created at Versailles. This inclination to grandeur was expressed after 1688 by work on Hampton Court and Kensington Palace.[25] Using the Huguenot exile Daniel Marot amongst others, an attempt was made for the first time to produce fully integrated ensembles of both the interiors and exteriors of the various royal buildings. In addition, the royal couple indulged their passion for gardens. That the sober William thought it worth his while to indulge in such artistic pretensions in spite of the cost is clear. Indeed the fact that he continued to embellish Hampton Court and Het Loo in the Netherlands even in the midst of an expensive war, while at the same time his great enemy was allegedly being forced to melt down the silver at Versailles to pay for his campaigns, shows the significance of the arts as propaganda if nothing else.

James II's creation of the new Chapel Royal did do some damage to the world of religious music.[26] After the Restoration musical life at court had been revived in the form in which it had been left in 1642. However, a direct imitation of Louis XIV's violin band was soon established and styled 'The Twenty-Four Violins', who were to play together on state occasions.[27] In other cases the musicians were split up and allocated their duties as and when required at balls and masquerades, as well as to provide the background music for other royal meetings of the monarch and his people. Under Charles II court and the Chapel Royal had provided a focus for many a composer's output and employment. Henry Purcell, the most noted composer of his age, was involved there. Charles II in his musical tastes preferred foot-tapping French dance tunes and he disliked the innumerable fantasias of the day. Indeed he was apt to 'whet … his wit upon the subject of the fancy-musick' when given the opportunity to do so.[28] However, one of the most common types of Restoration music, the anthem, was favoured, for it could be used for political purposes to push forward both the court position and state policy.[29] There is little doubt that the court music scene occasionally suffered from the political fallout of the period. Louis Grabu, master of the English Chamber Music until 1675, for example, was a Catalan violinist who had studied in Paris, came to England in 1665 and became Master of the Music in 1666. He was eventually replaced in an atmosphere of anti-French and anti-Catholic feeling created by the passing of the Test Act designed to eliminate Roman Catholics from the public scene. Nicholas Staggins, an Englishman who favoured the Italian style of music, succeeded him.[30] On his accession James II, unable to leave any part of his kingdom alone for very long, undertook a substantial overhaul of the musical world of the court and a number of Charles II's musicians were simply removed or retired. The Roman rites were also observed in the Chapel Royal and this led to music performed there not only by Gregorian monks, an innovation in itself, but the use of celebrated foreign musicians. James and his queen were not in any case very sympathetic to English musicians in general; they had pro-Italian musical tastes and invited G. B. Vitali to court, as well as the singer and eunuch Ciffeccio, whom John Evelyn saw performing in the Chapel Royal in January 1687.[31] As a result, under James musicians began to be forced into a more secular vein. Public concerts tended to become alternatives to royal institutions. Although Purcell undertook some notable royal productions, the court under William and Mary swiftly resigned its grasp on musical tastes. According to an early biographer, William was apathetic to anything but martial music and the musical centre of gravity was in any case gradually shifting away from his court to the theatre and concert hall.[32]

Charles II

If those who went to court and became courtiers were a distinctive group then they found themselves in a distinctive place. The court of Charles II was not only the royal household, as well as a place of government, it was a palace of enjoyment and its hothouse atmosphere inevitably meant lax moral standards. This was not assisted by the presence upon the throne of one of the most dissolute monarchs who ever ruled the country. Engaging though he sometimes was, this unruly monarch led a court which has become infamous in the popular imagination for its pleasure and licentiousness, where maidens seldom held on to their virtue for long and the young bucks, including the King, sought their pleasures where they could find them.[33] Amongst the so-called 'courtiers of pleasure' who surrounded the King on a daily basis, success or failure often depended upon amusing Charles and indeed the King was soon found to be a man who needed to be constantly amused. While cultivated in some respects, some of Charles's tastes did tend towards the base and there were more than enough courtiers who tried to cater to them. As a consequence sycophancy, fawning, flattery and dissembling were the day-to-day currency of his court. Those courtiers who were rational enough to comment upon this claimed to hate the degradation which court life involved, but invariably proved unwilling to avoid it by leaving.

The ideal Restoration courtier was intended to be the sum of particular virtues: noble, handsome, and expert in horsemanship and the martial arts, attentive to his prince, but not servile, and a trusted adviser. Unfortunately few courtiers at the later Stuart court, if any, matched this ideal. The most immediate circle around the King were far more likely to be the 'roaring roist'rers of Whitehall' than paragons of virtue. This circle of wits, with whom Charles seems to have spent large amount of his time, were usually members of his bedchamber and thus in close proximity to the King. In general they apparently abhorred all serious discourse in preference for drollery and other such pleasantries.[34] Certainly the intellectuals amongst this group tended to cultivate the arts of poetry and prose and use such skills as they had to make fun of the more serious-minded politicians. These wits happily spent their days attacking the foppish element at court, and engaging in rakish behaviour.

The meeting place of the wits included William Chiffinch's lodgings, the apartments of the King's current mistress, or those of Bab May, where the topics of conversation included sex, mockery and satire. Men such as George Villiers, duke of Buckingham; Charles Sackville, earl of Dorset; Charles, Lord Sedley; Henry Killigrew; Henry Savile; Henry Guy; Baptist May; John, earl of Mulgrave; and when he was in town, John Wilmot, earl of Rochester, all attempted, in their own way, to make Charles's life a little more pleasurable. It is clear that these men did not like the King, nor for that matter was he over fond of them; for example, although Charles was diverted by Rochester's antics and squibs, Burnet pointed out that 'there was no love between them'.[35] In fact more often than not they resembled the King's famous set of spaniels, a personal pack of dogs, indulged, snapped at, and barely kept in check by the cynical monarch who purported to lead them. In response to the King's attitude, the wits took their revenge in foul language, even more obscene verse, some of the best of which is about their erstwhile leader, and general trouble-making. Reading of their antics often makes one wonder why Charles put up with them. Of course he didn't always do so. Rochester was not alone in suffering banishment from the court for going too far with the King.[36]

An important part of the culture of the court for such men was the expression of their 'wit'. The *Oxford English Dictionary* helpfully defines wit as a 'Quickness of intellect or liveliness of fancy, with a capacity of apt expression; [a] talent for saying brilliant or sparkling things, esp[cially] in an amusing way'. We do know from a number of sources that many courtiers thought that they were wits or strove to be so by using verbal dexterity. As Robert Boyle put it, a 'subtlety in conceiving things ... a quickness and neatness in expressing them' was an important asset to any courtier.[37] The difficulties of recapturing such verbal repartee are significant, but it can tell us quite a lot about the culture of the court. One means of recapturing contemporary wit is via the literary productions of the court. Courtiers made those men and women wits who had some pretence to being a poet or critic or raconteur.[38] Even allowing for the fact that recorded wit was not always the same as wit expounded verbally and that contemporary wit does not always travel very well, we can gain some insights from such literature. Here, for example, is Thomas Shadwell's character Wildish in his play of 1689, *Bury-Fair*, expounding on contemporary wit:

> A Wit is always a Merry, Idle, Waggish fellow, of no understanding: Parts indeed he has, but he had better without 'em: Your solid fop is a better man; ... Your wit will either neglect all opportunities for pleasure, or if he brings his business into a hopeful way, he will laugh at it, or draw his wit upon some great man or other and spoil all.[39]

This pattern of the wit would undoubtedly fit, as we shall see, many of the real social butterflies that inhabited the court during the period. But Shadwell also obligingly gives us three other types of contemporary wit in the same play and which we know were current at the court from other sources. First, there was that wit which was displayed in extravagant compliments, affectation of learning and artificial methods of expression with an exaltation of the French style; secondly, that wit which appeared in horseplay, punning and practical jokes; and lastly, that wit which appears to have been produced in a cynical aversion to extravagance and was armed with a series of 'put-downs' to attack the other two. That such modes of wit actually existed in the real world and are truly reflected in the drama which society eagerly devoured can be further uncovered in the life and work of George Villiers, duke of Buckingham, and George

Savile, marquis of Halifax.[40]

Buckingham, whom we have already met above, was a classic court wit. He was often satirised and satirised others in his turn. The most notable witty attack upon him was that by John Dryden, who captured Buckingham's personality as Zimri in *Absalom and Achitophel*: 'A man so various, that he seem' to be not one, but mankind's epitome ... everything by starts, and nothing long'.[41] While Buckingham was damned by his rivals, as a wit himself he was capable of appalling puns, as in his play *The Rehearsal*, still very amusing. He also had a turn for literary savagery (his satire on Arlington, 'Advice to a painter, to Draw the Delineaments of a Statesman, and his Underlings' is a case in point) and physical buffoonery. In the latter case he often entertained the court by mimicking, amongst others, Clarendon, Arlington and Lady Danby, all of whose peculiarities he chose to exaggerate and amuse the court with, although never, as far as we know, in their presence. Buckingham was a violent, passionate man, prone to duels or the simple wanton thuggery that occasionally passed for aristocratic pleasure in the period. Taken together, all of this was to give Buckingham a notable reputation in court circles as a wit, and his career bears a more than passing resemblance to Shadwell's pithy comments about wits noted above.

On the other hand, the wit of Halifax, Dryden's 'Jotham of piercing wit, and pregnant thought', was of a different order. It also exists in written and anecdotal form. Halifax actually made clear what he thought was the proper expression of his wit, or wit in general, in both conversation and writing, and such expressions were common currency at court. Wit, he noted, should observe proprieties of time, place and subject and avoid excesses. Moreover, it should be doled out in 'drops and not by palefuls' and thus resemble a rapier rather than the bludgeon sometimes used by Buckingham. However, if some memorialists are to be believed even Halifax himself forgot these rules, and as Burnet pointed out 'he was endless in consultations: for when after much discourse a point was settled, if he could find a new jest, to make even that which was suggested by himself seem ridiculous, he could not hold, but would study to raise the credit of his wit, though it made others call his judgement into question'.[42] In short Halifax became every bit of a bar-room bore as his colleagues and would not let subjects off the hook. In this sense he was perhaps as bad as Shadwell's character Sir Humphrey Noddy, who also fancied himself as a wit:

Wildish: Why, you can make a Joque, Sir Humphrey upon any-
           thing.
Sir Hum: I seldom fail, thank God.

Wildish:	Let's hear now, upon the Wainscot.
Sir Hum:	Pshaw waw! 'tis weak wainscot.
Bell:	How so? ...
Sir Hum:	Ha, ha, ha; you know, the weakest goes to the Wall; the Wainscot goes to the Wall, ergo, weak Wainscot, Ha, ha ... I am ready again: Reprieving Wainscot.
Wildish:	How so? ...
Sir Hum:	Ha, ha, ha: why, [a] wainscot saves many a hanging ...
Wildish:	Upon the Looking-glass.
Sir Hum:	Why, 'tis an Ill-natur'd Looking-glass ... Because it makes Reflections; ha, ha.[43]

'Ha, ha' indeed. As this all-too-brief exploration has hopefully suggested, by using literary sources wisely we can illuminate certain aspects of the court culture otherwise lost to us.

Fleetwood Sheppard is a good example of those poets and wits that hovered around the King on a day-to-day basis.[44] Sheppard had a good Oxford education, although he promptly became a hanger-on, 'debauchee and atheist' at the court at the earliest opportunity. His verse satires gave him a reputation as a critic and wit, and the acquaintance of Charles, Lord Buckhurst, gave him entrée into court circles. There he proved an ardent votary of not only Apollo, but also Bacchus and Venus, swiftly rising to become one of the King's 'companions in private to make him merry'. Sheppard's reward was to be made steward of Nell Gwyn's affairs and manage her finances, which was rather after the fashion of setting the wolf to mind the sheep. His own irregular income, as well as the extravagant lifestyle the court demanded, meant he was very much dependent upon being there to survive. While he might, and indeed did, criticise the court openly, he certainly could not afford to leave. Only upon the accession of James II, who never liked him, was Sheppard forced to retire from court. It was the Revolution of 1688 that revived his fortunes. When his good friend Dorset was made Lord Chamberlain in 1689, a year later Sheppard himself became a gentleman usher to William III. Dull service in William's livery must have provided a stark contrast to the former rake, but Fleetwood seems to have taken it in his stride.

Evidence of the activities of such men is inevitably fragmentary, a mixture of gossip, verse and hearsay, the latter mostly from the ever credulous Pepys. This was inevitable, for while they were in the habit of dissecting their pleasure in verse, they did not keep a strict record of the time spent upon it. The main pastime of the wits lay in mockery – especially of the King's ministers, which Charles indulged. Indeed the sight of Buckingham or the others imitating Clarendon or Arlington seems to have given Charles particular pleasure; it became an 'in joke' which he refused to share with the victims themselves.[45] Palace watchers, such as the French ambassador, took to measuring a minister's standing by the amount of mockery he underwent. Both Clarendon and Arlington were easy targets, although the latter clung tenaciously on to power in spite of the wits; perhaps this was the 'in joke' in his case. The other targets for the wits were the fops and coxcombs, as well as the ladies, of the court. The former pretended to intellectual pursuits, as any gentlemen would, but were in reality merely like so many birds of display, whose feathers needed plucking from time to time. The latter not only suffered from scandal and censure, which was cruel, irresponsible and not always true, but given the notable misogynist atmosphere of the court it was to be expected. For the circle of wits were rakes to a man. Their literary bent, which appears to excuse much of their behaviour amongst some academics, could not disguise the fact that they were also insolent, hard-drinking, violent souls, whose other main pastimes were those of the Caroline court itself: gambling, 'whoring' and drinking. Indeed according to Rochester there were only 'three businesses of the age ... women, politics and drinking'.[46]

Gambling, invariably for heavy stakes, was something of a vice amongst the ladies of the court. Cheating, which gentlemen were expected to do, but not to get caught, only gave an added frisson to the activity. 'Whoring' led to widespread venereal disease. That the court was a place of disease, symbolically as well as in reality, was well known. We can find it reflected in the frequent emphasis in Restoration satire on the connection between sex, disease and bodily fluids, such as this vulgar verse on Nell Gwyn:

Whose cunt, arse, mouth and every hole
Has served for Rowley's prick's close-stool;
Torrents flow from Nelly's sluice,
Only Arundel can produce
An equal stock of wheyey juice[47]

That the 'pox' so often mentioned in the verse of Rochester and others was a reality at court, claiming among its victims the King and his brother, their mistresses and lesser courtiers, was well known. Having chased and finally caught Louise de Keroualle, Charles promptly gave his mistress a venereal disease, and was forced to placate her subsequent tears with a string of pearls.[48] Again the presence of such widespread venereal disease was also used symbolically by poets and commentators. The court itself was frequently portrayed as a disease upon the body politic which needed to be cured or, according to closet republicans, cut out in order to save the patient: the state.

Amongst the more legitimate pastimes of the court of Charles II were the dances, balls, masquerades and plays that took place upon a regular basis. Dancing was a favoured court pastime with various regular balls and 'ballets' in which the courtiers took part. Sir Joseph Williamson, who became Secretary of State in 1674, was notorious for his love of dancing and at one of the French ambassador's events was alleged to have danced for six hours without resting.[49] The winter of 1676 was especially notable for its balls and plays, and a 'grande ballett' in 1671 proved so popular that one of the inumerable Bertie clan, Lady Mary, was 'forced to goe by four a clock, though it did not begin till nine or ten'. The fashion for masquerades in 1670 became such a regular diversion for all at the court that Burnet pointed out that 'without being in on the secret none could distinguish' the participants. In short, as the French ambassador put it, one had to be 'a man of pleasure to get on here'.[50]

Of the court at play only a few glimpses can be given here: George Monck, duke of Albermarle, being challenged to a drinking contest and drinking his younger rivals under the table; the court at Tunbridge Wells, notoriously known as 'les eaux de scandale' with all of its sexual intrigues; Monmouth, addicted to horoscopes, losing money hand over fist at the races, as he relied increasingly on the wrong predictions of an Italian abbé; the Queen and two of her ladies, dressed as country girls, attending a fair only to be discovered by the crowds around them because of their strange accents. In the winter of 1676 Charles II even arranged to have a 'Muscovit' sledge built to pull him round the canals of St James's Park and he was soon joined in this activity by the new duchess of York, who, when not throwing snowballs at her somewhat austere husband that winter, was 'pulled up and down the ponds in [her sledge] every day'. The Twelfth Night revels were particularly popular, not the least because of the serious gambling which took place at that time of the year. The King himself began the gambling on these occasions with a small bag of gold coins. The groom-porter's lodge, the place for such activities throughout the year, became a place of 'vanity and monstrous excess of passion' with 'vast heaps of gold squandered away in a vain and profuse manner'.[51]

Upper-class hooliganism, also frequently to be seen at court, was mainly disguised under references to a code of honour, which for the courtier was a 'system of rules constructed by people of fashion, and calculated to facilitate their intercourse with one another'. The code of honour prescribed the proper behaviour of a gentleman, the means of settling infractions between them and regulating their manners. As such it was a code which revolved not only around self-worth, but also the assessment of the claim by outsiders, which in many senses was of more significance. Breaches of honour invariably needed to be satisfied, whether it was by Rochester punching a fellow groom of the bedchamber, or Dorchester and Buckingham pushing, shoving and wig pulling in the House of Lords.[52] More often than not honour meant violent and deadly duels, something in which young noblemen and army officers were all too prone to indulge. It is clear that the duel with all of its structure and ritual was an organised means of defending aristocratic honour in order to give 'satisfaction', as well as a demonstration of manliness and status. More often than not the matters which courtiers fought over seemed petty, albeit they were taken with deadly seriousness. Disputes over ladies' virtues, or lack of them, were a primary cause. Lord Peterborough tried to fight a duel over Mrs Johnson, 'a lady of pleasure under his lordship's protection'. However, even the King balked at this and prevented the affair. Nor were the women of the court averse to following their men folk in such matters. In 1676 Lady Sussex and Madame Mazarine privately learned to fence and then turned up in St James's Park to 'make severall fine passes ... to [the] admiration of severall men that was lookers on'.[53]

In fact 'giving the lie', attacking a gentleman's honour verbally, was the most serious blow a gentleman could suffer. It publicly impinged upon the honesty and integrity of the man concerned. In many senses, although duels were a bloody method of resolving differences they were also the outcome of the code by which aristocratic gentlemen lived. The developing system of manners and etiquette was an important force in the court system. Lord Chesterfield was later to note that politeness and good breeding were forced upon courtiers because otherwise court life would have been a 'seat of slaughter' as each individual sought to affront the other.[54] At court, politeness and etiquette were agents of social necessity and part of the civilising process. According to some, they also emerged from the deliberate policies of dissimulation and flattery adopted by the *habitués* of the court, which in the long term proved far more effective than violence.

More seriously, the pastime of drinking inevitably meant a brutal lifestyle which could lead to serious explosions of violence in brawls and duels. Heavy drinking appears to have been the norm. Lord Gerard, who was a 'great swearer, drunkard and very debauched', was to drop dead of drink aged twenty-two in the Rose Tavern, while Bishop Burnet relates the story that Rochester had been in an alcoholic stupor on and off for some five years.[55] The connection between alcohol and violence was obvious. Court life was always exhausting and full of tensions, it being easy to fall into disgrace, and courtiers tended to live on their nerves with odd hours and little sleep, so such tensions were never very far from the surface. While Charles II made various attempts to stamp out the resultant aristocratic violence, he met with little success.

In the end the court politician had of necessity to learn the new techniques of his trade and become a master of such arts as civility as he moved from being a medieval feudal retainer into the court community. A man who could use flattery, yet not appear to do so, and give off a sense of 'seeming negligence' and cheerfulness, which would mark him out from the crowd, was a man of note. Suppleness, versatility, easy and noble manners proved to be important factors in many a new courtier's rise. Above all one had to be seen with the proper devices, apt poses and witty inventions any courtier should have.[56] A successful courtier was in short the sum of many calculated poses.[57] The aspirant to power would also need patience, being forced to endure endless ceremony in cold rooms listening to the idle chit-chat of the bored and the boring with good humour. It was the versatility to endure such things that would get the man of mode noticed.

While most courtiers usually sought a sedate and profitable way through the maelstrom of court life, just occasionally the members of the aristocracy who went there were merely mad. A prime example was Philip Herbert, seventh earl of Pembroke, whose massive drinking bouts led him into psychotic rages and at least two killings in 1678 and 1681.[58] A child of the disruptive 1650s with its civil wars and domestic disharmony, Pembroke had finally succeeded to the family title in July 1674. Within days he was involved in a duel and had been twice run through. Labelled 'Boorish Pembroke brave' by Rochester, the earl followed a literal career of addiction to field sports, drinking and violent confrontations with all who came across his path. Naturally enough, few were at ease in his company and his notoriety often preceded him; because of this 'people were very apt to raise and credit, all reports to his prejudice'. Even so, Pembroke was imprisoned in the Tower in January 1678 for blasphemy, and later that year found guilty of manslaughter by his peers. A further killing followed in 1681, when the King pardoned him. He died, finally burnt out, aged thirty in 1683.[59]

A more typical Restoration fop was Robert Fielding.[60] He was nicknamed Beau Fielding by contemporaries and was descended from a good Warwickshire family. Upon his father's death Fielding came into £600 a year. Immediately abandoning the Inns of Court for a life of wine, extravagance and women, he came to Whitehall. The King nicknamed him 'Handsome' Fielding, as he always found Fielding surrounded by women and flamboyantly dressed. At court the fop's chief pastimes were to avoid business and creditors, to study the fashions and vices of the town, and endeavour to appear in a new suit of clothes each day. The only other interest of this profane, irreligious spendthrift was gambling. When in debt he lived off women to the extent of marrying three times, the last two bigamously, which landed him in jail. Under James II, however, Fielding seems to have temporarily reformed and swiftly became a Catholic, as a consequence of which he was given a regiment in the army. After the Revolution of 1688 he followed James II to Ireland and France. He soon tired of this and sought a pardon from the new regime, ending his days as the last surviving Restoration rake at the court of Queen Anne.

The average Caroline courtier was thus not very average. He was something of a social butterfly, constantly on the social round, prone to use the fashionable drawl that passed for conversation at court, as well as bad language. He kept a 'whore', indeed he was mocked if he didn't do so. He was often an expert gamester with loose morals and a violent temper, which meant he was quick to defend his honour. As a school for developing the worst aspects of human life, therefore, seventeenth-century courts could rarely be bettered. To succeed at court also meant much cogging and fawning, or so many contemporaries thought, and a necessary degeneration of character.

James II, William III and Mary II

There has been a view, no doubt derived from a reading of Macaulay, that the atmosphere of the court of James II, in comparison with that of his brother, was a gloomy, priest-ridden affair of dullness and mediocrity. Certainly at James's accession the court began to be moulded into a new image of frugality, sobriety and more refined ceremony. The number of posts at the court was cut by one-third, while more restraint and harder work were required of those who remained. In fact James II's move towards more respectability in court circles initiated something of a trend. It was seen at its fullest extent under William and Mary, both of whom were, in some respects, cast in a more puritanical mould than even James II had been.[61]

As James II settled into his government, ceremony at his court undoubtedly increased. Ambassadors, even those of France, were told that audiences had to be requested rather than expected. Barrillon noted of the new King that he had an intention to 'observe every formality and to preserve exactly all the externals of the royal dignity'. James II's parting shot to his brother's former mistress, Portsmouth, was to remind her to pay her debts before she left.[62] The new King's frugality was matched by an emphasis upon the divine nature of his kingship. The practice of the royal touch that had never declined under Charles II was given renewed emphasis under James. James 'cured' innumerable people and early in the reign he washed the feet of fifty-two of the poor at the Banqueting House. At Bath in 1687 he touched the sick. While James re-emphasised the more mystical side of his kingship, at his court there were some homely touches. He took to having a little table by his door at night with lights on it which 'growing duskish, he came out to take in the lights himself '. He also installed a weathercock on the roof of the Banqueting House, so that the 'old sailor' could see whether the wind was favourable, and in 1688, of course, it wasn't.[63]

Scandal, as well as the undercurrent of satire and violence, re- mained at the Jacobite court, but it was frequently out of sight. The libertines of Charles II's day were generally frowned upon, and many, but not all, left. In February 1688, for example, a lampoon, of a 'short but cutting nature', was even left pinned to the door of the anti-chamber of the King's bedroom. Occasionally fights between courtiers took place outside the King's chambers.[64] However, it was to be the King's policies rather than his personal behaviour which were to drive many away from the social ambience of the court. More than ever the gossip rang through the corridors of Whitehall about who was 'in' and who 'out' among the King's ministers. For all of this James set a trend for a new morality, which, if it did little else, re- stored some dignity to the monarchy, and may account for the still relatively full drawing room of courtiers at Whitehall on the eve of the Revolution. As John Evelyn commented, 'the face of the whole court [was] exceedingly changed [under his rule] into a more solemne and moral behaviour'.[65] Under pressure from his confessors and his wife, James even put away his mistress in January 1686. He had already let it be known that no duellists, drunkards or womanis- ers were to be admitted to his court, and that he disliked 'prophanesse [and] Buffoonery', probably because he did not understand most of it.[66] A programme of moral reform at court, stem- ming from either the King's strong self-righteous streak or his guilt complex (for he had indulged in sin as much as anyone in his broth- er's reign), appears to have been created to run alongside plans for the Catholic reformation of the Church and state. In an effort to keep up some appearances, James still acted as a patron of the arts. Plays were performed once or twice a week at court, even though accord- ing to one wag they merely gave the King an opportunity to catch up with his sleep.[67] Crucially, however, a religious atmosphere began to be fostered, not as much as was later to be seen in James's later exile at St Germain, but still sufficient enough to begin to stifle those who sought more robust pleasures. Moreover, at court it soon became essential to be a Roman Catholic, or at least openly inclined to Roman Catholicism.

Naturally the King engaged in rebuilding, pulling down the old Privy Gallery and buildings at Whitehall to replace them with new apartments for the Queen and a Roman Catholic chapel. The outside of these new buildings was created in the latest style and the interiors were lavishly furnished, with marble fireplaces, ceilings by Verrio, a great staircase in Portland stone and landings of black and white marble. The Catholic chapel of the King was rebuilt at Whitehall as part of a £35,000 renovation of the palace. All of James's buildings were either to be abandoned after 1688 or finally destroyed in the great fire at the palace in 1698, but for all of his faults James was committed to a baroque splendour in architecture as well as kingship. Money that emphasised the dignity of Catholic kingship was to James money well spent.

Social occasions still occurred on a regular basis. John Evelyn attended a 'solemn ball' on James's birthday in 1685 and talked to the King about music, of which James appears to have been fond; a magnificent entertainment was given for the Venetian ambassadors that same year at which the dinners were plentiful, with music, trumpets and kettle drums being sounded at every health.[68] The King spent many of his days hunting and moved from Whitehall to Windsor to Hampton Court to indulge himself in this pleasure. Visits to Bath, to allow his wife to drink the waters there, enabled James to make a progress through his lands.[69]

Yet there were still opportunities to be had at his court for the enterprising. The early career of John Churchill, the future duke of Marlborough, is perhaps the most prominent example of this trend.[70] In his early life Churchill was ambitious, grasping, calculating and 'too fond of pleasure, to discharge the duties of a colonel', and he was to prove time and again his familiarity with the crooked paths which a courtier was forced to tread. His loyalty to his patrons, James, duke of York, Barbara Villiers, duchess of Cleveland, and even Princess Anne, was never unconditional and he worked hard to exploit his good looks and charming manner. In the process he was chosen for a number of positions and clambered to the top of the court tree.

In his initial foray at the court of Charles II, Churchill arrived with a number of useful attributes for a courtier. He was young, personable, handsome, charming, something of a 'lady-killer' and willing to offer his services to his patrons in a number of ways. The fact that his sister Arabella was also mistress to James, duke of York, at the time gained him an entrée into the duke's circle. The post of a page of honour to the duke and a commission in the Foot Guards soon followed. In the early stages his military career ran parallel to that of a courtier, but the latter was possibly the more significant to him.

Certainly his next move was to bring its own rewards. Churchill's good looks attracted Barbara Villiers, duchess of Cleveland, the King's mistress, and as a man with an eye for the main chance he took the calculated risk of becoming her lover. It paid dividends in financial terms and in establishing his reputation at court. Marriage (for love, as it happened) to Sarah Jennings put an end to the future dalliances of the 'he-whore', as the wits labelled him, but by this stage Churchill had already abandoned Barbara, £5,000 the richer according to rumour. It was military service which really won Churchill the respect and friendship of James. Moreover, Sarah's place at the side of Princess Anne and Anne's faith in her friendship gave the Churchills a firm hold in her favour and the opportunity for self-aggrandisement. These actions bought criticism in their wake, but the Churchills were certainly no better or at least no worse than many others at the time. John Churchill's nature and activities have occasionally confused many of his biographers, who have sought in him only the virtuous military hero. In fact this characteristic was only partly there, but whatever his military gifts were, Marlborough was first and foremost a court politician. He remained infinitely pliable, especially where his own interests were concerned. He became a great favourite with the future King James and as a confidant of the new King's weak-willed daughter he seemed set fair for a prosperous career. Yet in 1688 he again gambled it all by turning against James to protect his own interests. A calculated, and never forgiven, abandonment of his former master brought him safely into the Orange camp.

Churchill's reputation, if not his pocket, did of course suffer from this exchange of masters. He became known as a 'Judas on both sides'. Yet seen in the light of his background it is neither as dishonourable nor as unlikely as it seems. The betrayal of James did nothing to gain the favour of William III, who while he was forced to use Churchill never trusted the smooth-talking Englishman. It did, however, gain more interest with Anne, with whom he seems to have decided his future lay. Even in the 1690s, however, Churchill was not to be trusted. Indeed he was briefly imprisoned in the Tower and lost his offices and favour as his latent Jacobitism brought him trouble, and his relationship with the Williamite court remained fraught until 1701. For all of his problems Churchill's career represents the epitome of the consummate court politician able to move with ease and little conscience from one patron to another. His amorality reflected his background and upbringing, his greed for tangible rewards reflected the uncertainty of life at court, and his ability to seize the main chance was a principal characteristic of the courtier's arts.

If in many senses the Revolution of 1688 attacked Roman Catholic ways, it also damaged the old style of court life which had emerged under Charles II and James II.[71] The 'softness and luxuriousness' of Charles II's court, which some said had spread like 'an infectious disease ... and broke the martial spirit of the English', was to be purged not only by war, but a more moral, even puritanical style, which left the court a duller place. Neither William's character, nor indeed that of Mary, was conducive to the active social side of the court that could attract much 'wit'. Early in the new reign John Evelyn had noted William's 'morose temper' when faced with the hordes of courtiers who expected a 'gracious and cheerful reception, when they made their court'.[72] Nor given his foreign origins was the new King particularly adept at patronage. Difficult to speak to, and not just because his English was poor, William also proved difficult of access. His brusque replies to petitioners were matched by an attempt to avoid them as much as possible, as he went about the business of governing the country, steadying an unsteady regime and preparing for the inevitable, and invariably unfortunate, new spring campaign.[73]

William's pleasures were few, and for the most part typically robust, mainly the military arts, hunting and shooting. The finer arts, however, held some attachment for William. The King possessed a good collection of porcelain that was subsequently shipped off to the Netherlands on his death. He was also fond of architecture, although mainly as an expression of power projection.[74] William even delighted in the popular formal gardens of the period and some art, although he patronised few painters during his life. For music he had little relish, his ear being, as Abel Boyer put it, 'tun'd to no other numbers than the Charge of the Trumpet, or the rattle of the Drum'.[75] Unfortunately the reputation of William as a cultural philistine pursues him still. His court style certainly left little room for the empty-headed hangers-on at the new court. Later in his reign he did try to create a social ambience and even occasionally let his somewhat severe demeanour slip, but on the whole a wave of cultural reform, grounded in William's case in a mixture of Calvinistic Puritanism and indifference, struck at the court.

Mary, a possibly more enthusiastic role player in the society of the new court, did try to keep up some appearances, but she also was a religious soul who was given to finding the court a 'noisy world full of vanity'.[76] She was also constrained by the method by which she had reached the throne in 1688 and forced for the most part to behave sensibly. She missed, as did William, the easier life left behind in the Netherlands. As William went off on campaign and Mary withdrew to religious contemplation, having no relish for 'lazy diversions', the face of the court changed. Fortunately alternatives to the lost social life of the court soon emerged in the clubs and coffee-houses of London. Certainly the couple's nearest in-laws were not much help in retaining the court as a society in which to play. Anne and George of Denmark were dull, argumentative and grumpy for much of the reign. When after Mary's death in 1695 a great con-course of prospective courtiers floated to them they must have been sorely tried at what they found there. In this respect the Churchills are perhaps to be admired for their persistence. However, a shift in sensibility was taking place. This was a continuation of change in moral attitudes that ultimately led to the reformation of manners and the decline of the court as a force in the cultural life of the nation.

Notes

1   Perhaps the best place to begin remains S. B. Baxter, *William III* (London, 1966). But see M. Ede, *Arts and Society under William and Mary* (London, 1979). Also W. J. Cameron, *Poems on Affairs of State: Augustan Satirical Verse, 1660–1714* (7 vols, New Haven, 1963–75), V, 1688–1697, and F. H. Ellis (ed.), *Poems on Affairs of State: Augustan Satirical Verse, 1660–1714* (7 vols, New Haven, 1963–75), VI, 1697–1704. H. Horwitz, 'The 1690s re-visited: recent work on politics and political ideas in the reign of William III', *Parliamentary History*, XV (1996), 361–77.

2   For one of the better popular interpretations see C. Hibbert, *The Court at Windsor: A Domestic History* (Harmondsworth, 1964), pp. 100–23.

3   Quoted in J. Sutherland, *Restoration Literature 1660–1700: Dryden, Bunyan and Pepys* (Oxford, 1990), p. 1.

4   A. Kernan, *The Cankered Muse: Satire of the English Renaissance* (Hamden CT, 1976), pp. 1–36. T. Hobbes, 'Answer to Davenant's Gondibert (1650)', in J. E. Springarn (ed.), *Critical Essays of the Seventeenth Century* (3 vols, Oxford, 1908), II, pp. 54–5. J. H. Wilson, *Court Satires of the Restoration* (Columbus OH, 1970), pp. ix–xx.

5   See T. Claydon, *William III and the Godly Revolution* (Cambridge, 1996), pp. 90–121. Also 'The reformation of manners: a satyr', in *Poems on affairs of state from the reign of K. James the first to this present year 1703 written by the greatest wits of the age* (2 vols, 1703), II, 340–77.

6   This is a vast area. See documents 4 and 16 for examples. For fur-ther reading see Wilson, *Court Satires of the Restoration*, pp. ix–xx. Cameron (ed.), *Poems on Affairs of State*, V, 1688–1697, pp. xxxvii–xliii. S. J. Owen, *Restoration Theatre and Crisis* (Oxford, 1996). R. D. Hume, *The Development of English Drama in the Late Seventeenth Century* (Oxford, 1976). D. Foxon, *Libertine Literature in England, 1660–1745* (New York, 1965). W. G. Marshall, *The Restoration Mind* (Newark, 1997), pp. 7–20. W. L. Chernaik, *Sexual Freedom in Restoration Literature* (Cambridge, 1995). J. H. Wilson, *The Court Wits of the Restoration: An Introduction* (London, 1967). *Poems on affairs of state from the reign of K. James the first to this present year*

Social and cultural life

1703 *written by the greatest wits of the age*. J. Powell, *Restoration Theatre Pro-duction* (London, 1984). T. A. Birrell, 'Roger North and political morality in the late Stuart period', *Scrutiny*, XVII (1951), 282–98. F. A. Nussbaum, *The Brink of All We Hate: English Satires on Women, 1660–1750* (Lexington, 1984). A. Bennet and N. Royle, *An Introduction to Literature, Criticism and Theory: Key Critical Concepts* (London, 1995).

7   R. Latham and W. Matthews (eds), *The Diary of Samuel Pepys* (11 vols, London, 1970–83), V, p. 60.

8   Kernan, *Cankered Muse*, pp. 1–36.

9   Ibid. See also Wilson, *Court Satires of the Restoration*, pp. ix–xx.

10   'A Satire on the Court ladies (1680)', in Wilson, *Court Satires of the Restoration*, pp. 36–40.

11   M. Thormählen, *Rochester: The Poems in Context* (Cambridge, 1995), pp. 2–8. B. Greenslade, 'Affairs of state', in J. Treglown, *Spirit of Wit: Reconsiderations of Rochester* (Oxford, 1982), pp. 93–106. K. Walker, *The Poems of John Wilmot, Earl of Rochester* (London, 1984). E. Burns (ed.), *Reading Rochester: English Texts and Sub-texts* (Liverpool, 1995). V. de Sola Pinto, *Enthusiast in Wit: A Portrait of John Wilmot, Earl of Rochester, 1647–1680* (London, 1962). F. H. Ellis (ed.), *John Wilmot, Earl of Rochester: The Complete Works* (Harmondsworth, 1994). H. Weber, *The Restoration Rake-hero: Transformations in Sexual Understanding in Seventeenth-Century England* (Madison WI, 1986), pp. 4, 6, 49.

12   J. Milton, 'A ready and easy way to establish a free Common-wealth (1660)', in C. A. Patrides (ed.), *John Milton: Selected Prose* (Harmondsworth, 1979), p. 335.

13   T. Hobbes, *Leviathan* (1651) (Harmondsworth, 1985), p. 183. See also K. Thomas, 'The social origins of Hobbes's political thought', in H. C. Brown (ed.), *Hobbes Studies* (Oxford, 1985), pp. 153–236. L. Teeler, 'The dramatic use of Hobbes's political ideas', *English Literary History*, III (1936), 140–69. Latham and Matthews (eds), *Diary of Samuel Pepys*, VII, pp. 228–9.

14   N. Elias, *The Court Society* (Oxford, 1983), pp. 146–213. N. Elias, *The Civilising Process* (2 vols, Oxford, 1982), II, pp. 258–70.

15   J. Hook, *The Baroque Age in England* (London, 1976). H. Trevor-Roper, 'The culture of the baroque courts', in A. Buck, G. Kaufman, B. G. Spahr and C. Wiedemann (eds), *Europäische Hofkultur im 16 und 17 Jahrhundert* (3 vols, Hamburg, 1981), I, pp. 12–23.

16   P. Burke, *The Fabrication of Louis XIV* (New Haven, 1992), pp. 5–19.

17   William Cavendish, duke of Newcastle, in T. P. Slaughter (ed.), *Ideology and Politics on the Eve of the Restoration: Newcastle's Advice to Charles II* (Philadelphia, 1984), p. 64.

18   G. Burnet, *A History of My Own Time* (6 vols, 2nd edn, Oxford, 1833), III, p. 12. W. G. B. Murdoch, 'Charles the second: his connection with art and letters', *Scottish Historical Review*, III (1905), 41–52.

19   J. Sutherland, 'The impact of Charles II on Restoration literature', in C. Camden (ed.), *Restoration and Eighteenth-Century Literature* (Chicago, 1983), pp. 251–63. Ede, *Arts and Society under William and Mary*. See also the important work of Owen, *Restoration Theatre and Crisis*. Hume,

Development of English Drama. B. Dobrée (ed.), *Five Heroic Plays* (Oxford, 1960). P. Hammond, 'Dryden's Albion and Albanius: the apotheosis of Charles II', in D. Lindley (ed.), *The Court Masque* (Manchester, 1984), pp. 171–5.

20   Hume, *Development of English Drama*, pp. 487–8. Also J. Brewer, *The Pleasures of the Imagination: English Culture in the Eighteenth Century* (London, 1997), pp. 9–18. S. B. Baxter, 'William III as Hercules: the political implications of court culture', in L. G. Schwoerer (ed.), *The Revolution of 1688–1689: Changing Perspectives* (Cambridge, 1992), pp. 95–106. Claydon, *William III and the Godly Revolution*, pp. 90–100.

21   Hook, *Baroque Age in England*, p. 45. R. W. Berger, *A Royal Passion: Louis XIV as a Patron of Architecture* (Cambridge, 1994), p. 2.

22   These paintings no longer survive in situ, but see D. Watkins, *The Royal Interiors of Regency England from Watercolours Published by W.H. Pyne in 1817–1820* (London, 1984), pp. 18–32, 40–1. Also Brewer, *Pleasures of the Imagination*, pp. 9–10.

23   *Dictionary of National Biography*, Antonio Verrio. See also A. S. Barnes, 'Catholic chapels royal under the Stuart kings: IV the later years of Charles II and the reign of James II', *Downside Review*, XXI (1902), 39–55. Dom G. Dolan, 'James II and the Benedictines in London', *Downside Review*, XVIII (1899), 94–103.

24   Baxter, *William III*, pp. 248–9.

25   Brewer, *Pleasures of the Imagination*, pp. 10–11. N. Robb, *William of Orange: A Personal Portrait* (2 vols, London, 1966), II, p. 230.

26   E. Halfpenny, 'Musicians at James II's coronation', *Music and Letters*, XXXII (1951), 103–14. P. A. Scholei, 'The Chapel Royal', *Musical Times*, XLII (1902), 88–92.

27   See P. Holman, *Four and Twenty Fiddlers: The Violin at the English Court 1540–1690* (Oxford, 1993). Also A. Ashbee (ed.), *Records of English Court Music* (14 vols, Aldershot, 1986–96), I, 1660–85 (1986), II, 1685–1714 (1987). R. King, *Henry Purcell* (London, 1994), pp. 23–4. F. B. Zimmermann, *Henry Purcell 1659–1695, his Life and Times* (2nd edn, London, 1983). One means to understand the musical life of the era is to listen to it. For this recommended listening would be The Parley of Instruments Renaissance Violin Band, 'Four and twenty fiddlers music for the Restoration Court Band', The English Orpheus Series, vol. 19 (Hyperion Records, 1993, CDA66667).

28   R. North quoted in Zimmermann, *Henry Purcell*, p. 67.

29   The King's Consort, 'H. Purcell, Complete odes and welcome songs volume 3' (Hyperion Records, 1990, KA66412) and Various, 'P. Humfrey, Verse anthems' (Harmonia Mundi, France, 1992, HMU907053).

30   Zimmermann, *Henry Purcell*, pp. 21, 24, 35, 37, 133, 136–7. J. C. Sainty and R. O. Bucholz, *Officials of the Royal Household, 1660–1837, Part I: Department of the Lord Chamberlain and Associated Offices* (London, 1997), p. 45.

31   E. S. de Beer (ed.), *The Diary of John Evelyn* (6 vols, Oxford, 1955), IV, p. 537.

32 King, *Henry Purcell*, pp. 142, 168–9. Zimmermann, *Henry Purcell*, pp. 154–79, 217.

33 R. D. Hume, 'The myth of the rake in Restoration Comedy', *Studies in the Literary Imagination*, X (1977), 25–55.

34 For contemporary impressions see *The character of a town-gallant exposing the extravagant fopperies of some vain self conceited pretenders to gentility and good breeding* (1675) and N. Williams, *Imago saeculi: the image of the age represented in four characters viz: the ambitious statesman, insatiable miser, atheistical gallant, factious schismatick* (Oxford, 1676).

35 G. Burnet, *A History of My Own Time, Part I: The Reign of Charles II* (2 vols, Oxford, 1897), I, p. 476.

36 Historical Manuscripts Commission (hereafter HMC), 12th Report, V, Rutland MSS (1899), p. 43, and *The life, amours, and secret history of Francelia, late duchess of Portsmouth favourite mistress to King Charles II* (1734), p. 52.

37 Robert Boyle quoted in *Oxford English Dictionary*, 'Wit'.

38 Wilson, *Court Satires of the Restoration*, pp. xi–xx.

39 T. Shadwell, *Bury Fair* (1689), in M. Summers (ed.), *The Complete Works of Thomas Shadwell* (5 vols, London, 1927), IV, p. 299. For Shadwell see also A. S. Borgman, *Thomas Shadwell, his Life and Comedies* (New York, 1989).

40 For the political activities of these men see chapters 3, 5 and 6.

41 J. Dryden, *Absalom and Achitophel*, in K. Walker (ed.), *John Dryden* (Oxford, 1987), p. 192.

42 G. Burnet, *A History of My Own Time, Part I: The Reign of Charles II*, I, p. 485.

43 Shadwell, *Bury Fair*, IV, pp. 332–3.

44 For Fleetwood Sheppard see Wilson, *Court Wits of the Restoration*, pp. 8–10, 37–8, 65–6, 216.

45 See documents 3 and 10.

46 Rochester quoted in V. de Sola Pinto, *Restoration Carnival: Five Courtier Poets: Rochester, Dorset, Sedley, Etheredge and Sheffield* (London, 1954), p. 17. Also Chernaik, *Sexual Freedom in Restoration Literature*.

47 Wilson, *Court Satires of the Restoration*, p. 61.

48 A. Fraser, *King Charles II* (London, 1980), p. 311.

49 H. Forneron, *Louise de Keroualle, Duchess of Portsmouth, 1649–1734* (2nd edn, London, 1887), pp. 155–6. HMC, 12th Report, V, Rutland MSS (1899), pp. 22, 96.

50 Forneron, *Louise de Keroualle*, p. 63, and HMC, 12th Report, V, Rutland MSS (1899), pp. 22–3. J. J. Jusserand, *A French Ambassador at the Court of Charles the Second* (London, 1892), pp. 89, 92–3.

51 HMC, 12th Report, V, Rutland MSS (1899), pp. 33, 34, 37–8. HMC, Montagu MSS (1900), p. 191. Forneron, *Louise de Keroualle*, pp. 45–6, 89, 92–3, 96–7.

52 E. Hyde, first earl of Clarendon, *The Life of Edward Earl of Clarendon, Lord High Chancellor of England* (2 vols, Oxford, 1857), II, pp. 338–9.

53 HMC, 12th Report, V, Rutland MSS (1899), pp. 34, 43.

54   C. Strachey (ed.), *The Letters of the Earl of Chesterfield to his Son* (2 vols, 2nd edn, London, 1924), I , pp. 354–5. Thomas, 'The social origins of Hobbes's political thought'. L. Stone, *The Crisis of the Aristocracy, 1558–1641* (abridged edn, Oxford, 1967), pp. 107–13.

55   G. Burnet, *A History of My Own Time, Part I: The Reign of Charles II,* I, pp. 476–7.

56   See for a number of examples B. Castiglione, *The Book of the Courtier* (Harmondsworth, 1981), pp. 113–14. Also *The character of a town-gallant.*

57   See E. C. Metzger, *Ralph, First Duke of Montagu, 1638–1709* (New York, 1987), pp. 24–9, 102–3. D. J. Milburn, *The Age of Wit, 1650–1750* (New York, 1966).

58   For Pembroke see A. Marshall, *The Strange Death of Edmund Godfrey* (forthcoming, 1999).

59   Ibid.

60   *Dictionary of National Biography,* Robert Fielding.

61   See below chapters 6 and 7.

62   J. Miller, *James II: A Study in Kingship* (London, 1989), p. 121.

63   T. Bruce, earl of Ailesbury, *The Memoirs of Thomas Bruce, Earl of Ailesbury* (2 vols, London, 1890), I, p. 178. British Library (hereafter BL), Additional MS 34510, fo. 50. BL, Additional MS 34508, fo. 12v. Dom G. Scott, *Sacredness of Majesty: The English Benedictines and the Cult of James II* (Huntingdon, 1984).

64   BL, Additional MS 34510, fo. 81v. De Beer (ed.), *Diary of John Evelyn,* IV, pp. 453–4. John Lord Viscount Lowther, *Memoirs of the Reign of James II* (York, 1808), p. 33. HMC, Frankland-Russell-Astley MSS (1900), p. 60. G. A. E. Ellis (ed.), *The Ellis Correspondence* (2 vols, London, 1829), I, p. 14.

65   De Beer (ed.), *Diary of John Evelyn,* IV, p. 415. HMC, Frankland-Russell-Astley MSS (1900), p. 60.

66   De Beer (ed.), *Diary of John Evelyn,* IV, p. 415. HMC, Frankland-Russell-Astley MSS (1900), p. 60. Also Burnet, *History of My Own Time* (1833), III, pp. 13–14.

67   'The court diversion (January 1686)', in Wilson, *Court Satires of the Restoration,* pp. 149–53.

68   De Beer (ed.), *Diary of John Evelyn,* IV, pp. 492–3.

69   Burnet, *History of My Own Time* (1833), III, pp. 189–90.

70   'The dear bargain: or, a true representation of the state of the English nation under the Dutch in a letter to a friend', in W. Scott (ed.), *Somers Tracts* (13 vols, 2nd edn, Edinburgh, 1809–15), X, p. 372. W. S. Churchill, *Marlborough, his Life and Times* (2 vols, London, 1966). Also J. R. Jones, *Marlborough* (Cambridge, 1993), pp. 10–56. H. J. Edwards and E. A. Edwards, *A Short Life of Marlborough* (London, 1926).

71   For the impact of the Revolution on the court see chapter 7.

72   De Beer (ed.), *Diary of John Evelyn,* IV, p. 620.

73   HMC, 12th Report, V, Rutland MSS (1899), pp. 125–6. G. Burnet in H. C. Foxcroft (ed.), *Supplement to Burnet's History of My Own Time* (Oxford, 1902), p. 312.

74   J. G. van Gelder, 'The Stadholder-King William III as collector and man of taste', in *William and Mary and their House* (New York, 1979), pp. 29–41. E. F. Strange, 'The furnishing of Hampton court in 1699', *The Connoisseur*, XIV (1906), 169–72.

75   A. Boyer, *The History of King William the Third* (3 vols, London, 1702), III, p. 517.

76   Document 29 and L. G. Schwoerer, 'The queen as regent and patron', in R. P. Maccubbin and M. Hamilton-Philips (eds), *The Age of William III and Mary II: Power, Politics and Patronage, 1688–1702* (New York, 1989), pp. 217–24. Ede, *Arts and Society under William and Mary*.

Part II

The court in three reigns

5

Court politics under Charles II, 1660–1685

Charles II and his court

Of Charles Stuart as monarch of his country it might be said that there are as many views as there are portraits of the King.[1] Even in his own lifetime Charles II was never an easy man to appraise. Yet understanding the King's character is essential for an understanding of his reign, for in an era of personal monarchy it was Charles who set the tone for much that happened around him at court and in the reign itself. Arguments over the King's personality and the politics of his reign began early in his rule and were to continue well after his death in February 1685. Following his brother's unfortunate reign and in the aftermath of the Revolution of 1688, Charles Stuart's character and actions continued to be seen in a critical light. His reputation declined in the more 'moral', upright and martial climate of the 1690s and he began to be seen as something of a blemish on the nation's past. The King was seen as a man prone to popery, if not an outright practising Papist, and few doubted that he had engaged in elaborate, albeit unsuccessful, absolutist schemes and plans. 'Merry monarch' or not, Charles had, noted one contemporary, brought the country into 'vice, softness and luxuriousness', and this disease, it was said, had spread throughout his kingdom, to the detriment of England's glory.[2] The reign was now to be portrayed as a technicolour scene of libertinism, sensuality and sexual dalliance, with a cynical King Charles presiding over a court of misrule.[3] These images of Charles have tended to devalue somewhat his actual character and the reality of his rule. In fact the King's reputation has been persistently caught up in a confusion of historical determinism, outright condemnation and even occasional rehabilitation as a result.[4]

One of the most formative influences upon Charles II's character was his day-to-day activities at his court. On one level Charles was actually as much a 'courtier' in the broadest sense of that word as any of those who surrounded him. He was a courtier king and the image of Charles as a courtier, adopting court tactics to suit his wider policies, is an eminently satisfactory one. It certainly explains his short-term view of life and events, as well as his often-crude political tactics. In addition, the King was a man who was somewhat careless of the future; he refused to commit himself to any political scheme for long, kept his actual beliefs as obscure as possible, and engaged in tactical alliances and schemes to remain on top of the political scene. He was in fact a participatory monarch in more than name.[5] He was also prone to those other court wiles: concealment and secrecy. These, as well as the theme of divide and rule, were ever present in all of his political manoeuvres. They led to ministers, courtiers, foreign potentates, mistresses and servants being set one against the other in a complicated balancing act which sometimes succeeded, but all too often simply failed to come off. On the other hand the view of Charles as a man who sought the easy life of wine and women is, at least in part, a misleading myth. Amongst those in the know the King possessed a deserved reputation for intelligence, complex political gerrymandering and even hard work when it suited him.

It has been relatively easy, and unfair, for armchair commentators to say that the King achieved little by his rule. Certainly in the long run Charles's foreign policy could be seen as detrimental to his country's interests, if not to his own. His domestic policy appears to have led to a series of emergencies and crises, mostly revolving around financial and religious questions. Additionally the King's personal life was chaotic and there were enough flaws in his psychological make-up, including an immensely cynical and occasionally downright nasty streak, to cause serious problems for both himself and those around him. But all of this becomes understandable in a court situation. That Hobbesian world of all against all, where trust was never given freely and life was always lived on the edge, not only reflected the King's personality, but in turn shaped both his personality and his rule.

The central core of Charles II's reign became the monarch's untrustworthiness in matters of religion. But Charles's tolerance for the beliefs of others, or even his personal inclination for the Catholic faith, was never really expressed by practical policies. Laziness, indifference, or fear of the consequences to himself kept getting in the way. This was equally true of the King's faith in an absolutist style of government, something clearly seen in his patronage of the arts, if not explicitly stated elsewhere. However, Caroline absolutism was never really put into practice.[6] Only twice does Charles seem to have channelled his energies into practical kingship: in 1669–72, when it led to war and disillusion, and in 1679–83, at the crisis point of his reign, when he defended his brother's right to succeed him. Otherwise Charles's main efforts in the course of his reign often seem to have gone into surfing the waves of government and preventing anyone, including his own ministers, from completing their own plans. Even so, government in the seventeenth century was not the easiest of tasks and while other monarchs' actions brought them to sticky ends, amongst them his own father and brother, at least Charles II died in his bed, confusing the issue to the last by alleged confessions of Roman Catholicism. In the end perhaps Charles is best summed up by his apocryphal rejoinder to Rochester's verse:

> God bless our good and gracious King,
> Whose promise none relies on;
> Who never said a foolish thing
> Nor ever did a wise one

Typically he shifted the blame, answering that 'My words are my own, but my acts are my ministers".[7]

Court intrigues, 1661–1674

The early years of the reign of Charles II found the English court and nation in a state of flux. The focus for much of the discontent both in the court and in the country at large soon came to lie at the door of the Lord Chancellor, Sir Edward Hyde, earl of Clarendon.[8] Rumours that Clarendon's political fortunes were in decline were frequent around the court in the early 1660s. Indeed court gossips such as Samuel Pepys, a ready, if sometimes fallible measure of the rise and fall of ministers, confidently and regularly predicted the Chancellor's political demise. Yet Clarendon's power was to prove rather more robust than many believed. It rested for the most part upon his past services for the monarchy whilst in exile, and upon a King who for the first few years of his reign at least was bent upon enjoying himself. With Charles at least on the surface leaving much of the tasks of government to his minister, the political facts of life appeared to bolster the Chancellor's position. There were apparently few opportunities for those who wanted to gain office other than on the Chancellor's terms. Unfortunately the number of Clarendon's enemies grew the longer he continued in power and they frequently sought solace in each other's company. Moves were soon afoot to band together to try to push him to one side. Such manoeuvres were to become commonplace in Restoration politics, as Charles allowed those who were 'out' to work hard to replace those who were already 'in' his favour. This system was to allow the King himself to play at 'divide and rule' amongst those around him. But as the court politics of the early 1660s developed they became something of a 'bear-garden', with individuals and groups jostling for attention and office, whilst policies rapidly coalesced and fragmented around the King.

For his part Clarendon controlled most of the levers of the new government. His own interests associated him with a group of men and clients who shared some of his ideals, and who may for convenience sake be labelled Clarendonians. James Butler, duke of Ormonde, Sir Edward Nicholas, and Thomas Wriothesley, earl of Southampton, proved to be the most prominent of his allies.[9] In the long run Southampton proved to be rather feeble in office as Lord Treasurer, while the duke of Ormonde was somewhat removed from the court's day-to-day politics by his post as Lord Lieutenant in Ireland. Conversely, although he was located at the court, Sir Edward Nicholas was a rather elderly gentleman, who proved unable to cope with life at court for long. This led younger men to stake their claim on the government and amongst these younger men no one man of the age better exemplifies the new court politics and its methods than Sir Henry Bennet, earl of Arlington.

The earl of Arlington was said by one contemporary to be 'a man bred from his cradle in the Court, [who] had no other business in the world than to be a good courtier'.[10] In fact his lengthy political career, which began in 1661 and only really concluded with his death in 1685, has meant that Arlington has suffered a poor press from friends, foes and not a few historians. No politician can be successful all of the time and Arlington's condemnation has taken many forms. He has been seen as a 'man of vanity'. He has been viewed as a dull, pompous, backstairs intriguer, who lacked not only the talent, but indeed the courage to bring him to real greatness. Yet while he was always obliging to his master's whims, with his fashionable clothes, polished manners and smooth tongue, Arlington was the court politician of his age: tactful, civil and ingratiating to his superiors, generous and obliging to his clients and inferiors. He sometimes found the rowdy atmosphere of the Caroline court distasteful and beneath his dignity as a gentleman, but he was also politician enough to know that to gain and retain power he had to stoop low and play the game. In the manner of his royal master, Arlington thus became a player of roles and he more than once managed to survive where others came to ruin.

In the late 1650s Bennet had been posted to Spain as a diplomat for the exiled Charles Stuart. There he had discovered not only the

Spanish court's formality, which stayed with him for the rest of his life, but the courtier's art: when to speak, when to remain silent, how to endure patiently, how to read men's faces and actions, how to make small talk.[11] His political manoeuvres in the reign itself appear to have been motivated by a genuine craving for power, which he seems to have shared with almost every politician of his generation. This was moderated by a fear of failure and a return to exile in Europe. There was unquestionably a genuine timidity in Arlington's character, which at least made him ever cautious in domestic as well as in foreign policy. His advice to his King always proved circumspect. When he had policies he was never 'wedded and glued' to them, to use that Cromwellian phrase. Indeed he proved to be a child of his age, being all too willing to cast policy aside where it conflicted with self-interest.

What then were the policies of Arlington? It is clear that he was personally in favour of religious toleration, but throughout his career he also thought it far too risky, both for himself and the government, to express this fact openly. He was in favour of efficient government and freedom from parliamentary influence. He hired some notable men to bring about the former and was only reluctantly cajoled into an attempt to influence the latter. 'Patience and shuffle againe', as he pointed out, became his philosophy towards not only Parliament but also life in general.[12] In foreign affairs Arlington was in favour of a pro-Spanish and anti-French line abroad, yet he was more than willing to move into a complete reversal of this policy in 1670. Indeed his slippery reversals of policy were such that to outside observers he quite often appeared to be on both sides at once, but none of this should be seen, as it so often has been, as hypocrisy. It was in the nature of a court artist such as Arlington to follow numerous lines of attack, to keep his options open, just occasionally all at the same time, and by so doing retain his position at court.

Time and again Arlington did show his cautious approach to affairs at court. He proved restrained in his comments in council, preferring 'opportunity in private whispers' as Clarendon put it. Some thought him arrogant, yet he was also believed by foreign ambassadors to be 'the most polite and obliging minister the English Court has'.[13] Indeed when faced with impeachment in 1674 he was able to win over even the sullen House of Commons with his subtle verbal dexterity and, it must be said, with some of the back room dealing which was his hallmark.[14] Even Clarendon, who hated him, was forced into admitting that Arlington had a winning way at times, particularly in private, 'where', the Chancellor noted, 'he frequently procured, very inconveniently, changes and alterations from public determinations'. Naturally his helpful nature and services to the young Charles II in exile had soon attracted the King's friendship. Thereafter Arlington used all of his skills of flattery to 'make himself acceptable to any man who loved to hear himself commended and admired'.[15] Religious faith, the core of many men at the time, was in Arlington redolent of all of the malleable qualities inherent in his temperament. While he was undoubtedly pro-Catholic, possibly due to his preference for social order, grandeur and stateliness (he still felt something of a parvenu), cautious to the last he refrained from declaring his religious beliefs until his dying moments.

Arlington thus remains the archetype of the ever-pliable politician on the make at the Restoration court: eager to retain office, resentful of enemies (Ruvigny, the French ambassador, said 'he would sell his soul to the devil to worst an enemy') and fearful of the consequences of his actions. His career also illustrates several other aspects of life there. One client of Arlington told Samuel Pepys that of all the 'great men of England, there is none that endeavours to raise those he takes in to favour [more] than my Lord Arlington, and on that score, he is more to be made one's patron than my Lord Chancellor'.[16] The men who crowded around Arlington in his years of power would doubtless have agreed, for Arlington proved to be a generous patron.

There is no doubt that the most momentous turn in Arlington's fortunes was his appointment as a Secretary of State. In 1662 he took control of this major office of state and was allowed substantial control of the foreign policy of the realm for the next few years. Being a Secretary also meant that Arlington was constantly in the King's eye, whether at the Council board, in the precincts of the bedchamber, or the outer court. Harry Bennet, the 'little gentleman', as Ormonde sarcastically called him, thus swiftly rose to become a major figure in the world of the court and government.[17] Naturally he had his detractors. If he was portrayed in satire and court lampoon as a vain 'arrant fop' and too formal for words, he lived up to this reputation in some respects. His nose, scarred from a skirmish in the civil war, he was to cover with a black sticking plaster, so that it could be noticed and it would emphasise his services to royalty. He always dressed in the height of fashion and fitted into his court role quite admirably, although it gave the wits wonderful scope for their satires.

Given his somewhat cynical view of life, on his arrival at court in 1661 Harry Bennet promptly decided to join the opposition to Clarendon led by the earl of Bristol. He was not alone in his choice, which seems to have been governed not only by his eye for the main chance, but also by the fact that one of Clarendon's besetting sins was his jealousy and obstruction of anyone who was younger and fitter for office than himself. As Bennet fell into both categories, and he had links with Bristol from the very beginning of his career, his decision becomes more obvious. In the early 1660s Bristol's court troops were to prove to be somewhat nondescript. They were made up from the 'little people' who collected around Charles at court and who sought to undermine Clarendon at every opportunity. However, taken in conjunction with other circumstances they could represent a powerful lever in the court to thwart the Lord Chancellor's designs. The faction, if it can be called such, included the King's 'companions of pleasure', the wits and hangers-on at court; Charles's current *maîtresse-en-titre*, Lady Castlemaine; as well as the Queen Mother and Lord Jermyn who had hated Clarendon in exile and were clearly resentful of his place in the Restoration government.

Being more mature and old-fashioned than most, Clarendon, even at the best of times, was reluctant to engage in daily court skirmishes with such individuals, and would not even attempt to placate them. His view of politics was that such matters had no role to play in the life of the state. In the long run this tactical error on his part was to cause him great difficulties. For it was soon clear that one of the more unpleasant aspects of the culture of the Caroline court was to take every opportunity to mock and ridicule the more sober members who worked there. As one later author pointed out

> The method they took in order to ruin any person, who was obnoxious to them, was to begin with raising a laugh at his expence by the mimicry, or rather the distortion of all his words and gestures. After frequently entertaining the King with these buffooneries, and placing ... [them] in a ridiculous light, they knew the transition would be easy from laughter to contempt; and then by continual, though almost imperceptible attacks, they widened the breach in a man's character, which was first effected under the show of mirth, so as to let in calumny and scandal enough to destroy the best built reputation.[18]

The 'little people' at least recognised where the true power lay, and being around the King most of the time, from his first waking moments to his mealtimes, in the bedchamber and especially during his leisure hours, they proved willing to use every opportunity to try to influence Charles's opinions for their own gain. They naturally took especial care to find fault with the Chancellor. How much effect this had upon Charles is a difficult matter to assess. At a later date the King became reluctant to be led by anyone and resentful of any that tried. But the constant sniping at the Chancellor's position must have given him food for thought. A callous cynic at the best of times, Charles would have doubtless weighed this fact alongside Clarendon's former and current services and the Chancellor's eagerness to take on the role of a nagging conscience to an otherwise amoral monarch.[19]

When Bennet became associated with Bristol, he did not neglect to secure his own route to Charles by gaining the King's confidence, and he sought other allies. While Charles liked Bennet's company, the courtier's engagement in the court politics of the era was initially similar to many others in his position. It began with a series of temporary tactical alliances to supplement his more strategic goal, his own *gloire*. As far as we can perceive, this was achieved in three ways: studied and circumspect advice to the King; the undercutting of rivals by astute conversational abilities, which even his enemies allowed was one of Arlington's main talents; and the gathering to himself of clients and dependants, who could then be placed into the strategic offices of the government to become reliable lieutenants. This would also have the effect of letting everyone know that he was a force to be reckoned with at court.

For his part Clarendon's personality was not one to win friends in the somewhat immoral court atmosphere in which he found himself. Rather old-fashioned, he tended to look down upon the King and his companions as rude, untutored and basically immoral. A shocked Clarendon later wrote that they were:

> confident young men [a crime in itself for the Chancellor]; who abhorred all discourse that was serious ... preserved no reverence to God or man, but laughed at all sober men, and even at religion itself; and ... the custom of this license ... would by degrees [give them] ... the presumption ... to enter ... into business.[20]

If Clarendon noted one method of entering into the real business of government, it was far from being the whole story. Most, if not all, of Charles's chosen ministers had some ability to offer: Thomas, Lord Clifford, and Sir Thomas Osborne, earl of Danby, were well versed in financial and parliamentary management, while Antony Ashley Cooper, earl of Shaftesbury, had his innate shrewdness, links to the City of London and tactical political skills to play with. James Butler, duke of Ormonde, who governed Ireland for the King for many years, was noted for his loyalty, while John Maitland, earl of Lauderdale, had extensive Scottish experience. Later ministers such as Robert Spencer, earl of Sunderland, possessed notable tactical court and management skills, while George Savile, marquis of Halifax, was a noted wit and orator. Arlington of course had his extensive knowledge of foreign affairs. Charles came to show ample evidence that he knew much more about his ministers' greed, weaknesses and talents than perhaps they did themselves. As Halifax was to point out, the King ultimately came to live with them 'as he did with his mistresses; he used them, but he was not in love with them'.[21]

Nor was Clarendon enamoured of Lord Arlington, as Bennet

became in 1662, for the latter took most easily to flattery and dissembling, as well as 'turning the gravest and most substantial discourses into ridicule', 'which', complained the Chancellor, 'was a wit much in fashion' at that time.[22] Although capable of ruthlessness himself, the Chancellor became increasingly reluctant, or unable, to immerse himself in the quicksand of court politics. Frequent illnesses led to his absences on crucial occasions. But he was safe as long as he retained the support of the King. As others were to find, Charles's support was at times a flexible commodity. While the King recognised Clarendon's former services, he swiftly grew to resent his pompous self-importance and rather brusque manners, which the Chancellor was later to pass off as delivering his opinions freely, usually on all subjects, whether they concerned him or not.[23] The other courtiers feared that Clarendon's obstructive views on government, and his connections by marriage to the duke of York, could in the end lead to his long-term domination of the regime. This would mean frustration for those who were not associated with him in what would become a closed patronage system.

In fact Clarendon's obstruction of Arlington's advice and policies in particular was only matched by his sometimes perverse blocking of the younger members of the court. This fortunately meant that Arlington found additional allies amongst them and he took every opportunity that came his way to undermine his enemy. As we have seen, the formation of a faction was one of the commonest ways in which a prominent man could become more prominent. Factions invariably had their connections in the court, in the administration, in Parliament and in local government. Arlington's most notable allies in his early years at court, albeit temporary, included William Coventry, one of the most abrasive men at court. Coventry was to gamble heavily in destroying the Chancellor, but eventually lost out because his personality came to irritate the King. Arlington also associated with the King's friend Sir Charles Berkeley, earl of Falmouth. A generally neglected figure in the histories of the time, the latter's flourishing influence was cut short by his untimely death in 1665.[24] More significantly Arlington was ever on the lookout for the best of the younger men at court to assist him. He was responsible for furthering the careers of a number of young hopefuls who became his clients in all the areas of government. Three men in particular stand out: Thomas, Lord Clifford, who was used in Parliament; Joseph Williamson, who assisted his patron in the secretariat; and Sir William Temple, who swiftly became part of Arlington's team of diplomatic contacts.[25] In fact the clients of Arlington eventually inhabited most of the major embassies of Europe: Temple in The Hague, William Godolphin in Madrid, Robert Southwell in Lisbon, John

Trevor and Edward Montagu in Paris. In domestic politics many of these men proved to be less sure-footed than Arlington himself, but the Secretary at various times in their careers used their genuine talents.

Arlington made himself a useful servant to Charles II, and his slow growth into the position of Secretary of State also assisted his claims on the King. Those who sought Arlington's patronage on the other hand invariably found themselves cold-shouldered by the Chancellor. But it was to be Arlington rather than Clarendon who was to survive the first real crisis of the reign. It must not be thought that Clarendon's position suddenly collapsed. A process of continual erosion, which proved to be the norm in most ministers' careers in the period, had taken place. Clarendon seemed to play a negative role in all of the events he touched in the period: the marriage of his daughter Anne to the heir to the throne in September 1660, which initially provoked much opposition in the royal family; the King's marriage to the barren Catherine of Braganza; the sale of Dunkirk; as well as the failure of Charles's plans for religious toleration. In his autobiography Clarendon attributed his fall to the envy of others, but generally it was as much due to his acts of omission as his acts of commission. His refusal to assert his authority and the influence he still had with the King, other than in a manner Charles began to find irritating, did his cause more harm than good. His inability to deflect criticism from the acts that, whether correctly or not, carried his name meant that in the end he was held accountable in popular opinion.[26]

By the spring of 1663 it was generally believed once more that Clarendon was on his way out as a force in politics. Failures in Parliament, as well as diverse groups of opposition to him, which had continued to emerge, clouded his successes. Also the opposition to the Chancellor now included the gloriously dangerous figure of George Villiers, duke of Buckingham. Buckingham was a figure who, as we have seen, appeared at various points in the history of the court and politics of Charles II, usually trailing ill-will behind him for all concerned. To those in the know, of course, Charles's opinion of his most wayward minister, which he openly expressed to the French ambassador, was that Buckingham was the most useless of men when in power and the most dangerous of men when out of it.[27] The King evidently shared with President Lyndon Johnson of later years the somewhat crude politician's view that it was better to have such an unstable man 'inside the tent pissing out, than outside [the tent] pissing in'.[28] In fact these new advisers appeared to some to be gaining increased strength in the King's councils. But once again Clarendon survived, mainly due to his good fortune rather than his own energies.

The opposition to him continued to revolve around Barbara Villiers, Lady Castlemaine, the King's mistress, and George Digby, the earl of Bristol, both of whom were Clarendon's mortal enemies. Castlemaine, whom Clarendon in his biography always referred to as the 'lady', and never by name, was entirely hostile to his interests, and it was her rooms which provided a meeting place for those who wanted the Chancellor eliminated as a force in politics.[29] As Charles also tended to spend his leisure time with Barbara, it seemed there were golden opportunities to criticise Clarendon, mock his attitudes and undermine his position. These happy hours came under a cloud, however, with the arrival of a new beauty on the scene: Frances Stuart. The arrival of Frances at court and her subsequent pursuit by the King somewhat dimmed Barbara's star. Enterprising courtiers, who had previously fluttered around Barbara in the hopes of patronage, sniffed a new mistress in the offing and soon began to abandon her. Unfortunately for Charles, Frances was reluctant to play the role of mistress; so much so that both Arlington and Buckingham became part of the legendary committee set up to get Frances into bed for their lord and master. In Arlington's case Frances was merely amused by his attempts to pimp for his master and laughed at him. But Castlemaine's position as a force at court was diminished by these antics and one source of the baleful influence on the Chancellor was, if not removed, somewhat lessened.[30]

Away from these sexual frolics, whose political aspects should never be underestimated, a more significant collapse occurred. In late June and early July 1663 the earl of Bristol's obsessive hatred of Clarendon finally overstepped the mark with a plan to engineer the impeachment of his opponent in Parliament. A furious Charles, still supportive of the Chancellor for his own reasons, was enraged at action taken without his authority, and banished Bristol from the court. The earl's further antics ensured his subsequent political demise.[31] As these events strengthened Clarendon's hand, others were forced to shift their ground and allegiances. Arlington and Buckingham had kept themselves aloof from Bristol's actions and Pepys was not alone in pointing out that 'My Lord Chancellor grows great again'.[32] With the drift towards the disastrous war against the Dutch in 1665, however, the court once again became torn with faction.

Although Clarendon was one of the few in the government who were actually against the Dutch war, the weaknesses and rifts in the regime were soon to be exposed under the pressure of the war. In this period war illuminated many areas of the regime which were in need of reform, and in the case of the Dutch war of 1665–67 one of the obstructions to a reform of the English government, which Charles came to favour, appeared to be Clarendon. The Lord Chancellor's view of the government system was generally a conservative one. It was based around his belief in a strong Privy Council composed of a few men, which would serve to 'restrain the encroachments of parliament, while respecting its privileges, and … to check the undue influence of official favourites'.[33] He was also reluctant to involve the monarchy too deeply in parliamentary management, favouring an old-style balanced constitution of a pre-Civil War vintage.[34] Of course management of Parliament, which held the purse strings, became an essential part of financing the war. At first Clarendon was only reluctantly cajoled into letting Arlington, William Coventry and Clifford make an attempt at this most difficult of questions. Moreover, his reliance on the old-fashioned virtues of the Privy Council also led to problems. Throughout his reign Charles preferred working in smaller cabinet councils, as it enabled the secrets of state to be kept amongst a small group of personally selected advisers and allowed the King to play at divide and rule amongst them.[35] Clarendon's stand against the war also alienated many of the young bloods at court. Led by the King's brother James, duke of York, they were attracted to war like most aristocrats by the wealth, glory and martial valour it would bring in its wake.

Charles himself, preferring an easier life and not at all a martial prince of the old school, was decidedly lukewarm about the conflict that broke out on 22 February 1665. Clarendon, the nominal head of the government in others' eyes, if not his own, also soon proved that he was not a war minister. He later argued, somewhat disingenuously, that strategy was 'so much [out] of his sphere, that he never pretended to understand what was fit and reasonable to be done: nor throughout the whole conduct of the war was he ever known to presume to give an advice; but presum[ing] that all whose professions it was advised what was fit, he readily concurred'.[36] Unfortunately for him the conflict went badly wrong from the beginning – no allies, other than the feeble forces of the bishop of Munster, failures at sea, the ravages of plague, fire and a corrupt administration culminated in the final shame at the Medway when part of the English fleet was destroyed at anchor.[37]

As is the nature of such things, if Clarendon claimed not to want to run the war, others were not so reluctant to be seen to be involved. The younger men at court took the opportunity to stake their claims for power, and the pack was led by Arlington, Buckingham, Antony Ashley Cooper, the former Cromwellian and future earl of Shaftesbury, John Maitland, the earl of Lauderdale, who controlled Scotland for the King, and the aggressive William Coventry. Of these the re-emergence of Buckingham proved a pointer for things to come. At least the duke's constant belief in his own abilities never flagged. By 1666, disappointed at not getting the lion's share of the glory of war, he began to make overtures to various disgruntled factions in Parliament and those with 'levelling principles'.[38] At first Charles regarded these dabblings with vague amusement. He saw Buckingham as a political butterfly that was never constant for very long. However, as the need to finance a failing war rapidly became more problematic, the duke's interference soon got him into trouble. His attacks on Ormonde, via the Irish Cattle Bill, led to a scuffle with Ossory, Ormonde's son. The emergence of tales of his involvement with astrologers and republicans, revealed by a helpful Arlington, infuriated the King and led to Buckingham's brief incarceration in the Tower of London in 1667. As the war went from bad to worse, all of the King's advisers began to position themselves for the aftermath of the conflict. Naturally when faced with a difficult Parliament some scapegoat would be required for the war's misfortunes. So Buckingham feverishly sought to build up links with parliamentary groups, while Arlington stuck ever closer to the King, and the anger of the nation began to focus on Clarendon, the 'kingdom's broker' with his 'Pride, lust, ambition, and the people's hate'.[39]

Clarendon himself believed that his destruction in 1667 was more personal than political, and it must be asked how far he was right in this respect? The reasons for his fall in 1667 are certainly to be found in the disasters of war, the failures in Parliament and a background of misfortunes from Dunkirk to the regime's religious policies. But he also failed to manage the court. Certainly the Lord Chancellor's criticism of the King's personal life rapidly begin to irritate Charles. Clarendon's obtuse, and sometimes perverse, obstruction of the younger courtiers whom the King began to favour also led to their alienation. His reluctance to flatter the men of wit, mistresses and hangers-on around the King ensured their hatred and ridicule. This was also fuelled by their fear that he might finally succeed in dominating court office and patronage and block them out altogether. Most importantly, however, Charles himself grew tired of the old man's rule and needed a scapegoat to placate a disgruntled nation. When the King himself came to accept that Clarendon would have to be removed, the Chancellor's fate was sealed.[40]

In fact Clarendon's fall came in two stages: first his dismissal from his office as Lord Chancellor and then moves for his impeachment by Parliament. The first of these events was the result of the persuasion of Charles by William Coventry, Arlington and the newly released Buckingham that someone would have to fill the role of scapegoat, and as they did not wish to fill the role, Clarendon was the most suitable candidate. Charles eventually agreed that the Chancellor had to go. He was to write to the ever-loyal Ormonde that: 'The truth is, his [Clarendon's] behaviour and humour was grown so unsupportable to myself, and to all the world else, that I could not longer endure it, and it was impossible for me to live with it', and more significantly he went on to say that to 'do those things with Parliament that must be done [he must go], or the Government will be lost'.[41] Persuasion and hints at resignation having proved ineffectual, Charles was finally forced to take the seals from Clarendon in August 1667. At that point the old man's fall could have led to a mere graceless retirement from the scene, but Buckingham was not content to let the ex-Chancellor off so lightly. His fear was that although Clarendon was out of favour for the present, he could well come back at some stage into the King's plans, and if possible he had to be completely removed from the scene. Leading a group of ambitious younger politicians, most of whom were piqued at Clarendon's former rejection of their services and frustrated that his allies still held on to the offices they so desired, Buckingham persuaded Charles that he alone could raise supply in Parliament, but that the cost would be the destruction of Clarendon by impeachment. In fact Clarendon had only been forced out of office with great reluctance, and still continued to protest his innocence. The Pilate-like Charles had hoped that the old man would now take the hint and leave the country voluntarily. However, it soon became clear that faced with intransigence Charles could and would turn viciously against those he saw as opposing his will and did nothing to prevent the impeachment of Clarendon proceeding along its course. Indeed Charles, riding out the approaching storm, began to encourage the impeachment himself. As the ex-Chancellor's enemies closed in for the kill, Buckingham's men such as Sir Edward Seymour made 'inflammatory speech[es in Parliament] on the late chancellor's corrupt practices and pernicious counsels' and Clarendon, fearing for his life, was forced into exile in November 1667.[42]

What can the Lord Chancellor's fate tell us about the nature of court politics in the early part of the reign? In effect the variety of challenges a minister under Charles II now had to face to survive are illuminated by Clarendon's fall. Even without the war, the difficult assignment of managing Parliament, the court and the government to the satisfaction of all concerned, and particularly the King, was to prove an almost impossible task. Moreover, the reluctance of any minister to involve himself in the activities of the court could prove fatal to his survival. To hang upon the King's word, enjoy his confidences and whisper advice into his ear now seemed to be the norm if a minister wished to succeed. Yet even this was not enough. An awareness of the backstairs intrigues and a sixth sense for the complexities of the political situation would highlight two other elements in court politics after 1667. The first was the role played in Clarendon's destruction by the King himself. With his cynical disregard for the old man's services, Charles had for the first time openly set out his stall for the rest of the reign. For now he would involve himself in making his own policy, either above that of his ministers or, as it turned out, behind the backs of most of them. Should they fail him he would have little hesitation in allowing them to be cut down. Secondly, the use made by ambitious rival courtiers of the spectre of Parliament uncovered another potentially dangerous route into office. Such ambitious men would subsequently try to raise Parliament itself against ministers, and, like Buckingham, claim that they could raise supply for the King as 'undertakers'. In reality whether any man could marshal the disparate forces of court and Parliament in the face of the calculations of the wily Charles Stuart was to become one of the great problems of the age.

It is alleged that at the fall of Clarendon, Baptist May, one of the 'little people' at court, flung himself at his master's knees and declared that Charles was now truly a king. And in the wake of the Lord Chancellor's removal, it does seem that for the first time in his reign the King was more than ready to assert himself both at home and abroad.[43] The period from 1667 to 1674 has a mythology of which no element is more enduring than the idea of the 'Cabal' ministry. In reality the King's often disparate group of ministers of these years had little in common aside from the urge to eliminate one another from the political scene and an inclination for toleration in religion, to varying degrees and for a variety of motives. In fact if the policies of this period of the reign reflect the ideas of anyone then it is those of Charles II himself. Freed as they were from the shackles of Clarendonian management, these new schemes included a number of significant elements which were to set the tone for the rest of the reign: the management of Parliament; toleration for his Roman Catholic subjects and, as a by-blow to this, the non-conformists; an assertion of the monarchy's prerogative powers; and new attempts to correct the regime's finances. But the scheme that was ultimately to cause most trouble of all was the creation of an alliance with the France of Louis XIV for it led to another failed war. Out of this war would come a return to an old form of politics with the King's reliance upon one minister to dominate the political scene. So the mid-1670s were to be dominated by a 'flaming meteor, above our horizon', the pale-faced Lord Treasurer with a bad stomach and blackened teeth: Sir Thomas Osborne, earl of Danby.[44]

The Danby ministry, 1674–1679

It was not an auspicious beginning for the new Lord Treasurer, as Osborne became in 1673. He had been called to the helm of government amidst the raging storms of a dissolving ministry and in the wreck of a lost war. His subsequent struggles to remain afloat in this sea of troubles were to be increasingly hampered by the ambitions of a foreign king, Louis XIV, a factious and uncooperative Parliament, and the envy and malice of his rival courtiers. In turn Danby, as we should now call him, set himself the impossible task of reconciling the irreconcilable. He sought to make Charles II, whose methods and activities were naturally secretive and whose aims were not those of his minister's, journey along with a nation which by the 1670s had acquired an intense prejudice and distrust of the court itself, and saw it as a nest of popery and French influence.

In order to achieve his purpose Danby hoped to create a policy of coupling loyalty to the monarchy with the Anglican religion, thereby bolstering the Cavalier interest and establishing some of the basis for winning financial security, whilst treading as carefully as possible through the minefield of the court. Certainly John Evelyn thought the new earl 'haughty & [of a] far less obliging nature & [someone] from which I could hope for little'.[45] Indeed throughout his years of power Danby was never to be noted for his personal generosity. The earl of Shaftesbury, his greatest enemy, called him a man of 'art, power and interest. I wish (and so we all have reason) that we were rid of him [and] ... deliver ourselves from this meteor that hangs over us.'[46] Moreover, with his rough Yorkshire manners Danby was still very much the outsider at court. Recently ennobled and all too aware of it, he was the archetypal country gentleman made good. This fact of life may have brought even more urgency to his attempts at consolidating his position by a variety of means.

The newly promoted Lord Treasurer did not lack ambition. As the second son of a relatively recent minor gentry family, he had effectively made his own way in the world. Lacking the social connections of a Buckingham or even an Arlington, he initially used the marriage market to maintain his social position on the county scene. His marriage to Lady Bridget Bertie in May 1653 was a good one for a promising young man to make and according to Dorothy Osborne he looked upon the affair with a cool eye, as 'nothing tempted him ... [to marriage] so much as that she was an earl's daughter'.[47] Bridget was the second daughter of Montague, earl of Lindsey, and for Osborne this marriage provided him with a wife with links to a considerable part of the noble houses of England. His wife's relations, the Berties, were subsequently to prove both innumerable and grasping, but in the end he turned them into his political allies. Not surprisingly, the marriage market subsequently proved a major pillar to Danby's career. In ever-increasing circles as he rose to power, he used relatives, sons and daughters to create a family network. Making socially brilliant or financially successful matches, the Osbornes, with their multitude of connections, were often compared to the Habsburg House of Austria by their rivals.

In order to protect and expand his new ministry, in 1674 the Lord Treasurer sought to use practical management techniques upon those most troublesome elements of the constitution: Parliament and the court. Danby attempted to create a solid core of followers. In the case of Parliament he thus became one of the first of the real 'undertakers', men who guaranteed the monarchy supply by undertaking to manage the House of Commons for the crown's benefit. In many ways the foundation material was already available for this strategy. Danby already possessed the personal loyalty of his family and friends, and to this was added the 'party' loyalty of those in the old Buckingham group who had come over to him. To the local loyalty of Osborne partisans in Yorkshire and Bertie partisans in Lincolnshire, were added an inheritance of Lord Clifford's former partisans from the south-west, a group who now owed allegiance to Edward Seymour. He was Speaker of the House of Commons by 1673, and possessed a strong influence in Devon.[48] Danby's activities led to the formation of a 'party' in the broadest sense of the word, but the reliability of his followers was in fact very dubious. And however hard Danby worked, he met with obstacles at every turn. As a result, his ministry was exemplified by the number of annotated lists of wilful members of Parliament that are to be discovered in his personal papers, and by the continual struggle to sustain both his policies and position.[49]

Some of these connections, however, are worth briefly exploring for the light that they throw on the new system. During the course of the 1670s, for example, Danby's familial connections to holders of the Lords Lieutenancy in the various counties are particularly noticeable. On the local level this office interested Danby because it was an office which could be used to influence elections. A brief survey of the connections he made there opens up a world of sub-groups and familial ties. In a survey of the holders of the office of Lord Lieutenant in the 1670s Danby's brother-in-law the earl of Lindsey was located in Lincoln, and was also Lord Great Chamberlain at court. Danby's other relatives were scattered around the country: his wife's half-brother Lord Norris in Oxford; his wife's brother-in-law Viscount Campden in Rutland; his wife's brother-in-law's eldest son, Edward Noel, in Hampshire. Even distant relatives were dragged into the Danby fold. His fourth daughter's cousin by marriage, the earl of Pembroke, was to be found in Wiltshire, and was also married to the sister of his ally, the duchess of Portsmouth; his fifth daughter's father-in-law, the earl of Bath, had control of Cornwall. In addition, by 1678 Danby had two of his sons, three brothers-in-law, one brother, one son-in-law and a host of lesser relatives established in the House of Commons.[50] Unfortunately the Danby clique's obvious enthusiasm for honours, cash and favours made both them and their master hated. This antagonism grew as Danby's power increased.

At court Danby had other problems. The earl was never a 'companion in pleasure' able to enjoy the King's society and so he remained very much the outsider there. In an attempt to compensate for this, Danby began to associate with some of the King's mistresses, making an early alliance with Portsmouth and using his wife to try to influence Elinor Gwyn, in order to influence the King.[51] According to Sir John Reresby, Danby's wife also assisted him in a 'secret trade of taking bribes for good offices'.[52] Nor was he above keeping a mistress himself and drinking hard in order to establish himself as a courtier of the old school. To this end Bishop Burnet noted that like many another courtier Danby was 'a very plausible speaker' and 'gave himself great liberties in discourse [but] did not seem to have any great regard for the truth'.[53] Certainly the Lord Treasurer's insinuating manner could make men who wished to believe that he was their staunch ally and friend convinced he was so. Sir Henry Goodricke's comments to Sir John Reresby in December 1674 illustrate his methods, especially the techniques used to ensnare his own Yorkshire folk: 'My Lord Treasurer increases daily in favour and consequently has so great a Court att his house, as is scarcely credible, [but] hee is the same man to his Countrymen as ever, full of civility and ready to oblige'.[54] Positive and reassuring, with his thin pale face and blackened teeth, the result of a constant stomach problem, Danby even seems to have given the wary Charles Stuart the confidence that 'all things would go according to his mind in the next session of Parliament'. And after his hopes failed him, 'he had always some excuse ready, to put the miscarriage upon that'.[55] Despite this, Charles did not enjoy his minister's company as he had that of Arlington. The minister was demanding. William III later noted Danby's aggressive stance towards monarchical patronage and stated 'l[or]d Danby did never speak of anything but to recommend men ... [and] Did not ask of things as favours but as his right. This was his style with Charles 2d ... [indeed] Charles 2d incouraged him to use that method.'[56]

In the long run this need not have mattered, for after all it was Danby's abilities which finally kept him in power. Yet perhaps even these have been exaggerated. Certainly the earl never forgot an enemy and his rapacious nature meant that those who would not totally subordinate themselves to his will, or were simply too able, were often brutally thrust aside. It was his belief that the great men at court came at too high a price for their allegiance and thus he favoured gaining 'ten ordinary men cheaper then one of these'.[57] In part this was due to his innate jealousy of anyone with too much credit with the King other than himself. Many of the courtiers were also appalled by the financial retrenchments Danby began to institute and even the duchess of Portsmouth was jokingly advised by Charles to 'make a friendship with the Treasurer' if she wished to keep up appearances.[58] At the same time, as the earl of Essex's informant put it, Danby was prone to 'laye about him & provide for his family'. It was suggested that this was a double-edged sword in the end, 'for if he comes to be out with ye King his enemies will [certainly] maul him'.[59]

On one level Danby was undoubtedly motivated by a fear of what had happened to his predecessors. Amongst his other activities, therefore, he made a conscious attempt to control the sources of patronage, or a least run the bulk of them through himself and his clients in order to make those around the King come to him for favour. He had apparently learned much from the fall of Clarendon, especially that the 'companions of pleasure' around the King could be dangerous given their ready access to Charles's person. This degree of danger of course varied with the King's moods, but Charles certainly allowed his immediate entourage great licence to turn his ministers 'en ridicule', as Ralph Montagu put it. It was said that Buckingham was soon prone to performing accurate and satirical impersonations of Lady Danby before the King.[60] The danger to those at court from the all-powerful Lord Treasurer was equally apparent: if Danby and his lackeys won control over everything then those not in his favour would lose out. So the struggle which resulted was intense. Not that the Treasurer took the easy road. He was 'bold … in making enemies, depending wholly on his credit with the King, which all people wonder at, he having seen so many effects of [the King's] inconstancy'.[61] Danby's brother-in-law, the earl of Lindsey, later noted that the situation could not last for ever, for 'I always thought the court of no good complexion towards your Lordship and that if such small things as Bab May, Chiffinch, Godolphin and others had influence enough with their master to have removed you, it had long since been effected'.[62]

Danby's reputation as a politician in this first phase of his career was based upon his financial skills. In this, the ultimate base of his power, the Lord Treasurer proved both able and efficient, rather than brilliant. Although an expansion of trade and prosperity in the 1670s gave him some advantage, Danby was hampered by an obvious reluctance to prevent the extravagance of a King whose expenditure rose in proportion to the money available. Retrenchment indeed proved virtually impossible to achieve, for prestige as well as personal reasons. Not only would it have damaged Danby's own interest at court, it would have threatened his relationship with the King and the duchess of Portsmouth, as parsimonious treasurers, then as now, were never popular. However, Danby's policy of 'management' in the coils of revenue and expenditure, allied to the patriotic 'Church and King' stance of his ministry, did bring in some extra cash. He was also friendly with many of the City of London bankers, although he tended not to encourage men cleverer than himself in financial matters. Yet on his fall in 1679 he bequeathed a debt to his successors of £2.4 million. In part this was due to his adoption of certain political tactics to which we must now turn.

As we have seen, the creation of a court party based on family ties was one aspect of Danby's policy. There is also little doubt that in one form or another Danby sought to win over minor MPs through a policy of 'compensation'. His techniques, previously unused according to contemporaries, were also to proffer titles, land and cash to those whose services he thought worth buying.[63] Should they fail to honour the deal, or reject it out of hand, it was said that Danby's answer was to give out that his victim could have been bought in any case and thus his reputation became odious to his party and either way the Lord Treasurer gained his point.[64] Alternatively, the accepted offer of land, title, office, gifts, pensions, straight cash or a combination of all of these elements meant the recipient was then under some obligation to the giver. This arrangement was strengthened by the fact that the receiver at any moment might be deprived of it should they fall into disfavour. Danby's use of the Excise to engage individuals and entangle them in the pensions system proved a significant novelty in this sense. With the payment of certain secret service monies through the hands of his minion Charles Bertie in the Treasury, a machine of management was being effectively tried out for the first time. It would be revived again in the 1690s. Lengthy lists of supporters were drawn up and various approaches made, mostly dependent on the personality involved. Opportunity certainly knocked for many an MP thereafter.[65]

Unfortunately, the unstable foundations of the ministry were there for all to see. Not only did Danby have to face a continual struggle with ambitious courtiers and recently favoured ministers such as Arlington, but also his tendency for widespread interference in domestic, foreign and Irish affairs increased his enemies. The idea that a 'Church and King' policy would lead to a reconciliation not only with the Church of England, but also with Anglican Royalists in Parliament, was eventually to prove a momentary dream. Nevertheless the Danby ministry was quick to emphasise its support for Cavalier doctrines and the well-being of the Church of England against Roman Catholics and dissenting toleration interests, as well as those 'anti-prerogative'. By so doing Danby hoped he could lead the nation into a genuine reconciliation of King, Parliament and Church, provide supply and thus establish his dominance in the King's councils for some time to come. That these policies were at least in part those of Clarendon revamped and that Danby's success would depend upon his already notoriously unreliable master were of course matters of current debate at court.

Charles II was head of the Church of England, but he also held tolerant religious views, and because of these clashes with his episcopal lieutenants were frequent and inevitable.[66] In the early years of the reign the archbishop of Canterbury, Gilbert Sheldon, took the lead in church matters. In general Sheldon and the hard-liners of the Church greatly disliked the King's pro-tolerationist stance, even to the extent of questioning Charles's motives. Sheldon's blunt response to the indulgence policies of the 1660s was to warn of the threats of popery and the suspicions such activities could raise in Parliament. Indeed Sheldon, taking the opportunity of the confusing signals from Whitehall, went so far as to instruct his subordinates to carry out the letter of the law. While Sheldon and the bishops took their lead from Clarendon over the next few years, this obstructive policy had a cost at court. Clarendon noted with some dismay that men of the cloth were frequently greeted with mockery there.[67] Indeed while the archbishop attended the Privy Council, he carried little weight and his relationship with the King was strained. Sheldon's relatively mild comments on his monarch's morals only fostered the feeling of 'cold war' between Lambeth and Whitehall, especially after the fall of Clarendon in 1667.

Little changed until Danby's ministry, for the ministers in power until that point had their own religious agenda. It was in fact Danby who launched a form of rapprochement with Lambeth Palace. His scheme was to draw in all of the prominent members of the clergy and thereby use the Church to bolster the ministry's policies. In return for becoming his allies, the clergy would receive the benefits of protection against dissenters and Roman Catholics. For their part the bishops, although they did not always speak with one voice, saw the offered alliance as a chance to re-build their influence. Bills to enforce the penal laws, suppress conventicles and emphasise the doctrine of non-resistance were soon attempted. The alliance with the bishops, who were also useful cannon fodder in the lobbies of the House of

Lords, was bolstered by some sentimental and practical action, which Andrew Marvell was sarcastically to call 'window-dressing'. This included money for the re-building of St Paul's, and the promotion of the myth of the martyr king Charles I.[68]

Danby's main ally in this 'new deal' for the Church proved to be Henry Compton.[69] While Compton shared many of Danby's views, he was particularly aggressive in his suppression of popery. Appointed bishop of London in 1675, he was well placed to assist Danby and the ailing archbishop Sheldon. Compton was brought into court life by his appointment as dean of the Chapel Royal in July 1675. This gave him influence over the education of the Princesses Mary and Anne, and as Gilbert Burnet noted it was common knowledge that he was 'a property' of the earl of Danby in church affairs.[70] On Sheldon's fatal illness in 1677, therefore, it was fully expected that Compton would be promoted to archbishop of Canterbury, but the forces ranged against him were too strong even for Danby to overcome. Charles merely tolerated Compton, while James, whom he had offended in a number of ways, not the least by his persecuting anti-popish stance, was actively opposed to him. While Danby 'all along caresse[d] him as secure of [the archbishopric] for himself', he soon realised that he could not deliver and the post finally went to the saintly William Sancroft, dean of St Paul's.[71] On another point Danby also could not deliver. His attempt to enforce a new Test Act in 1675, in order to institutionalise the alliance of court and Church through an oath which would have purged all but the most loyal of Anglican Royalists from national and local government, failed miserably.[72]

For all of his good intentions and notable propaganda exercises, Danby and his ministry were still hampered by the general lack of belief and trust in the government's dealings. Moreover, the presence of rivals in the government and the well-known potential switch-back inclinations of Charles II meant uncertainty. Forever an uncertain quantity in Danby's schemes, the King's own views had to be taken into account at all stages, and although Danby could humour Charles when things appeared to be going well, the monarch was still capable of vacillation and dissembling. Danby faced additional obstruction from the duke of York and Lauderdale. Both men had their own programmes and followings, and although Danby's plans coincided with those of Lauderdale until 1677, James was always unimpressed by the 'Church and King' policy and in 1675 even seriously looked to Danby's opponents for support for his own scheme of toleration.[73]

Of Danby's rivals, Ormonde was at best dispassionate about the ministry, and Buckingham, when in favour, could still use his talents for mimicry and mockery to undermine his old client, while the duchess of Portsmouth had to be bought off with numerous gifts. Arlington spent much of his time after the Dutch war re-positioning for future struggles at court. As part of the repercussions of the war, he swiftly abandoned any attempt at religious toleration, dropped the secretaryship and took up the post of Lord Chamberlain, which he hoped would enable him to remain close to the King whilst freeing him from the onerous business of administration. The new Lord Chamberlain's manoeuvres thereafter saw him stealthily skirting the fringes of opposition politics as a response to the ever-increasing power of Danby, whose rise he resented. Arlington not only sought to retain the friendship of the now outcast Shaftesbury, he attempted to damage the Lord Treasurer, Lauderdale and York by his scheming. While using his clients in the Commons to launch impeachment proceedings against Danby, Arlington also sought to undercut his new rival by attempting to forge a new link with William of Orange in an engineered marriage between the Prince and Mary, James's eldest daughter. At the same time rumour also had Arlington taking up the cause of the ambitious Monmouth. Unfortunately, the fact that Arlington's eventual negotiations with William did not go particularly well merely compounded his problems. Sent on an embassy to Holland in November 1674 to negotiate the marriage, an act which itself merely exasperated Danby, Lauderdale, York, and the French, his arrogant manners also managed to offend the easily offended William.

In the meantime, as Arlington laboured abroad, at home his opponents swiftly undercut his credit with Charles. For a while Charles clung on to his old minister, still engaged in his usual balancing act, but in the course of 1675 the Lord Chamberlain's actions were to cost him dearly. Standing aloof from the attacks upon the new premier minister in the House of Lords in public, and seeking to use his influence in private to promote the destruction of Danby in the House of Commons, Arlington was finally damned in the eyes of Charles.[74] Such actions convinced the King (and there were many who sought to convince him) that Arlington was in league with those who wanted to tie the issue of supply with Danby's destruction. Relations between Danby and Arlington only worsened as Arlington hurled 'himself at all doors in the effort to re-enter affairs' and his situation only declined still further. The attempt to place the duchess of Mazarin in the King's arms as a rival to Portsmouth also proved a disappointment to the minister, if not to Charles. Gradually Arlington's power faded away as that of his rival grew and ultimately the once proud minister was left to intrigue fitfully with the opposition in 1678, his only real aim being the destruction of Danby.[75]

Back in 1674, however, Danby began to 'move boldly', as one contemporary put it, and the departure of Ormonde for Ireland in the same year removed at least one potential threat.[76] As the campaign for Church and King began to move forward, the programme for 1675 also became clearer: no dissolution of Parliament, support for the Church of England, a strict enforcement of the law in matters of dissent and recusancy, and a link between redress of grievances and supply. Equally hopefully the inevitable attacks on Danby and Lauderdale in Parliament were beaten off, although the business there soon shuddered to a halt as the Lords and Commons fell out with each other in the *Shirley* v. *Fagg* case. This ruined another proposed Test bill. During the recess Danby undertook to build up his forces in the Privy Council. In foreign affairs the Lord Treasurer pinned his hopes on an anti-French policy, which was to result in the one real achievement of his ministry: the marriage of William and Mary in 1677. However, his removal of opponents such as Shaftesbury from the King's councils was more than matched by the feeding frenzy of his numerous and grasping relatives, which brought him into further disrepute. His unwieldy domestic alliance was forced to stagger along achieving little by way of forward momentum.[77]

Throughout the 1670s Danby's financial plans were eclipsed by the increasingly ill-tempered Parliament he strove to control. Viewing events with his usual jaundiced eye, Charles II even slid back towards the French in order to finance his lifestyle, especially as Danby, faced with a possible shortage of cash, was finally forced to embark on a policy of retrenchment. Charles once more entered into secret negotiations with the French ambassador for money over the head of his minister, who, once he was made aware of the situation, was only reluctantly dragged into ever more baroque schemes. Danby's counter-move was an attempt to make sure that the next parliamentary session was more profitable. Once again exhaustive lists of supporters were drawn up and approaches made to various individuals in order to strengthen the court's hand. Attempts were also made to suppress the London coffee-houses as centres of opposition, but after a brief struggle in January 1676 this also failed. Failure meant that Danby turned on his rivals and their underlings. Individual opponents such as George Savile, marquis of Halifax, who had defended the coffee-houses, were struck off the Privy Council for their opposition.[78] Sir Stephen Fox, an Arlington man, was ousted from his office as Paymaster of the Forces and replaced by a Danby nominee.[79] The local magistracy also became a target for new modelling foreshadowing the events of the 1680s. With secret service money now securely passing through Charles Bertie's hands, an attempt was also made to remove Shaftesbury from the London scene.[80] Here Danby did not have all his own way and the scheme again misfired.

In the latter half of the 1670s Danby's problems increased. His own position, while it seemed secure, was dependent on securing the House of Commons and thus gaining supply mainly through an anti-French and pro-Church policy which had already failed to secure anything thus far. As Danby hammered away at the King, he wrote to Charles in a memorandum of June 1677: 'Till he [the King] can fall into the humour of the people he can never be great nor rich, and while differences continue prerogative must suffer, unless he can live without parliament'. This, as Danby frequently pointed out, was not possible, as the condition of the crown's revenue would not permit it. A French alliance on the other hand was to Danby merely 'good words'. His not very original answer to the problem was to secure supply through a Protestant foreign policy, the marriage of William of Orange to the Princess Mary, an alliance to the Protestant powers and even war with France.[81] And so in 1677 Danby's hopes were still resting upon his preparations for a compliant Parliament, the attractiveness of his policies to the Anglican Royalist mentality and an organised party to push through legislation. Already, however, the structure of his ministry was being eaten away by the activities of the King in Europe.

The crisis, 1678–1685

Ralph Montagu had originally been a client of Arlington and had assisted in Arlington's attack on the new Lord Treasurer in the mid-1670s. Montagu was a thorough courtier and he soon perceived that with Arlington's star setting it was time to look around for new opportunities to make himself useful. Like many other courtiers, Montagu always possessed an inflated sense of his own worth and self-importance. Never a handsome man, he was still urbane, suave and ambitious, with the appropriate background for moving in the highest circles. His foray into the more limited world of diplomacy was in the end merely part of his plan to spring into power and position at Whitehall and he had certainly used Arlington cynically enough for such an objective. As a result, he had become a Privy Councillor and Master of the Great Wardrobe in 1671, although even King Charles had balked at the ambitious courtier's request for a Garter. Montagu's astute marriage to Elizabeth Wriothesley, daughter of the earl of Southampton and widow of the earl of Northumberland, which had brought with it both prestige and wealth, had somewhat compensated him for his disappointment and in 1676 he finally succeeded in obtaining the prestigious post of ambassador to France.

This immediately flung the resourceful Montagu straight into the intrigues of Charles II and Louis XIV – an ongoing saga of secretive dealings whose ramifications and obscure by-ways were uncertain even to the two main principals.[82]

At this time Louis XIV was still engaged in the war that he had launched against the Dutch in 1672. Charles II's position, as usual, was an uncertain one in this conflict. While Charles had been forced out of the war in 1674, he was reluctant to give up the game entirely and indeed saw the role of mediator between the antagonists as the most likely avenue for his peculiar needs. He came to believe that by using his good offices he could earn the respect and friendship of Louis XIV and even some cash. In turn Louis merely sought English neutrality. Danby's view of the European situation was, as we have seen, locked into his domestic concerns and he continued to pester the King to follow a Protestant Dutch alliance and thereby assure his potential Anglican Royalist supporters that all was well in foreign affairs. Playing the anti-French card, however, had its problems. The King's susceptibilities to French persuasion were well known and the failures of his first minister in Parliament soon convinced Charles that there should be at least one escape route available to him should Danby fail yet again. As a result, Charles eventually forced his minister's hand by ordering him to enter into the ongoing negotiations with France. While the Lord Treasurer was not convinced such activities would ever lead anywhere, under orders to do so he reluctantly entered into the negotiations. His motives were various, either to prove to the King that deals with Louis were always futile, or more cynically to squeeze as much cash as possible out of the French.

Montagu's part in these schemes was to hope that his good service with all the parties involved would mean he could have some claims on Charles, the Lord Treasurer and Louis when the time came for his own advancement. He had also set his sights upon a secretaryship. With an eye for the main chance, he hoped to cut a deal with the French which would benefit the King. He was soon persuaded that the Lord Treasurer would not sanction his promotion to the secretaryship, and he concluded that Danby had to be moved out of office before his own ambitions could be fulfilled. Loyalty was an unknown in Montagu's vocabulary, and he became deeply involved in schemes to remove Danby. Alongside Arlington, he found himself with a part in the plot to replace Portsmouth with the duchess of Mazarin, and when this fell through he proclaimed to the King that he could gain a better subsidy from Louis. Charles forced Danby into this new device.[83]

In the meantime in the spring of 1678 Montagu was preoccupied with more romantic notions and conceived a lust for Lady Sussex, the daughter of Charles II and Barbara, duchess of Cleveland. Having already fallen out with Cleveland herself (he was one of her former lovers), this new scheme was again to cost him the secretary-ship of state, which he had already arranged to buy from Henry Coventry. Cleveland reported his antics to the King and learning of this Montagu hurriedly returned to England, without permission, which lost him his embassy.[84] Montagu blamed Danby for his loss of fortunes and, already bearing a grudge, agreed with the French to ruin his former patron for 100,000 crowns. Before entering into this venture, however, he sought to protect himself by election to Parliament. Distracted by the widening ramifications of the so-called Popish Plot, Danby only realised at the last moment what was going on and attempted a pre-emptive strike by the seizure of Montagu's incriminating documents. In revenge on 19 December 1678 Montagu revealed the Lord Treasurer's reluctant French dealings to the House of Commons. These letters told much of Danby's dealings, but little of Montagu's involvement, and moves to impeach the Lord Treasurer soon followed.[85]

The storm that broke over the country in 1678 was the result of a combination of Danby's tactics, Titus Oates's lies, Montagu's papers and Charles II's blunders. Danby's regime had already hit the metaphorical buffers when the underclass of society, who sparked off the political hysteria against popery, came along in August 1678 to blow up both the engine and the driver. With each passing session in the 1670s Parliament seemed to grow more and more troublesome, and the game of hazard which was Caroline politics seemed more and more problematic for the minister. The 'proofs' which Montagu gave to the Commons finally blew apart Danby's carefully staged vision of Church and King. But the crisis of the early 1680s was anyway too complex for Danby to control, as we shall see. Factional rivalry, and the rottenness of the corruption which seemed to inhabit the court and the dealings of Charles II, all added to the picaresque scene which now developed and to many contemporaries seemed merely evidence of a much deeper malaise at the heart of Stuart government.[86]

The crisis of 1678–83 engaged with all of the problems of the regime since at least the Restoration and it has been variously interpreted.[87] The question of a popish successor undoubtedly loomed large as a result of Charles's failure to produce a legitimate heir. But the failure of religious toleration, fears for English liberties in the face of the monarchy's prerogative powers, the secret dealings with France in the 1670s, war in Europe, factional rivalry, and the corruption which seemed to inhabit the court of Charles II, all added to the crisis which now developed. A primary focus for this crisis undoubtedly lay in the religion of the heir to the throne. Indeed it might be argued that there would have been no crisis without the duke of York's conversion to the Roman Catholic faith. The latter had been a long-drawn-out affair, and when the rumours of his conversion were finally confirmed in 1673 the fear that a future Catholic monarch would introduce arbitrary government and overthrow English liberties raised the hackles of many a staunch country squire. James himself did nothing to dispel a growing belief in his violent and bloody nature. He was seen as a man who would, if given the opportunity, take the worst of counsels in all his affairs.[88] Perceived by many as a threat to the state, the heir to the throne was at best indifferent and at worst aggressive in his opinions about the matter. The feeling grew that the answer to the problem might well lie in excluding this wayward man from his right of succession.

While the crisis of 1678–83 has thus been frequently labelled an exclusion crisis, it was not all about exclusion; other important elements existed in the debate. It was clear that to some the secret (and not so secret) deals made with Louis in the late 1670s were as much a threat to the nation as James. They were thought to be part of the undermining of Protestantism itself as well as damaging to English trade interests. The widespread abuse by Danby of the parliamentary system was also perceived as a threat to English liberties. As a result, new political patterns were now developing which would lead to the formation of political 'parties' following the dissolution of the Cavalier Parliament in 1679. Country beliefs and staunch Protestantism, concerned with liberty and hostile to prerogative notions and court corruption, were to re-emerge in a Whig 'party'. The old Anglican Royalist beliefs of 'Church, King and hereditary right' were to produce the 'Tories'.[89] Thereafter the divided political nation was to pursue the banners of exclusion, limitations, legitimacy, divorce and re-marriage or simple loyalty with equal force. Hand in hand with this were the widespread fears of court corruption and waste, of hidden court Catholics and their influence, and of the increasing power of France. The catchwords of 'popery and arbitrary government' seemed to exemplify the fears of the nation and the revelations of Titus Oates, Ralph Montagu and the other informers only crystallised fears that were already in place. Time and again in the pamphlet literature of the period there was an ache for a more comfortable, more stable golden age.[90]

The crisis itself went through three phases: the polarisation of the political nation through the events of the Popish Plot from 1678 to 1679, the attempts to settle the succession from 1679 to 1680, and the winning of the initiative by the crown from 1680 to 1683. Two elections were fought on exclusion in 1679 and 1681 and two exclusion bills went through the Commons. The first was quashed by Charles II's prorogation of Parliament in May 1679 and the second by the rejection of the House of Lords. The Oxford Parliament of 1681 put an end to the question in Parliament. Thereafter the politics of the nation seemed once more to resolve into a former mode. At court Charles played at divide and rule with his ministers. He also dabbled in foreign intrigues to produce more cash, and sought revenge on the Whigs in general, while sustaining the loyalists with the right noises on the established Church and hereditary right. But the crisis, as we shall see, had not gone away and was only really resolved by the events of 1688.

In 1679 Danby, floored by the repeated attacks on his position, was more than willing to fight back against his enemies. Revelations of the plot, however, had destroyed what little balance and credibility remained in his government. The subtle Charles sought to protect himself, as ever, and with his dissolution of Parliament on 24 January 1679 effectively cut the minister's feet from under him. A new phase began with attacks, sponsored by Shaftesbury and others, on the duke of York's position and upon Charles's own queen. These were also bolstered by fresh revelations from the odious Titus Oates, and further undermined by the fabian tactics of Charles. Charles seems to have hoped that by playing for time in the end the whole crisis would eventually blow over. In fact the elections of February 1679 brought further disaster. Danby's understandable reluctance to re-enact Clarendon's role and run for cover in Europe led to his confinement in the Tower and temporarily brought his career to a halt. As the crisis switched gear, however, new opportunities for the men impatiently waiting in the wings of the court were opened.

With the fall of Danby there were now various factions at court with whom Charles was now forced to deal. His brother James, duke of York, began to assert himself, and although this caused Charles many problems he at least had the courage to defend James's position. To get him away from the crisis and give Charles some breathing space, however, James was packed off into temporary exile in Flanders, where he fired off various disgruntled missives on the political scene. The emergence of a country opposition, who refused to be managed, corrupted or bribed (at least by Danby, if not by Louis XIV), and the development of a new political grouping in the form of the Whig party, had in the meantime raised the stakes in domestic politics.

The leaders of the Whigs were to have a number of aims, and quite often some of them danced to the old court tune of believing that if they could oust the current incumbent ministers then they might just be able to replace them.[91] Led in the main by Shaftesbury and Essex, with Buckingham sometimes in the van and sometimes the tail, depending on his mood, the Whigs were now believed by many to have the upper hand in political life. Their tactics varied, and their leadership and followers were never as unified as many believed, but the main concentration of this group of politicians lay in trying to use the Parliament and the press to impose either limitations on a popish successor, the divorce and re-marriage of Charles himself to a Protestant, the legitimising of Charles's eldest illegitimate son Monmouth, or the exclusion of York from the succession. Each of these policies had their own supporters, but each depended upon Charles giving way, something that in the end he proved unwilling to do. Ultimately defeat would return the Whigs in 1683 to that old political standby in English political life: conspiracy. But other groups also existed that were even more problematic in their allegiance than the Whigs.

Of the newly prominent men at court after the fall of Danby one was Robert Spencer, earl of Sunderland, who was prone to reckless gambling both at the card table and in his life. Sidney Godolphin was another of a more sober mind and although a courtier in his background he was to prove just as able at administration. Both men began to become prominent in the new order. Another group, represented by George Savile, marquis of Halifax, and the rather timorous and eternally pessimistic Sir William Temple, was more temperate in its leanings, hoping for a compromise and even 'trimming' solution to the country's problems. On the other hand James himself sponsored the court 'Tories', and his right-hand man was Lawrence Hyde. Hyde, the second son of the ex-Lord Chancellor Clarendon, had only recently emerged as a figure in the political life of the court. The fact that he was his father's son and York's former brother-in-law assisted his rise into office. Hyde also staked his claim for office on his financial abilities. Roger North was not alone in noticing that Hyde's infirmities were his 'passion, in which he would swear like a cutter, and the indulging himself in wine'.[92] But Lory, as he was nicknamed, was also capable of great industry and was to prove an adroit courtier, as well as a supporter of the established Church and James's succession.

In the divided court that greeted the King after Danby's removal, new changes soon swept away the minions of Danby. Sir William Temple advised the King to refurbish the Privy Council and clear it of the Lord Treasurer's 'creatures'.[93] Members of the opposition to Danby were thus brought into the government to sit alongside moderates and loyalists in a clear attempt to placate them. Shaftesbury was appointed Lord President of the Council. Revelations from informers and trials for treason, however, continued to roll over the regime in waves and at court matters settled down into a sullen stale-mate. Charles, believing himself surrounded by his enemies on every side in the new Privy Council, returned to his old caballing and gradually drew in Temple, Sunderland and Halifax to advise him. These men favoured an offer of limitations on any future successor. But the introduction of a bill of exclusion in the Commons led to the prorogation and dissolving of Parliament in May 1679, which in turn meant further elections. The summer and autumn of 1679 witnessed more changes in the political world. James, duke of Monmouth, the King's eldest illegitimate son, seized his chance to stake his claim to the throne, and joined the opposition. He was removed from his prominent position as Commander in Chief and sent out of the country for his temerity. Shaftesbury was ousted from the now misfiring Privy Council. And Essex resigned from the Treasury and was re-placed by Lawrence Hyde. Halifax made one of his periodic retire-ments to his country estate and the other Whigs on the Privy Council were to resign in January 1680 disgusted with yet another proroga-tion of Parliament. The hapless Sir William Temple abandoned the whole situation and also retired from the scene. Sunderland, Hyde and Godolphin, collectively, and ironically, known as the 'Chits', were now given more prominence in the King's councils.[94]

It was at this point, in winter 1679–80, that the crisis deepened still further. The discovery of the so-called 'Meal Tub' Plot rekindled popular excitement to new intensity. To many it seemed that 1641 would come again and the country would once more slide into what seemed an inevitable civil war as the parties began to organise. Monmouth returned without permission from the continent and Charles refused to see him and ordered him abroad once more. Now advised by his 'evil genius' Shaftesbury, Monmouth began to play the popular card with a royal progress through the West Country. On the other hand the return of James from Scotland in January 1680 stiffened the resolve of the supporters of the crown. Excitement, cre-ated by numerous petitions on one side and counter-petitions on the other, was raised to fever pitch. Indeed the terms Whigs and Tories soon replaced 'petitioners' and 'abhorrers' as terms of abuse. A series of pamphlet wars took place as writers of every political shade and hue sought to explore every possibility of the political scene.[95]

In the meantime at court Sunderland appeared to have the upper hand in his association with Hyde and Sidney Godolphin. The new ministry, inexperienced or not, took care to prepare for a Parliament, whenever Charles decided to allow it to sit, and engaged in a foreign policy of sorts. In 1680 Charles and Sunderland made overtures to Holland, Spain and the Holy Roman Emperor for an alliance. Their sincerity, or at least Charles II's sincerity, in the schemes was doubtful. He may have gone along with it to persuade Louis XIV that his government was worth buying off. Sunderland and his ally the duchess of Portsmouth soon began to lose confidence in the solidity of the ministry and in the firmness of Charles on the question of exclusion. Sunderland, fearful of what might happen should the exclusionists persuade the King to give in to their demands, miscalculated and began to make overtures to the opposition. Godolphin also believed that exclusion would carry in the end. While Hyde remained loyal, Essex had returned to the opposition and Halifax sat on the political fence.

The Parliament of October 1680 proved even more hostile to the regime, and as even the moderates began to swing over to exclusion, alienated by poor government tactics, a further introduction of the exclusion bill in November led to uproar. It was believed that the country was now close to civil war. Shaftesbury stood ready with his 'brisk boys' to hand, but in the end the dog failed to bark in the night. At heart the Whigs remained disunited, fearing above all the potential horrors of civil war. The fact that the King stood firm in face of all the pressure to assent to exclusion, and in spite of the defections of Sunderland and Godolphin in the House of Lords, bolstered his support. It was left to Halifax to sway the House with his rhetoric.

If in his opinions George Savile, marquis of Halifax, has been traditionally depicted as a man before his time, he himself was, or claimed to be, a moderate in politics and religion, a 'trimmer' by nature and principle, albeit with Tory leanings. Although he held 'country' principles in the 1670s, he had also been an enthusiastic royalist in his youth and this mixture produced a man more typical of his times than later historians have made out. In his dislike of the regime led by Danby, for example, there had been a strong personal cause. There was also an air of self-righteousness about Halifax – a refusal to believe that he could ever be in the wrong. His sense of self-worth was certainly matched by some ambition. In the end, however, he proved more than willing to go along with the reaction against the Whigs. Recommended by Temple after many debates with Charles, his return to the Privy Council and high office left him close to a King who neither understood him nor liked him. In general Halifax returned the complement for he held a poor opinion of monarchy itself. He thought that Charles was ever unsteady and 'what he seems to approve [of in] the council you gave him he harkened to other councils at a backdoor, which made him wavering and slow to resolve'.[96] In the end, however, Charles had the last laugh, whatever Halifax's view of him, for the King seems to have used his minister as a sop to any opposition groups while at the same time keeping him from any real power.

Halifax's opinion of the crisis, if we are to believe Lady Russell, was to 'hear all sides, and then choose wisely'. But if his view on exclusion was generally negative he also believed that any exclusion bill would lead to civil war as James would fight for his rights. In preference to this the road to limitations on a future successor was Halifax's choice. Not that this pleased James in any way, but for his own part Halifax prided himself on his independent spirit and noted 'I neither am nor will be under any obligations that might restrain the freedom of my opinions concerning him; but yet if there is any possibility of making ourselves safe by lower expedients, I had rather use them, then venture upon so strong a remedy, as the disinheriting the next heir of the Crown'.[97] If the problems of succession divided the court in 1680, in the end faced with a final choice Charles expressed his determination not to yield in November 1680 and it was this that decided Halifax to stick with the duke. Despite attempts to coerce Halifax, the debate between him and Shaftesbury in the Lords marked a turning point. Halifax's powerful eloquence won the day and he took his stance against Monmouth and expressed confidence in his own ability to land limitations and fear of the peril of civil war. It was the wayward and diffident minister's finest hour. As he became the King's new favourite and hate figure to exclusionists, he was driven to 'cast about for a new set of friends'. These proved to be the Hydes, Reresby and the Musgraves, with whom he in fact had little in common. Finally Charles in January 1681 dismissed the Parliament and called a new one at Oxford, while Sunderland, Essex and Temple were struck off the council and Sunderland was removed from his office.

After a short lapse into private life Halifax returned to London in May 1681 to confer with the King as to the advisability of York's return from Scotland. He was soon enlisted as a minister in the regime from May 1681 to March 1682 and was now regarded as a chief councillor. Notwithstanding appearances, however, his apparent predominance in the regime was superficial, for underground influences soon worked against him and neutralised his councils. The Oxford Parliament of 1681 had now ruined the Whigs, as it removed their platform and left them stranded and voiceless. In addition, many moderates now saw just how close the threat of civil war had been. As new Toryism began to prosper, Shaftesbury was charged with treasonable conspiracy and placed in the Tower. In all of this Halifax continued his policy of moderation, but he was against both James's recall or Monmouth's re-admission to favour. On the continent the peace negotiations which were taking place at Nijmegen to end the European war were on the verge of collapse, but more secret agreements still floated around the English court.

Three polices now appeared open to Charles. First, he could return to Danby's schemes of 'Church and King' and strengthen the links of the crown with the Church, in addition to persecuting dissenters and adopting a popular anti-French foreign policy. Hyde and Sir Edward Seymour, as well as Sir Leoline Jenkins, the Secretary of State, supported these ideas. A second possibility, however, having withstood the exclusion crisis, was to move for conciliation, by freeing Danby and the Popish Lords from the Tower, relaxing the penal laws and thus cutting the ground from under the remaining Whigs. Halifax favoured something of this sort. Lastly was the view of the duke of York, who wanted no Parliament, a French alliance to safeguard the prerogative and severe punishments on all the crown's opponents. As usual Charles decided to mix his policies: he supported the Church with penal persecution, but kept up his beloved French alliance while forcefully persecuting his enemies. With York apparently back in favour and the way to power clear, Halifax was forced to stick with the new regime. However, the visit of the Prince of Orange offered an alternative policy. Halifax urged an alliance with the Dutch and their allies, but as this would mean a war with France, it was something Charles was not willing to risk. Nor would the King risk a new Parliament.[98]

In fact the ascendancy of York and the revival of Hyde at court and in the King's councils led to Halifax's further decline as a force to be reckoned with. While outwardly his power was the same, to those in the know at court it was entirely superficial. His influence was further reduced by the return of the errant Sunderland to office. Being polar opposites in character and policy, the two men hated one another, but Sunderland had sought out the favour of the duchess of Portsmouth in order to return to office. Once more he proved that very little was beneath him in the search for power. In the meantime Halifax was made Lord Privy Seal, which gave him precedence and gratified his inordinate vanity, while carrying little administrative weight, and this suited him as he had little taste for this type of work. However, the return of York meant an abandonment of any form of conciliatory policy by the regime. As a result, in 1682 attempts to break the Whigs as a force in local government were begun. Halifax, while giving his consent to such purges, was in reality little involved in the practical details. Danby was also released from the Tower and the star of Halifax appeared in decline. The re-appointment of Godolphin at the behest of Hyde, now made earl of Rochester, was also considered a blow to Halifax's fortunes. There was, however, a hint of revolution in the air in 1684. Charles, as was his wont, began to rebel against the guidance of both James and Rochester and sought to revive Halifax as a counterweight. In July 1684 Rochester was even 'kicked upstairs' to the honourable but rather negligible post of Lord President. The ministerial revolution of divide and rule that should have followed, however, was never really effected. Intrigues to move James back to Scotland, recall Monmouth and Halifax's own links to William were halted by Charles's death in February 1685.[99]

Notes

1   The standard modern biographies for the King are: R. Hutton, *Charles II, King of England, Scotland and Ireland* (Oxford, 1989), J. Miller, *Charles II* (London, 1991), J. R. Jones, *Charles II, Royal Politician* (London, 1987). See also R. Hutton, 'The religion of Charles II', in R. Smuts (ed.), *The Stuart Court and Europe: Essays in Politics and Political Culture* (Cambridge, 1996), pp. 228–46.

2   A. Boyer, *The History of King William the Third* (3 vols, London, 1702), I, pp. 4–54.

3   At least according to the court satires, see above chapter 4.

4   See Hutton, *Charles II*, pp. vi–x, 446–58. Miller, *Charles II*, pp. xiii–xv. Jones, *Charles II*, pp. 1–10.

5   D. Starkey (ed.), *The English Court from the Wars of the Roses to the Civil War* (London, 1987), pp. 8–9.

6   See above chapter 4

7   Rochester, 'On King Charles', in K. Walker (ed.), *The Poems of John Wilmot, Earl of Rochester* (London, 1984), p. 122.

8   For Clarendon see G. E. Miller, *Edward Hyde, Earl of Clarendon* (Boston, 1983). H. Craik, *The Life of Edward, Earl of Clarendon* (2 vols, London, 1911). T. H. Lister, *The Life and Administration of Edward, First Earl of Clarendon* (3 vols, London, 1838).

9   For these men see E. Hyde, first earl of Clarendon, *The Life of Edward Earl of Clarendon, Lord High Chancellor of England* (2 vols, Oxford, 1857), I, pp. 269–73. See also J. C. Beckett, *The Cavalier Duke: A Life of James Butler, First Duke of Ormonde, 1610–1688* (Belfast, 1990).

10   For Arlington, who still has no modern biography, see E. Hyde, first earl of Clarendon, *State Papers collected by Edward, Earl of Clarendon* (3 vols, Oxford, 1786), III, p. lxxxi. M. Lee, 'The earl of Arlington and the treaty of Dover', *Journal of British Studies*, I (1961), 58–70. V. Barbour, *Henry Bennet, Earl of Arlington, Secretary of State to Charles II* (Washington, 1914). Also of note is P. Milton, 'Hobbes, heresy and Lord Arlington', *History of Political Thought*, XIV (1993), 501–46.

11   Barbour, *Henry Bennet*, pp. 29–45.

12   Bodleian Library, Carte MS 221, fo. 52.

13   *Calendar of State Papers Venice*, 1671–1672 (London, 1939), pp. 61–8.

14   Barbour, *Henry Bennet*, pp. 219–38. O. Airy (ed.) *Essex Papers, 1672–1679* (London, 1890), I, pp. 163–4.

15   Clarendon, *State Papers collected by Edward, Earl of Clarendon*, III, pp. lxxxii–lxxxiii.

16   R. Latham and W. Matthews (eds), *The Diary of Samuel Pepys* (11 vols, London, 1970–83), VIII, pp. 185–6. H. Forneron, *Louise de Keroualle, Duchess of Portsmouth, 1649–1734* (2nd edn, London, 1887), p. 327.

17   Barbour, *Henry Bennet*, pp. 46–60.

18   C. MacCormick (ed.), *The Secret History of the Court and Reign of Charles the Second by a Member of his Privy Council* (2 vols, London, 1792), I, pp. xi–xii.

19   Clarendon, *Life of Edward Earl of Clarendon*, I, pp. 270, 309, 320, 358–9.

20   Ibid., I, p. 355.

21   Halifax, 'A character of King Charles the Second', in J. P. Kenyon (ed.), *Halifax: The Complete Works* (Harmondsworth, 1969), p. 255.

22   Clarendon, *State Papers collected by Edward, Earl of Clarendon*, III, p. lxxxiv.

23   Clarendon, *Life of Edward Earl of Clarendon*, I, pp. 89, 97.

24   Ibid., I, pp. 105–6, 131–2. B. D. Henning (ed.), *The History of Parliament: The Commons, 1660–1690* (3 vols, London, 1983), I, pp. 630–1. C. H. Hartmann, *The King's Friend: A Life of Charles Berkeley, Viscount Fitzhardinge of Falmouth, 1630–1665* (London, 1951).

25   Barbour, *Henry Bennet*, pp. 77–8. For Arlington's faction see Henning (ed.), *The History of Parliament*, I, pp. 622–3, 630–1; II, pp. 21–6, 71–3, 175–6, 515–17, 547–8, 728; III, pp. 85, 136–7, 256–7 323–5, 426–7, 504–6, 592–5.

26   See G. de Lord (ed.), *Poems on Affairs of State: Augustan Satirical Verse, 1660–1714* (7 vols, New Haven, 1963–75), I, 1660–1678, pp. 158, 419.

27   J. H. O'Neill, *George Villiers, Second Duke of Buckingham* (Boston, 1984). G. D. Gilbert (ed.), *Marie Catherine d'Aulnoy, Memoirs of the Court of England in 1675* (London, 1913), p. 118. C. Phipps (ed.), *Buckingham, Public and Private Man: The Prose, Poems and Commonplace Book of George Villiers, Second Duke of Buckingham (1628–1687)* (New York, 1985), pp. 40–2.

28   Lyndon B. Johnson quoted in T. Augarde (ed.), *The Oxford Dictionary of Modern Quotations* (Oxford, 1991), p. 114.

29   Miller, *Charles II*, pp. 123–4. A. Fraser, *King Charles II* (London, 1980), p. 253.

30   Bodleian Library, Carte MS, 46, fo. 286; Carte MS 222, fo. 81.

31   Miller, *Charles II*, pp. 102–4.

32   Latham and Matthews (eds), *Diary of Samuel Pepys*, IV, p. 213. Pepys observed Clarendon's fortunes fluctuate throughout his diary. See for examples *Diary*, III, p. 290; IV, pp. 115, 123, 137, 195, 196; V, pp. 73, 345.

33   Miller, *Edward Hyde*, p. 20.

34   Ibid., pp. 20–1. J. R. Jones, 'Court dependants in 1664', *Bulletin of the Institute of Historical Research*, XXXIV (1961), 81–91.

35   See J. Ferris, 'Official members in the Commons, 1660–1690: a study in multiple loyalties', in J. Morrill, P. Slack and D. Woolf (eds), *Public Duty and Private Conscience in Seventeenth-Century England: Essays Presented to G. E. Aylmer* (Oxford, 1993), pp. 277–303.

36   Clarendon quoted in Miller, *Edward Hyde*, p. 19.

37   Hutton, *Charles II*, p. 248.

38   Phipps (ed.), *Buckingham*, pp. 41–2. B. Yardley, 'George Villiers, second duke of Buckingham and the politics of toleration', *Huntingdon Library Quarterly*, LV (1992), 319.

39   Anon., 'Downfall of the Chancellor (1667)', in de Lord (ed.), *Poems on Affairs of State*, I, 1660–78, p. 158; see also p. 419.

40   J. S. Clarke (ed.), *The Life of James II, Collected out of Memoirs Writ of his Own Hand* (2 vols, London, 1816), I, pp. 433–6. MacCormick (ed.), *Secret History*, II, p. 323.

41   Charles II quoted in Miller, *Edward Hyde*, p. 21. Also Bodleian Library, Carte MS 35, fo. 737; Carte MS 220, fo. 301.

42   MacCormick (ed.), *Secret History*, II, p. 336. C. Roberts, 'The impeachment of the earl of Clarendon', *Cambridge Historical Journal*, XIII, (1957), 1–18.

43   See Hutton, *Charles II*, pp. 255–86. Miller, *Charles II*, pp. 142–74. M. Lee, *The Cabal* (Urbana, 1965). Also A. Browning, 'The stop of the exchequer', *History*, XIV (1930), 333–7. C. L. Grose, 'Louis XIVs financial relations with Charles II and the English Parliament', *Journal of Modern History*, I (1929), 177–204.

44   For Danby the standard biography remains A. Browning, *Thomas Osborne, Earl of Danby and Duke of Leeds, 1632–1712* (3 vols, Glasgow, 1951). See also J. Ralph, *The History of England during the Reigns of King William, Queen Anne and King George I with an Introductory Review of the Reigns of the Royal Brothers Charles and James* (2 vols, London, 1744–46), I, pp. 270–1. G. Burnet, *A History of My Own Time, Part I: The Reign of Charles II* (2 vols, Oxford, 1897), II, pp. 14–15, 79. J. Le Neve, *Lives and Characters of the Most Illustrious Persons British and Foreign who Died in the Year 1712* (London, 1713), pp. 145–6.

45   E. S. de Beer (ed.), *The Diary of John Evelyn* (6 vols, Oxford, 1955), IV, p. 20.

46   Shaftesbury quoted in K. H. D. Haley, *The First Earl of Shaftesbury* (Oxford, 1968), p. 508.

47   G. C. Moor Smith (ed.), *The Letters of Dorothy Osborne to William Temple* (Oxford, 1928), p. 97.

48   Henning (ed.), *History of Parliament*, I, pp. 639–43. Burnet, *A History of My Own Time, Part I: The Reign of Charles II*, II, p. 79. See also British Library (hereafter BL), Additional MS, 28054, fo. 1. A. Browning, 'Parties and party organisation in the reign of Charles II', *Transactions of the Royal Historical Society*, XXX (1948), 29–30.

49   M. K. Geiter and W. A. Speck (eds), *Memoirs of Sir John Reresby* (2nd edn, London, 1991), p. 145. Browning, *Thomas Osborne*, III, pp. 71–86.

50   Browning, 'Parties and party organisation', 29–33.

51   Browning, *Thomas Osborne*, I, p. 236; II, p. 40. D. Allen, 'Bridget Hyde and Lord Treasurer Danby's alliance with Lord Mayor Vyner', *Guildhall Studies in London History*, II, pt 1 (1975), 11–22. Historical Manuscripts Commission (hereafter HMC), 9th Report, Alfred Morrison MSS

(1895), pp. 450–1.

52 Geiter and Speck (eds), *Memoirs of Sir John Reresby*, p. 172. R. D. Blencowe (ed.), *The Diary of the Times of Charles the Second by Henry Sidney* (2 vols, London, 1843), I, pp. 6–7.

53 Burnet, *A History of My Own Time, Part I: The Reign of Charles II*, II, pp. 14–15.

54 Sir Henry Goodricke quoted in R. Carroll, 'The by-election at Aldborough, 1673', *Huntingdon Library Quarterly*, XXVIII (1964–65), 173.

55 Burnet, *A History of My Own Time, Part I: The Reign of Charles II*, II, p. 15. Also see Le Neve, *Lives and Characters of the Most Illustrious Persons*.

56 Halifax, 'Spencer House Journals', in H. C. Foxcroft, *The Life and Letters of Sir George Savile, Bart., the First Marquis of Halifax* (2 vols, London, 1898), II, p. 210.

57 Burnet, *A History of My Own Time, Part I: The Reign of Charles II*, II, p. 79, 101.

58 Airy (ed.), *Essex Papers*, I, p. 199.

59 Ibid., I, pp. 258–9, and Ralph, *History of England*, I, pp. 270–1.

60 See document 3.

61 Airy (ed.), *Essex Papers*, p. 279. Browning, *Thomas Osborne*, II, p. 40.

62 See document 15.

63 Browning, *Thomas Osborne*, I, pp. 154, 162–3, 175–81.

64 Ibid.

65 Henning (ed.), *History of* Parliament, I, pp. 639–43. Burnet, *A History of My Own Time, Part I: The Reign of Charles II*, II, p. 101. J. W. F. Hill, *Tudor and Stuart Lincoln* (Cambridge, 1956), pp. 183–5. S. B. Baxter, *The Development of the Treasury 1660–1702* (London, 1957), pp. 182–90. C. D. Chanderman, *The English Public Revenue, 1660–1688* (Oxford, 1975), pp. 231–8, 244–5. W. A. Shaw (ed.), *Calendar of Treasury Books* (London, 1904–), IV, 1672–75, pp. lxvii–xix; V, pt I, 1676–79, pp. ix, xxxvii, xi. Carroll, 'The by-election at Aldborough', 157–78.

66 V. D. Sutch, *Gilbert Sheldon, Architect of Anglican Survival 1640–1675* (The Hague, 1973), pp. 91–147. J. Spurr, *The Restoration Church of England 1646–1689* (London, 1991), pp. 68, 73–4.

67 Sutch, *Gilbert Sheldon*, p. 99.

68 *Reflections upon a paper intitled, some reflections upon the earl of Danby in relation to the murder of Sir Edmund Bury Godfrey in a letter to Edward Christian* (1679), p. 2. Browning, *Thomas Osborne*, I, pp. 148–9. Burnet, *A History of My Own Time, Part I: The Reign of Charles II*, II, p. 100.

69 E. Carpenter, *The Protestant Bishop, Being the Life of Henry Compton, 1632–1713 Bishop of London* (London, 1956), pp. 28–9.

70 Burnet, *A History of My Own Time, Part I: The Reign of Charles II*, II, p. 100.

71 Carpenter, *Protestant Bishop*, pp. 37–8.

72 Browning, *Thomas Osborne*, I, pp. 152–4.

73 Ibid., I, p. 152.

74 Barbour, *Henry Bennet*, pp. 244–5. Browning, *Thomas Osborne*, I, pp. 126, 141–5.

75 Barbour, *Henry Bennet*, pp. 244–5.

76 Airy (ed.), *Essex Papers*, p. 279.

77 Browning, *Thomas Osborne*, I, p. 283.

78 Ibid., I, p. 195

79 C. Clay, *Public Finance and Private Wealth: The Career of Sir Stephen Fox, 1627–1716* (Oxford, 1978), p. 103.

80 Baxter, *Development of the Treasury*, pp. 182–90. Haley, *First Earl of Shaftesbury*, pp. 404–5.

81 Browning, *Thomas Osborne*, II, p. 70.

82 E. C. Metzger, *Ralph, First Duke of Montagu, 1638–1709* (New York, 1987), p. 24. *The court in mourning being the life and worthy actions of Ralph duke of Montague* (1709). M. Petherick, *Restoration Rogues* (London, 1951), pp. 103–82.

83 Metzger, *Ralph, First Duke of Montagu*, pp. 96–7, 102–3, 125, 169.

84 Ibid., pp. 163–5. Petherick, *Restoration Rogues*, pp. 103–82.

85 Metzger, *Ralph, First Duke of Montagu*, pp. 163–5. Petherick, *Restoration Rogues*, pp. 103–82. Browning, *Thomas Osborne*, I, pp. 286, 305.

86 Geiter and Speck (eds), *Memoirs of Sir John Reresby*, p. 174. *The sentiments, a poem to the earl of Danby in the Tower by a person of quality* (1679), pp. 3–5. A. M. Evans, 'The imprisonment of Lord Danby in the Tower, 1679–1684', *Transactions of the Royal Historical Society*, 4th series, XII (1929), pp. 105–35.

87 Hutton, *Charles II*, pp. 357–404. Miller, *Charles II*, pp. 288–346. Jones, *Charles II*, pp. 135–61. M. Knights, *Politics and Opinion in Crisis, 1678–81* (Cambridge, 1994). J. Miller, *James II: A Study in Kingship* (London, 1989). J. R. Jones, *The Revolution of 1688 in England* (London, 1984). W. A. Speck, *Reluctant Revolutionaries: Englishmen and the Revolution of 1688* (Oxford, 1988). J. Israel (ed.), *The Anglo-Dutch Moment: Essays in the Glorious Revolution and its World Impact* (Cambridge, 1991). L. G. Schwoerer (ed.), *The Revolution of 1688–1689: Changing Perspectives* (Cambridge, 1992).

88 Miller, *James II*, pp. 121–4.

89 See J. R. Jones, *The First Whigs: The Politics of the Exclusion Crisis, 1678–1683* (Oxford, 1961).

90 See document 22.

91 Knights, *Politics and Opinion in Crisis*, p. 112. Jones, *First Whigs*, pp. 9–18.

92 R. North, *Lives of the Norths* (3 vols, London, 1890), I, p. 302.

93 Knights, *Politics and Opinion in Crisis*, p. 45.

94 J. P. Kenyon, *Robert Spencer, Earl of Sunderland, 1641–1702* (London, 1958), p. 25. H. C. Foxcroft, *The Character of a Trimmer, Being a Short Life of the First Marquis of Halifax* (Cambridge, 1946), pp. 62–109. T. Bruce, earl of Ailesbury, *Memoirs of Thomas, Earl of Ailesbury* (2 vols, London, 1890), I, pp. 23–4.

95 Knights, *Politics and Opinion in Crisis*, pp. 184–92.

96 BL, Additional MSS 17677, fo. 347. Geiter and Speck (eds), *Memoirs of Sir John Reresby*, p. 210. And see Halifax, 'Character of King Charles the second', pp. 247–67.

97 Geiter and Speck (eds), *Memoirs of Sir John Reresby*, pp. 205, 210. Foxcroft, *Life and Letters of the First Marquis of Halifax*, I, pp. 233, 241. BL, Additional MS 17677, fo. 347.

98 Geiter and Speck (eds), *Memoirs of Sir John Reresby*, p. 395. Foxcroft, *Life and Letters of the First Marquis of Halifax*, I, pp. 269–70. Foxcroft, *Character of a Trimmer*, pp. 136–210.

99 Foxcroft, *Character of a Trimmer*, pp. 136–210.

6

The crisis and James II, 1685–1688

Although a relatively short period of some four years, the reign of King James II has always been seen as a crucial turning point in the history of the British monarchy and state. In fact the series of problems revolving around the King's personality, his religious policies, ministerial rivalries at court, as well as outside intervention, were eventually to result in a revolution in 1688, but their origins can be traced to the 1670s and even the 1660s.[1] The 'Glorious Revolution' itself, whether it is seen as a national response to a religious and political crisis, or a mere palace *coup d'état*, was to have a number of consequences. James II's forced desertion of his throne in 1688 would lead to his eventual replacement by the joint monarchy of William and Mary. Another direct result of the Revolution of 1688 was the emergence of Parliament as a real force in the state and the refinement of party politics. Eventually this was to lead to the creation of a modern constitutional monarchy, while the nation's entanglement in a major European war in the course of the 1690s led to the creation of Britain as a world power.

Contrary to popular expectations, which had predicted a Protestant bloodbath at his accession, James II's reign began quietly enough in February 1685. The winter weather cut England off from most of Europe, and a cautious new government immediately closed the ports in a bid to clamp down on intelligence of events in the country. In his first days the new King proved to be sober in his bearing, strong-minded, and, more importantly, preached religious tolerance, good government and the protection of the law and established Church. He also appeared to confront the main problem of his reign head on by claiming that 'I have been reported to be a man fond of arbitrary power, but that is not the only falsehood which has been reported of me'.[2] Yet James's initial statements appeared to set the benchmarks by which he now wished to be measured throughout his reign: the defence of the established Church, the monarchy working through the law, and the protection of property. At court all employment in office ended with the death of the old king. While there were some changes (those close to James when he had been duke of York finally came into their own), rumour, a frequent inhabitant of the corridors of Whitehall, was soon marking out those who would founder and those who would survive the change of monarch.

Of all of the politicians from whom James had to choose in February 1685, Halifax was believed to be one of the prime targets for dismissal.[3] The new King James II did not approve of Halifax's wit or his subtle mind, these being two elements which soon proved to be sadly lacking from James's own character. Nevertheless after a secret discussion between the two, in which James generously claimed to forget the marquis's past and only to remember Halifax's defence of the succession during the exclusion crisis, Halifax survived for a time. In reality any truce between monarch and minister was unlikely to last for very long and Halifax was soon sidelined in the government. Indeed James said as much to the French ambassador Barillon, and when Halifax was kicked upstairs into the Lord President's office, his robust comments on royal policy and Roman Catholicism, as well as his inability in 'feign'd confidences and politic managements', marked him out for removal.[4]

It thus became apparent that the lesson that could be drawn from Halifax's fate was that only those who could anticipate the new King's wishes unreservedly could expect his favour. Naturally the brothers Hyde hoped to prosper more than most from their former brother-in-law's accession. At the end of of Charles II's reign, Lawrence Hyde, earl of Rochester, the second son of the ex-Lord Chancellor Clarendon, had been close to both the court and the duke of York.[5] As we have seen, he had only recently emerged as a figure in the political life of the court. Hyde now staked his claim for office on his financial abilities. Lory, in spite of his passion, drinking and swearing, was also capable of great industry and was to prove an initially adroit courtier, as well as a supporter of the established Church. He was rescued from the potential ministerial graveyard of Ireland and made Lord Treasurer, effectively making him a first minister of the crown. His brother Henry, earl of Clarendon, was also favoured by James and was made Lord Privy Seal. The choice of the Hyde brothers appeared to mark James's support for the established Church. Both of the brothers were the leaders of that faction at court, and James's royalist followers were comforted by his openness in claiming that as their monarch he would take care to 'defend and support' the Church.[6] In reality the Hyde brothers' promotion marked the first stage of James's plan for religious toleration by reaching agreement with the establishment.

The ever-pliable Sunderland appeared to have most to lose from the change of monarch. Given his recent slippery dealings, Sunderland was soon marked out as the most likely victim of a purge. Not only did he have a past, in that he had voted for exclusion, but the good offices of the duchess of Portsmouth, his most reliable ally, were also lost to him.[7] James, with a poor reputation for forgiveness, may well have thought twice about retaining Sunderland as a minister, but the great survivor managed to insinuate himself into a position where he could attempt to persuade the King of his point of view. What Sunderland's actual strategy was seemed at first to be unclear, but the need for a friendly Parliament, as well as a neutral France, and what one contemporary called the 'violent and boisterous nature' of Rochester at court, gave him some hope for the future. Short-lived plans to push him into Ireland as Lord Lieutenant were soon frustrated by Sunderland's own tactical move of suggesting Clarendon as eminently more suitable for the post.[8]

In the meanwhile, as with any new reign, all sorts of courtiers generally floated toward to the new King. One observer informed the aged and soon-to-be-removed Ormonde that the 'Court is crowded as much as it was at the Restoration, the ministers seem to be in as great a hurry of business, and the promoters of the Bill of Exclusion come in as fast as others'.[9] Those with shady pasts were soon rebuffed. James took to purging the Augean stables of his brother by speaking out against lewdness and drunkenness; in doing so he shocked the cynics as these were but two of the major vices in his brother's court in which he, as much as anyone, had recently indulged. James, however, appears to have been something of a reformer by nature and he soon set about him with a will. Sobriety and decorum, in addition to hard work, were to be his watchwords, offices were cut back at court and the new King spent many hours in council and at the Treasury and Admiralty until he had at least acquired a reputation for action and business. His effectiveness in such matters was quite another matter and leads us to the character of this most puzzling of our monarchs, who although given golden opportunities at the beginning of his reign was wilfully to cast them aside.

King James II

In 1685 James was fifty-two years of age. He possessed some twenty-five years of experience as a politician from his brother's reign, but it is doubtful whether he had really learned anything in that time. His reputation at his accession was certainly suspect, but he was neither

Macaulay's melodramatic villain, twirling his moustache as he forced England back to Rome, nor F. C. Turner's syphilitic incompetent.[10] In fact, although James's career as a soldier and sailor had occasionally given him a short-lived popularity, this had not survived his open conversion to Roman Catholicism in 1673. Indeed, as we have seen, the primary focus for the crisis of the early 1680s lay in the religion of the heir to the throne. Despite his fortunes, the new King had acquired little real understanding of the peculiarly vexed relationship between the English and popery over the years. In spite of his comments to the French ambassador about 'l'aversion que le peuple d'Angleterre avoit pour la religion catholique', he appeared to have held to rather simplistic views. Dissenters were to James republicans, while the Church of England men were merely lapsed or even closet Catholics who, with a push in the right direction, would soon join him in the glories of Rome.[11] If this view was deluded, it was certainly understandable. The immense personal satisfaction that James drew from his religious beliefs has led John Miller to argue that after the execution of his father, it was undoubtedly the most important experience of his life.[12] And like so many converts to a new faith, James naturally wanted to share his new-found religion with others. He became fervent in the promulgation of his faith, as well as hostile to those who sought to change his mind. Much to the distress of the Pope and his papal nuncio to England, James the zealot was rather old-fashioned in his views of Roman Catholic thought and teaching and in the long run he caused his Church more trouble than was thought befitting in a Catholic monarch. A rather humourless man of simple beliefs, the new King was never the pragmatist that his brother had been. Marked out from an early age as obstinate, narrow of mind, with a rigidity and lack of imagination, to James all opposition appears to have stemmed from the worst of motives. Having said this, he was to show some of his supporters a loyalty which perhaps went too far at times, and increasingly he had come to believe in a form of providentialism which goes some way to explain his gloomy reactions to the Dutch invasion of 1688.[13]

In his attitudes to kingship, however, James was clear enough. He was a divinely appointed patriarch who hoped to rule through a staid council of state, and a docile as well as tranquil Parliament. Such bodies, where possible, were to be filled with representatives of a godly and satisfied people which would increase his *gloire*. James was also one of the most English of the Stuarts, and a mulish patriot of sorts; indeed his courtiers were soon claiming that the country now had 'a martial prince who [not only] loved glory, [but] who would bring France into as humble a dependence upon us, as we had been formerly on that court'.[14] While James was to prove a hesitant ally of France on his accession, he immediately followed his late brother's line and asked the French ambassador for money, although his relationship with Louis thereafter cooled somewhat.[15] In spite of all these problems, there is little doubt that James would in time have made a good king, but whatever his other merits ultimately it was his devout Roman Catholicism that always stood in the way of his total acceptance by his people.

James II's objectives for his fellow Catholics have been subject to continual debate since the seventeenth century. The revisionist orthodoxy argues that James understood, if not very well, the difficulties facing the minority religion of English Catholicism. He simply wanted equal rights for Roman Catholics to be followed in time by secure civil rights, if, as seemed likely up until June 1688, his Protestant daughter Mary was to succeed him.[16] However, the King's plans seem also to have been based on three illusions: that royalists in general would prefer a more autocratic regime, as he certainly did; that the doctrines of non-resistance which permeated the belief system of the King's Anglican supporters would prevent them from ever objecting to toleration if the idea came from James himself; and that latterly the dissenting community would make a devil's bargain with James to support the abolition of the penal laws for Catholics in exchange for toleration for themselves. Unfortunately for his plans James was faced with the aggressive Protestantism of the majority of the English nation, and in his haste to achieve something for his co-religionists he often appeared to go out of his way to alienate his most significant supporters. The loyalty of the Church of England and the Tory Anglican Royalists was thus stretched to breaking point. And when they failed him James chose to create an improbable coalition of Catholics and dissenters to force a form of permanent security for the Catholics against the Anglican establishment's wishes. Thus his attempts to persuade the Anglicans in the first phase or his reign (1685–86) and the dissenters in the second phase (1687–88) simply did not work. Moreover, James became increasingly prone to tunnel vision, unwilling, or simply unable, to reverse his objectives as his reign progressed.[17]

The King's apparent hastiness in matters religious has been frequently put down to his age, but it is equally likely to have been the product of some twenty-five years of frustration in playing second fiddle to the man of convenience that was his brother Charles. His brother's fabian tactics often frustrated James. He wrote in nautical terms in January 1679 of how Charles should have followed 'bold and resolute councells, and [stuck] to them ... measures must be taken and not departed from [and a King] should steer another course, and looke out for another passage, which no doubt may be found, to gett on's port'.[18] Now that James was king he may well have thought that at last he was able to do the things his brother should have done, or would have done, had not Charles been so weak-willed. Above all else a visible support for his Church was now in order. It should have been obvious to all that this was going to happen, for he had previously written, and openly expressed the view, that 'I cannot be more Catholic than I am'. James's wife was also aware of how immovable his beliefs were, noting in 1674 that he was 'firm and steady in our holy religion … [and] he would not leave it for anything in the world'.[19] Having said that, the King's religious policy seems to have come as something of a surprise to most of his subjects.

In his new position James openly sought to express his loyalty to his Church through a high-profile court Catholicism and by publicising conversions where possible. Building works were also put into action, such as the lavish new Catholic Chapel Royal and the establishment of 'mass houses' in London (at least eighteen by 1688), emphasising that this was now an openly Catholic monarchy. A diplomatic shift in foreign policy could also be observed by the open embassy sent by the King to the Pope in 1686; although typically of James it was somewhat dubiously led by the former cuckold the earl of Castlemaine.[20] The King's actions at court, where for example he requested the new resident of Cologne, an English Benedictine monk, to appear in his public audience in his habit, 'astonished and bewildered' the courtiers and caused numerous mutterings. The public reception of a papal nuncio, d'Adda, led to the sacking of the duke of Somerset when he refused to attend the ceremony. The throwing open of the doors of the Chapel Royal so that his subjects could see the mass, as well as James's invitation to his ministers to attend him there, caused yet more dismay.[21] While all of these actions were open enough, they were sufficient to lead to increasing erosion of Anglican Tory support that would be crucial in 1688.

At the court itself James saw his new ministers and courtiers as being obliged to do his bidding, but the King was not particularly well served. Despite his claim that 'he was king and would be obeyed', more and more his policies meant frequent absences from his court and he came to be surrounded by second-rate men, time-servers, flatterers, and extreme Roman Catholics even more out of touch with the country than he was himself. They in turn, by their seizure of office, began to exclude the traditional, if greedy, supporters of the crown. Even Lord Churchill, raised from nothing by James and assured of his favour, began to feel the pressure from the Romanising policy.[22] The idea that one faction, and a Catholic one at that, could finally win in the game of court politics appears to have disturbed many at court. Sir John Reresby noted on 5 March 1685 that:

> Though it could not be said that there was as yet any remarkable
> invasion upon the rights of the Church of England, yet the King
> gave all the encouragement he could to the encrease his own, by
> putting more papists in office here (but especially in Ireland); by
> causing or allowing popish books to be printed ... sold and cried
> publicly; by publishing some popish papers found in the late
> King's closet, and the declaration of his dying a papist ... and many
> other such things; which made all men expect that more would fol-
> low of a greater concern.[23]

If this were to happen then the losers would almost certainly begin to
turn elsewhere for favour. Indeed foreign observers also began to
notice the potential consequences. Terriesi, the Modenese ambassador, pointed out in August 1687 that:

> His Majesty is at the worst with his principal subjects, who will not
> agree with his government. Therefore, such of the nobility as have
> any credit, standing, or power in the kingdom are rarely to be seen
> at Court; they remain alienated and are constantly in conference,
> consulting how to prevent the abolition of the test and the Catho-
> lics from gaining ground.[24]

If the result was a court divorced from many of the realities of life by
1688 and split because of the misunderstandings between James and
the political nation, these misunderstandings began soon after the
crushing of the rebellions of Monmouth and Argyle. For one after
another the troublesome areas of ministers, toleration, the army, prerogative powers, royal authority and the role of the Catholics in the
English and Irish administration were all marked out for James's
blundering tactics.

Rochester and Sunderland, 1685–1687

As has been noted, in the early days of the regime Lawrence Hyde,
earl of Rochester, held office as the King's premier minister.
Rochester had at least some advantage in his relationship to the new
King as a former brother-in-law, but he soon found little else to sustain him. 'Lory', the 'Chit of state', found himself the representative
of the Church party in government, and in spite of his views James
made him Lord Treasurer in 1685. Rochester was regarded with distaste, followed by hostility and suspicion, by the many Romanists
who now flocked to James's court. As with his brother Henry, earl of
Clarendon, he also found himself caught in the trap between the
Tory creeds of loyalty to the monarchy and loyalty to the established
Church, and found that neither could be reconciled under James. He

later explained his position in the regime by claiming that both he and his brother Clarendon had remained in office as long as they did 'as honest men' with a purpose of doing as much good as they could.[25] Increasingly, however, the Hydes found themselves left out of the inner circle of rule. In fact Rochester's rise to office through diplomatic channels, as well as the treasury commission in the late 1670s, although it had given him a taste for power, had also exposed his inability. He had a temper, and enormous amounts of nervous energy that emerged in foul language when provoked. His natural arrogance also made him disliked and resented by those around him. As it turned out, Rochester's great rival Halifax was not to be his main opponent in these years, but the most unprincipled man at court: Robert Spencer, earl of Sunderland.

If Rochester was regarded with distaste, and few at court were to regret his fall, all contemporaries were well aware that Sunderland was a 'bad man'. As the future Queen Anne noted to her sister Mary, 'this man turned backwards and forward in the late king's reign; and now to complete all his virtues is working to bring in popery'.[26] Fittingly labelled by one court satirist as the 'Proteus Sunderland', the earl was at times pliant, unprincipled and even a knave.[27] He was a character whose slipperiness and arrogance had become proverbial even by 1685. Abel Boyer noted him as a man 'cut out by nature for a politician' and in doing so he was not being complimentary.[28] As a well-educated young man of a prominent royalist family, Sunderland had first emerged in diplomatic circles as an Arlington appointee to various diplomatic posts, including an embassy to France. Whilst there he had gained some knowledge not only of the French modes of government, but of the workings of power. His reputation on his return to England in 1679 was somewhat uneven, but sufficient enough for him to obtain the secretaryship of state in 1679 replacing Sir Joseph Williamson. Following this appointment his rise was rapid and as we have seen he soon became part of Charles II's inner cabinet alongside Essex, Halifax and Temple. The withdrawal of Halifax and Temple, a regular occurrence for both men, as well as Essex, who went into opposition, left Sunderland on his own with new opportunities to make allies in August 1679. As one of the 'chits', alongside Godolphin and Lawrence Hyde, he was most directly responsible for Charles's government in the last years of his reign.

Sunderland's power in this period always remained insecure. It rested upon his dubious political tactics, his ingratiating manners, and a close alliance with the King's mistress: Louise, duchess of Portsmouth. Only Arlington, whose career Sunderland's to some extent resembles, could match this opportunist politician and gambler. Sunderland craved office for the power and wealth that it brought with it. He also took bribes from the French like many another in the era, but at the same time was perfectly willing to maintain contacts with William of Orange. Only his fervent desire to stay in office can really explain the miscalculation of February 1681 when he misread the signs and voted for exclusion. Louise and the French ambassador engineered Sunderland's return to court in August 1682 following overtures to Charles. Once back in favour Sunderland soon renewed his rivalries with Halifax and Rochester and took care to make his peace with a previously unfriendly duke of York. But the death of Charles in February 1685 appeared once again to have wrecked his career. Fortunately Sunderland, for all his affected speech and fine clothes, was an absolute realist in all he did and was willing to do anything to cling on to power. If the 1680s had taught him anything then it was the futility of following a policy that was diametrically opposed to his monarch's wishes.

Sunderland had some advantages over his rivals: he was capable of savage sarcasm, he was also an absolute master of political trickery and, where necessary, sycophancy. Suave, sophisticated and urbane, confident in his decision-making and administration, he was willing to take responsibility and became the first real 'undertaker': an intermediary between the monarch, the factions at court and Parliament.[29] It was a role that he was to develop into a fine art in the succeeding reign of William III. In the struggle which opened out at James's court, Sunderland was to prove himself the great survivor, playing a decisive role in wrecking James's regime as a result, although whether this was as deliberate as Sunderland later made out is open to debate. If it was utility that kept Sunderland in office in 1685, it was Sunderland's ingratiating manner that made James choose him as Lord President on 4 December 1685. By this stage, however, he was already deep in the confidences of James. In exile James later regretted the licence which he had given to his minister, although at the time he seems to have believed that the earl was the best man for the tasks ahead. As to their relationship, one insider, Princess Anne, noted that Sunderland was 'perpetually with the priests and stirs up the K[ing] to do things further that I believe he would [not do] of himself'.[30]

Naturally the main target on the minister's horizon in the early days of the new regime was the elimination of his rival Rochester and his minions from a court which, as usual, was beginning to settle into factional struggles. Sunderland hoped to gain the confidence of James by his identification with the Catholic clique at court. In fact Sunderland does not appear to have felt any real sympathy with any of the factions that emerged at James's court. By late 1685 these were becoming clear. The first of these factions was the somewhat 'fabian'

Catholic clique, which was backed by the Spanish ambassador Ronquillo and led by old Catholic aristocrats such as William Herbert, marquis of Powis, and the 72-year-old John, Lord Bellasyse. Bellasyse was later to tell Sir John Reresby that 'he had been very adverse (though a papist) to the measures used in that reign for promoteing that religion … but his counsel was suspected as comming from a man that … was old and timerous, and that haveing a good estate was in fear to hazard it'. Another Catholic grouping, the so-called 'hott party', was more extreme in its demands. This was basically the Queen's party headed by Mary herself, as well as Henry Jermyn, Lord Dover, whom Reresby called 'a papist and great favourite', and the papal nuncio, Ferdinand, Count d'Adda.[31] There was also a Jesuit party led by Father Petre, the King's confessor, and an Irish grouping of swordsmen, adventurers and priests led by Richard Talbot, later earl of Tyrconnel and a prime actor in the King's romanising policy for Ireland; Colonel John Fitzgerald, an Irish catholic soldier, Sir Richard Bellings and Robert Brent were also part of this group. The 'Court Tories' led by men such as John Churchill, Sidney Godolphin and John Grenville, earl of Bath, were another group. Of course the Hydes and the Church of England group also had their own agenda. On the lower rung of the administration were groups of moderate and generally apolitical civil servants and courtiers, men such as Samuel Pepys, William Bridgeman and William Blathwayt. Sunderland, as one of the few political lone wolves of his generation, ambled his way merrily through them all. He took a French pension of some 6,000 livres, undermined any opposition to his schemes, created tactical alliances as he saw fit, reconstructed the council to suit himself, openly expressed his authority on all matters, and finally took care to maintain his influence with the only man who really mattered in all of this, the King.

Despite the increasingly more open Roman Catholic stance of the monarch – James took to attending mass within a week of his accession – and the increasing presence of Romanists at his court, the political elite stuck to the King through the rebellions of Argyll and Monmouth in June–July 1685. With these rebellions against him crushed, James's Parliament, traditionally called at the beginning of any new reign, lost much of its initial compliance. It was thought that widespread interference in the elections to the House of Commons had made it a secure and ostensibly loyal body, if somewhat resentful, and that fear of fanatics in Scotland and the West Country increased this loyal tendency. However, this loyalty was soon found to have its limits. Once the rebels were disposed of, the Commons in particular became increasingly ill-natured over the familiar problems of the 1680s: finance, the expanding army, many of whose recruits were apparently Catholic, and events abroad. Louis XIV, who was to have a major role in James's downfall, chose this moment to purge France of its Protestant Huguenot population. Moreover, Louis XIV's plans for Europe continued apace and stirred up yet more problems for James. In any European conflict James would be forced to take some stance and it was unclear whether he would be drawn into an alliance with Catholic France or the Protestant Netherlands. In addition, James's attitude to the established Church (he quickly ordered it to desist from anti-Catholic preaching) as well as his insistence on attending mass in public raised the political temperature. New policies, which sought not only the repeal of the Test Act, but also Habeus Corpus, created a second stormy session in Parliament in November 1685. Opposition soon broke out over the idea of removing limitations on Roman Catholics and matters were not assisted by the arrival of Huguenot refugees in London with their horror stories of Roman Catholic persecution. The Parliament's disagreements ensured its prorogation on 20 November. It was never to meet again.

Unease also began to grow in court circles. Halifax refused to go along with the ideas for repealing the Test Act and was removed as an example. James's policy of toleration by any means, virtually a test of loyalty to himself, began to move into overdrive within the court as the balance of the ministry began to shift. Indeed Owen Wynne, writing in July 1686, noted that there were already 'some warm feuds amongst the great ones at Court' and for those circling the two ministers involved, Rochester and Sunderland, it made life a little more difficult than usual. Sir William Trumbull declared that it was 'next to impossible to have a friend of one and not an enemy of the other'.[32] The conflict between the two occupied much of that year and Sunderland's unscrupulous nature was always likely to give him the upper hand over his rival. Despite Rochester's close links to the Church of England and his fellow Anglicans, once James had set his course for a new type of government the minister's days in office seemed numbered. Rochester's protestations that he wished to remain true to his Church were simply met by various attempts to convert him, through debates with ecclesiastics, and 'evidence' of Charles II's conversion to the Roman faith. This soon came to a crisis point. The Lord Treasurer's last interview with the King in December 1686 only confirmed Rochester's greatest fears of what had been going on behind the scenes but his own inability to combat it. James, weeping as he spoke, bluntly told Rochester than 'no man must be at the head of his affairs that was not of his own opinion ... that it was impossible to keep a man in so great a trust, in so ... eminent a station, where there was so much dependence, that was of an interest so contrary to that which he must support and own and advance'. These were words that undoubtedly echoed Sunderland's private mutterings in the King's ear. Nor had James forgotten Rochester's advice in 1685 'not to make a public profession of his religion', a damning thing in itself he thought, and after Monmouth's rising 'not to take any more persons into employment of the catholic religion'. 'No man of sense', thundered James, 'could have been [of Rochester's] opinion, but a Protestant.'[33]

Persuaded of the difficulties of calling another useful (by which he meant packed) Parliament while Rochester was still in the government and apparently caballing against the Roman policy, James had eventually promised to dismiss him if the Lord Treasurer did not change his religious views. Moreover, the Lord Treasurer's tactical skills in court politics had proved to be woefully inadequate, especially in comparison to those of his main rival Sunderland. The attempt to use the King's mistress Catherine Sedley as a way to influence James was a case in point.[34] For while this rebounded upon all of the ministers, James had a sudden attack of morality, Sunderland had persuaded a hostile Queen of the luckless Treasurer's part in the intrigue. In addition Sunderland, a total cynic in such matters, could always trump his rival in the religious stakes which mattered so much to the King by his own conversion to Roman Catholicism. As yet he had held his hand in this matter, but he had managed to give out subtle hints to the King of his inclinations. Rochester on the other hand followed in his father's footsteps as a staunch supporter of the established Church and indeed *de facto* head of that party at court, so that he ultimately found it impossible to succumb to the blandishments of James to turn Catholic in return for power. His subsequent diminishment led to his final fall in January 1687, which was only slightly softened by a pension.[35]

Henry Hyde, earl of Clarendon, who had been made Lord Lieutenant of Ireland in September 1686, was also in difficulty. Clarendon was handicapped throughout his administration by the presence of Richard Talbot, earl of Tyrconnel. Tyrconnel had had soon acquired a separate power base in Ireland as commander of the Irish forces. He had a long history as a courtier and was noted for his petty violence, 'cunning' and enormous vanity. It was certainly believed that Tyrconnel 'would stick at nothing' to reach his end and he was the archetype of those Roman Catholic Irish courtiers who had once clustered around James when he was duke of York seeking his protection and favour. Although James was a natural defender of any Catholic interest, especially after his open conversion in 1673, he sometimes saw the Irish Catholic interest in a different light, for as Roy Foster has noted 'Irish Catholics were "different" for reasons of strategy as well as property'.[36] Having said this, James had much in common with those Irishmen who collected around him, as he too was an old soldier, and even though their needs often crossed his own self-interest in seizing Irish land, he was willing to help them out. When he became their monarch James took care to build up the Irish army and to allow Tyrconnel to purge these troops of Protestants, direct a Roman Catholic association which ultimately wished to reverse the settlement of the 1660s, and undermine Clarendon's more moderate Protestant stance. At court few could compete with Tyrconnel's blustering authority in matters Irish, while Clarendon's activities were criticised as 'Whiggish' or even, without a sense of irony, 'Cromwellian'. To those at home in James's court such opportunities were not to be missed and Sunderland, as intent upon bringing down Clarendon as anyone else, saw in Tyrconnel an ally, albeit a rather dangerous one. In exchange for his support and some perks in land and cash he was also willing to go along with the remodelling of Ireland. The more moderate Catholics disagreed. They were hostile to Tyrconnel's ambitions (Powis indeed wanted the post of Lord Lieutenant for himself), but the more extreme Catholics, such as Petre and the Queen, supported Tyrconnel and so Clarendon was pushed out of his office.

The reverberations of the Hyde brothers' fall were soon observed elsewhere. Those of a 'depending interest' on Rochester and Clarendon were to be forced to follow them into the wilderness; the opportunity to change patrons, the usual course in such circumstances, did not appear to exist in a regime where without a conversion to Roman Catholicism nothing was possible. Roger North visiting the court at this time noted how the 'times began to grow sour, all favour leaned towards the Catholics and such as prostituted to that interest. We who were steady to the laws and the Church were worst looked upon … I thought my person was no agreeable object, and it was better court to keep it away.'[37] Although James himself appeared to have hoped that the lesser figures at his court would now be frightened into co-operation with him by the removal of the Hydes and that 'closeting' would pick up others, a stream of dismissals resulted.

The road to revolution, 1687–1688

With Rochester and Clarendon both eliminated from the court scene, a further shuffle took place in Whitehall. Minor functionaries were removed or left. Newport lost his post as Treasurer. The Comptroller of the Household Maynard also went out of office. Lord Lumley's regiment was taken from him and he turned Protestant in disgust, while Admiral Herbert, a great friend of James, was ousted for refusing to be intimidated and replaced with the Catholic Roger Strickland.[38] With the removal of the King's old allies, and more were to follow, James began to become more and more isolated. Only men such as Dartmouth, Feversham, Mulgrave and Churchill, as well as the apolitical civil servants led by Samuel Pepys and Godolphin, were able to remain around him. Ormonde, now in his last days, removed himself, while the other great magnates of the land were to be seen only occasionally and then with reluctance at James's court.

In any case James was already moving away from such men. Visiting the court one day in 1687, a shocked Sir William Trumbull found James in his 'night-gown at the fireside with a company of Irish and unknown faces' around him.[39] In fact the King had already established an unofficial Roman Catholic council to advise him. Sunderland, unlike Rochester, not only managed to intrigue his way onto this, but to dominate its proceedings. He worked hard not only to cultivate those friendly to the King, but to maintain his stance as the 'Queen's man' in government, while at the same time he was able to parade his administrative and diplomatic experience and exploit the ignorance of those around him. This small Catholic clique, which consisted of Father Petre, the Catholic lords Bellasyse, Powis and Arundel, all of whom had been implicated in the Popish Plot, and Lord Dover, was brought together with the object of obtaining toleration and office for Roman Catholics, as well as the suppression of the penal laws. They emerged as the King's most intimate advisers and offices continued to shower on Roman Catholics. Lord Arundel was made Privy Seal; Lord Bellasyse was made First Lord of the Treasury; Lord Powis and Lord Dover became Privy Councillors; while the Lord Chancellor was the ever obsequious, but still Protestant, George Jeffreys. The more moderate Catholics in the regime moved for a cautious amelioration of the penal code, but the three most significant members of the regime after Sunderland proved to be extremists: Father Edward Petre, Tyrconnel and John Drummond, earl of Melfort.[40]

Edward Petre, a native Londoner, of 'a fair smooth tongue, and a very affable way of flattery', was a man whose advancement was to cause James a great deal of trouble. This self-seeking gentleman – Dalrymple called him 'puffed up with ... vanity and ambition' – had been introduced to James during the Popish Plot. He was soon looked upon as an intimate with James, who not only made him Clerk of the Closet, but also lodged him in his old apartments at Whitehall, eventually making him a Privy Councillor in 1687.[41] The Jesuit's major ambition was to be a cardinal of his Church, and James was not hostile to this plan. Indeed he tried to achieve it, much to the distress of the Pope. The Dutch ambassador certainly thought that

Petre could well become a 'second Stephen Gardiner ... namely either archbishop or bishop and at sometime Lord Chancellor of the kingdom' given half the chance. At the least Petre was able to become a broker at the court and a man whose 'antechambers [there] were crowded with Petitioners, for they found by experience if he undertook their business it seldom failed to prosper'.[42] While Sunderland unquestionably played on Petre's vanity in the early years of the reign, mainly in order to use him to gain even more of James's confidence, eventually Petre slipped from his patronage and sought to become a power himself.

Pressure by James on various institutions grew in 1687. Further dismissals from the court occurred. The raddled wit Henry Savile, an unlikely victim of closeting, was removed as Vice-Chamberlain, while even Christopher Musgrave, whose family could never be accused of disloyalty to the crown, was removed from the Ordnance, but the greatest obstacle to the grand design was the established Church. A Commission for Ecclesiastical Causes set up in 1686 was used to govern the Church. James also chose to put pressure on another area of religious life: the universities. When the president of Magdalen College died, Oxford became the new battleground between James and the political nation. When the fellows resisted an attempt to install a Catholic as their President, they were expelled to allow the King to get his own way. This move was followed by a Declaration of Indulgence on 4 April 1687.[43] The Indulgence, alongside a general suspension of the Tests, made a compromise solution to the religious question increasingly unlikely. At the same time, in the civil sphere a board of regulators was established to purge the corporations, and the Lord Lieutenants were ordered to frame suitable lists of dissenters for the Commission of the peace and the militia, as well as put the three questions to every justice of the peace. This led to much breast-beating and hedged answers. These local reforms also led to dismissals. The earl of Oxford as Lord Lieutenant of Essex was told by James to 'use his interest ... for the taking off the penal laws and the test[, but] told the King plainly he could not persuade that to others which he was a[d]verse to in his own conscience'.[44] Derby of Lancashire, Northampton of Warwick, Scarsdale of Derby and Winchelsea of Kent were all removed.

While the government continued to try and create a new force in political life, the older political nation, or disgruntled ex-courtiers, depending on one's point of view, were beginning to stir. We can trace the conspiracy against James at least back to 1687 when as a result of Dykevelt's mission to England William of Orange finally activated his latent interest in English politics that had been there since 1672. Relations between William and James had in fact been deteriorating for some time over a number of matters, not the least the King's religious policies, for which James had sought the approval of William and Mary in such a manner that if it had been anyone other than James it must have been thought a trap. William's opinions on a repeal of the penal laws had been cleverly hedged about so that his answers did not lose any favour with the English establishment. However, the time for intervention in English affairs appeared to be fast approaching.

In the end William's decision to intervene in English affairs rested on three factors: the state of Europe, religion and his interest in the succession. The discord that occurred with his father-in-law was a minor part in his scheme of things. Foremost in his mind were the diplomatic uncertainties into which Louis XIV was throwing Europe, where a new war seemed to be entirely possible. We must also add to this William's fears that the Catholic zealots might well persuade James to cut Mary out of the succession, although given James's previous stance on hereditary succession and exclusion this was an unlikely event. But William always feared the possibility. In fact William's view of English matters was as much obscured by his European outlook as dynastic considerations, and was inevitably linked to his great duel with Louis XIV. Not knowing which way James would jump in any future conflict with Louis made for one of life's uncertainties and William was a man who above all disliked uncertainty. Thus it was that a natural community of interests had soon begun to form between the Prince of Orange and the emergent, albeit reluctant, opposition in England which William took care to foster.[45]

In February 1687 William sent his ambassador, Dykevelt, on a mission to England. As a covert part of this mission, Dykevelt had a series of meetings at the house of Charles Talbot, earl of Shrewsbury, thereby opening direct contacts between William and the English leaders for the first time. These contacts were subsequently maintained both by correspondence and by Zuylestein's visit in the following year, but as yet there was no concerted plan. There was certainly no thought of replacing James with William, for the activists involved were more interested in talks about talks, in addition to using William to put pressure on James to reverse his policies, while William was himself testing the waters. Certainly pains were taken by William and Mary to reassure many of their supporters but little else came of the contacts. Both Rochester and Clarendon were in mourning for their loss of power, while Halifax, as usual, trimmed his sails and refused to be drawn out. Lord Churchill declared, on behalf of Princess Anne and himself, his frustrations, while Nottingham cautiously lamented the whole situation. Only Danby, ever eager to regain his lost power, went further in his dealings with the Dutch, but then he had less to lose in one sense as his re-employment by James was highly unlikely.

Throughout the reign while Danby had been treated outwardly with some civility there was little chance of him serving the new King or of ever completing the grant of the marquisette which he coveted and which Charles had promised.[46] Greed, ambition and a return to political life can explain his part in the schemes which followed. In any case his links with William went further back than most to the part he had played in the marriage of William and Mary. By March 1688, given the Queen's imminent confinement, Danby was at least clear that some form of resistance was becoming necessary and that the action party could wait no longer, and others were beginning to be of the same mind. Edward Russell, an associate of Shrewsbury, had been despatched to the Netherlands in April 1688 to ask the Prince of Orange his intentions and he received the cautious reply that if William were invited to intervene he would do so, but vague promises of support were insufficient. As a consequence Henry Sidney, the most active of the conspirators and the man in 'whose hands the conduct of the whole design was chiefly deposited by the prince's own orders', then put out proposals about William's intervention to Danby, Devonshire and Bishop Compton, as well as the army officers Charles Trelawny, Percy Kirke and Churchill. Daniel Finch, earl of Nottingham, was approached, but wavered at the last and refused to join. Churchill confidently accounted for Anne and some of the army and was to write to William in August 1688 his archetypal courtier's response to the situation: 'Mr Sidney will let you know how I intend to behave myself: I think it is what I owe God and my country. My honour I take leave to put in your royal Highness's hands in which I think it safe.' In fact in William's eyes Churchill and the army commanders were the most significant addition to the scheme, for by this he took it for granted that the English army would not fight and that desertions from the army would ultimately wreck James's chances of military resistance.[47]

As the preparations for an invasion began in earnest in the Netherlands, James heedlessly continued his action against the establishment with the trial of the seven bishops who had petitioned him over his ideas for liberty of conscience. He also celebrated the birth of the Prince of Wales on 10 June 1688. For the conspirators this was the final blow and it resulted in the invitation from the so-called 'immortal seven' for William to come to England.[48] Of these seven all had a court background of some sort and we may assume that whatever their fine words, to some extent their minds were governed by the traditional courtier's self-interest. Only Danby was of any real substance and he, of course, was tainted by his ministry of the 1670s. Indeed there is some reason to think that Danby's presence may have kept other discontented ex-courtier's such as Halifax from joining the invitation. William Cavendish, earl of Devonshire, had been fined and thrown out of James's court for brawling in 1687, since when he had sulked in Derbyshire. Lord Richard Lumley was a convert from Rome who resented the loss of his regiment. Charles Talbot, earl of Shrewsbury, in many ways the most interesting of the seven, was an uncertain soul throughout his career. In 1688 he was still a young man and debt-ridden, but of a Whiggish enough persuasion to join the scheme, and both he and Lumley may well have been under the influence of the more boisterous Charles Lord Mordaunt, who himself had openly criticised James in the last Parliament. Bishop Compton of London had of course risen through the assistance of Danby as well as his own high birth. His influence at court had extended to the education of the Princesses Mary and Anne, and presiding over their respective marriages. Compton had opposed exclusion, but was openly hostile to Roman Catholic interests. He was dismissed from the Privy Council in 1685 for the defence of one of his clergy who had been preaching anti-Catholic rhetoric. As he was suspended from his office, communication with William and Mary was a logical next step and Compton was in any case hardly a typical Anglican bishop. Henry Sidney and Edward Russell were younger sons of noble houses. Russell, a discontent from the early 1680s, was a useful naval contact whose intrigues were such that they turned him against James in the 1680s and against William in the 1690s. He had withdrawn from court in 1683 after the death of his cousin. Henry Sidney was a younger son of the Leicester clan easily estranged from James as he had known disappointment at court and lack of the rewards there that he felt were his due and thus was taken much into William's confidences.[49]

At court in the meantime the struggle continued. While few were capable of matching Sunderland's tactical skills and he still seemed to be retaining his strong position, he began to lose ground to the more extreme Catholics. Problems arose over the matter of another Parliament, which under the circumstances Sunderland wished to delay, and he continued to attempt to curb James's ardour for the Catholic design. The Queen's pregnancy, however, had put all into disarray and the trial of the seven bishops raised the political temperature to fever pitch. The moderate Catholics and Sunderland were now caught between two fires. They were to be forced to gamble on sustaining their support for James's plans, which if the child were a girl would effectively finish them with William, but if the child proved to be a boy and they had not been supportive enough of

James he would also be displeased. Sunderland, gaining courage from his gambling instincts, speculated on the latter, appearing to believe that should James die before a majority he would be well placed to manipulate the child's regent the Queen. Beneath his feet the more extreme Catholics at court were sapping and mining at his position. So much of a gambler had Sunderland become that he played his last card in July 1688 by declaring his Catholicism. Insincerity being the earl's forte, this was undoubtedly a tactical manoeuvre, which was meant to leave Sunderland well placed to undercut his main Catholic rival Melfort. Although the latter was both conceited and inadequate in office, he had been using his winning ways with the Queen and was closer to the Jesuits at court. Additionally his role as Scottish secretary gave him the unrestricted access to James's person which few, other than Sunderland, possessed.[50]

In the meantime, as summer merged into an ever more gloomy autumn, those with a more temperate view in the regime continued in their attempt to persuade James to moderate his actions. By August, news of William's invasion fleet massing in the Dutch ports was common knowledge. This, and moderate persuasion, soon put James into a poor temper, but as yet there was no hint from the King of the real problems facing him. Only with the proclamation issued on 21 September did he begin to show the first signs of retreat from his position. As the writs for a new Parliament were issued and then withdrawn, the indecisiveness at the heart of his government began to be palpable. James began to move from one extreme to another, pleasing no one in the process. Some attempts were made to regain the allegiance of the court's rejects. Rochester was summoned to Newmarket, Seymour had a private audience, Nottingham kissed hands and even Danby was approached. But Hoffman the Imperial ambassador noted that 'not one of the great nobles is to be seen at court, except those ... forced to it by their charges; all are in the country which is considered a very bad sign'.[51]

By mid-October, however, the situation appeared to have changed once more. The extremists amongst the Roman Catholics, who Rizzini noted were the 'priests and friars [who] have spoiled everything [with] their inopportune zeal' at court, insisted that James hold firm.[52] The States General of the Netherlands rejected James's half-hearted attempts at an alliance, intended to split Orange from his supporters, while Louis XIV offered assistance and was rejected. He engaged himself in the affair of Cologne and William saw his opportunity. A series of court manoeuvres then took place. Sunderland was finally dismissed from his office on 26 October 1688. The minister had fallen for his opposition to the King's policy, his treasonable contacts, and mostly for losing his nerve in the face of the almost certain invasion now facing the country. Damned in James's eyes, Sunderland's moves to advocate concessions gave his enemies a chance to undermine him. With William's fleet in disarray after a storm, some breathing space was gained, but his intent was clear enough. A subsequent declaration from William called for a redress of national grievances, a Parliament and an attack upon the veracity of the birth of the young Prince of Wales. James's attempt to get his peers and bishops to declare their abhorrence of this failed. In the meantime William landed in England on 5 November.

At first the King hoped the invasion would play into his hands and enable him to make an appeal for the loyalties of the political nation. In fact as James left to join his army on 17 November, the political nation, where it did not desert him, seems to have stood aside. James himself was at first determined to fight the invader, but as news came of trouble in Cheshire and the north, and of the desertions of his courtiers, his resolution began to crumble. James, unlike the Job to whom Sir John Reresby compared him, soon had his confidence and health undermined by trial and adversity.[53] By 26 November the somewhat broken King was back in a Whitehall which was already deserted by many of his subjects and even his own immediate family. He met with fifty peers of the realm the very next day to discuss the monarchy's difficulties, but James soon found himself browbeaten by these men as no king had ever been before. Led by Halifax, Nottingham and Clarendon, they called for a Parliament, the dismissal of papists from office, a repudiation of any alliance with France, amnesty for opponents and the appointment of a commission to negotiate with William.[54] James soon conceded these points and Halifax, Nottingham and Godolphin were appointed to treat with William. But as the commissioners went off to William to be wrong-footed by the wily Prince of Orange, events in London moved on to their conclusion.

The publication of William's Third Declaration, which he was later to claim was a forgery, panicked the remaining Catholic courtiers as well as their monarch, for it appeared to offer little compromise.[55] Already the court had dwindled to a handful of devotees and minor diplomats. In his plight and fearful of falling to his father's fate, James became desperate to ensure his son's safety and arranged for both his son and queen to go abroad on 9 December. On 10 December he himself prepared to leave. Having already destroyed the parliamentary writs that had not gone out, the King made arrangements to flee from the country. He retired for the night having written a number of justifications for his actions. In these he stated his preference to 'reserve himselfe safe for a better juncture', plainly thought to see the 'ambitious views of the Prince', and additionally wrote to the commander of his army a letter ordering the earl of Feversham not to resist a 'foreign army and a poisoned nation'. With that, and in spite of some courtier's entreaties, James fled from Whitehall in the early hours of the morning of 11 December. The King's first flight from London was ultimately fatal for it transformed what could have become another ministerial alteration at court into a fully fledged political crisis, a revolution in the state's monarchical, domestic and foreign policy, which was to have profound effects on the British Isles.

Notes

1   Standard works on the period include: J. Miller, *James II: A Study in Kingship* (London, 1989). J. R. Jones, *The Revolution of 1688 in England* (London, 1984). W. A. Speck, *Reluctant Revolutionaries: Englishmen and the Revolution of 1688* (Oxford, 1988). J. R. Jones, 'James II's revolution: royal policies, 1686–92' and J. Morrill, 'The sensible revolution', in J. Israel (ed.), *The Anglo-Dutch Moment: Essays in the Glorious Revolution and its World Impact* (Cambridge, 1991), pp. 47–71, 73–104. L. G. Schwoerer (ed.), *The Revolution of 1688–1689: Changing Perspectives* (Cambridge, 1992).

2   James II quoted in Speck, *Reluctant Revolutionaries*, pp. 43–4. See also G. Burnet, *A History of My Own Time* (6 vols, 2nd edn, Oxford, 1833), III, p. 8. Historical Manuscripts Commission (hereafter HMC), Franklin-Russell-Astley MSS (1900), p. 60.

3   H. C. Foxcroft, *The Character of a Trimmer, Being a Short Life of the First Marquis of Halifax* (Cambridge, 1946). J. P. Kenyon (ed.), *Halifax: The Complete Works* (Harmondsworth, 1969). D. R. Benson, 'Halifax and the trimmers', *Huntingdon Library Quarterly*, XXVII, (1963–64), 115–34. M. N. Brown, 'Trimmers and moderates in the reign of Charles II', *Huntingdon Library Quarterly*, XXXVII (1973–74), 311–36.

4   M. K. Geiter and W. A. Speck (eds), *Memoirs of Sir John Reresby* (2nd edn, London, 1991), p. 395. A. Boyer, *The History of King William the Third* (3 vols, London, 1702), II, p. 144. Burnet, *History of My Own Time*, III, p. 8.

5   S. W. Singer (ed.), *Correspondence of Henry Hyde, Earl of Clarendon and of his Brother Lawrence Hyde, Earl of Rochester with the Diary of Lord Clarendon from 1687–1690* (2 vols, London, 1828), I, pp. 93–6.

6   Ibid. Miller, *James II*, p. 148.

7   Burnet, *History of My Own Time*, III, p. 8.

8   Ibid., III, pp. 8–9. J. P. Kenyon, *Robert Spencer, Earl of Sunderland, 1641–1702* (London, 1958), pp. 111, 120.

9   HMC, Ormonde MSS, VII (1912), p. 327. Burnet, *History of My Own Time*, III, pp. 11–12.

10   See F. C. Turner, *James II* (London, 1948). See also M. Ashley, 'King James II and the revolution of 1688: some reflections on the historiography', in H. E. Bell and R. L. Ollard (eds), *Historical Essays, 1600–1750, Presented to David Ogg* (London, 1964), pp. 185–202. For a contemporary opinion on the King see Burnet, *History of My Own Time*, III, pp. 2–8.

11   Miller, *James II*, pp. 126–7.

12   Ibid., pp. 126–7.

13   Ibid., pp. 125–6. Dom G. Scott, *The Sacredness of Majesty: The English Benedictines and the Cult of James II* (Huntingdon, 1984). N. Genet-Rouffiac, 'Le Jacobites a Paris et Saint-Germain-en-laye', *Reve de la Bibliotheque Nationale*, XLVI (1992), 45–9.

14   Burnet, *History of My Own Time*, III, p. 13. R. H. George, 'The financial relations of Louis XIV and James II', *Journal of Modern History*, III (1931), 392–413. HMC, Frankland-Russell-Astley MSS (1900), p. 60.

15   George, 'The financial relations of Louis XIV and James II', 392–413.

16   Burnet, *History of My Own Time*, III, p. 102–3. Miller, *James II*, pp. 125–7. G. Bredvold, *The Intellectual Milieu of John Dryden: Studies in Some Aspects of Seventeenth-Century Thought* (Ann Arbor, 1956), pp. 160–80.

17   HMC, Dartmouth MSS, I (1887), p. 48. See also E. Corp, *James II and Toleration: The Years in Exile at Saint-Germain-en-laye* (Huntingdon, 1997).

18   Ibid., pp. 45–6.

19   M. Haile, *Queen Mary of Modena, her Life and Letters* (London, 1905), p. 44. HMC, Dartmouth, I, p. 31. Dom G. Nolan, 'James II and the English Benedictines in London', *Downside Review*, XVIII (1899), 94–103.

20   Haile, *Queen Mary of Modena*, p. 126. John, viscount Lowther, *Memoir of the Reign of James II* (York, 1808), p. 2.

21   British Library (hereafter BL), Additional MS 34510, fos 42–43v, 78v. *Calendar of State Papers Domestic, James II*, February–December 1685 (London, 1960), p. 41. Burnet, *History of My Own Time*, III. p. 195. A. de Mejer, 'James Willemart OSA at the court of James II, the fourth attempt to re-establish the English Augustinian province', *Analecta Augustina*, XLI (1978), 113–55.

22   J. R. Jones, *Marlborough* (Cambridge, 1993), pp. 36–8.

23   Geiter and Speck (eds), *Memoirs of Sir John Reresby*, pp. 416–17.

24   Terriesi quoted in Halie, *Queen Mary of Modena*, p. 167.

25   Singer (ed.) *Correspondence of Henry Hyde*, I, pp. 120–1. Also *Poems on affairs of state from the reign of K. James the first to this present year 1703 written by the greatest wits of the age* (2 vols, 1703), II, p. 215.

26   Document 25.

27   There is a definitive account of Sunderland's character in Kenyon, *Robert Spencer*.

28   Boyer, *The History of King William the Third*, I, p. 94.

29   G. Holmes, *British Politics in the Age of Anne* (revised edn, London, 1987), p. 189.

30   Document 25.

31   Geiter and Speck (eds), *Memoirs of Sir John Reresby*, pp. 425, 561. HMC, Downshire MS, I, pt I (1924), p. 182.

32   HMC, Downshire MS, I, pt, I (1924), p. 193.

33 Document 26.

34 Burnet, *History of My Own Time*, III, pp. 11–14.

35 Miller, *James II*, p. 163.

36 R. F. Foster, *Modern Ireland 1600–1972* (Harmondsworth, 1989), p. 140. Also Burnet, *History of My Own Time*, III, pp. 72–3. S. S. Webb, 'Brave men and servants to his royal highness the household of James Stuart in the evolution of English imperialism', *Perspectives in American History*, VIII (1974), 55–82. G. A. E. Ellis (ed.), *The Ellis Correspondence* (2 vols, London, 1829), I, p. 64.

37 Document 23.

38 Burnet, *History of My Own Time*, III, pp. 101, 122. Miller, *James II*, p. 164.

39 Trumbull quoted in Miller, *James II*, p. 173.

40 *Dictionary of National Biography*, Edward Petre, Richard Talbot and John Drummond.

41 'An account of the life and memorable actions of Father Petre the Jesuit (1689)' in *The popish champion or a complete history of the life and military actions of Richard Earl of Tyconnel generallisimo of all the Irish forces now in arms* (1689), pp. 47–58. E. Marquise Campana de Cavelli, *Les Derniers Stuarts à Saint-Germain-en-laye: documents inédits et authentiques* (2 vols, Paris, 1871), II, pp. 113, 127. Ellis (ed.), *Ellis Correspondence*, I, p. 240. BL, Additional MS 34510, fos 40v–41, 64.

42 BL, Additional MS 34510, fos 40v–41, 64. 'An account of the life and memorable actions of Father Petre the Jesuit (1689)', pp. 47–58.

43 See R. E. Boyer, *English Declarations of Indulgence, 1687 and 1688* (The Hague, 1968).

44 Geiter and Speck (eds), *Memoirs of Sir John Reresby*, p. 487. BL, Additional MS 34510, fos 10v–11.

45 Speck, *Reluctant Revolutionaries*, pp. 218–20.

46 A. Browning, *Thomas Osborne, Earl of Danby and Duke of Leeds, 1632–1712* (3 vols, Glasgow, 1951), I, pp. 321, 449.

47 Speck, *Reluctant Revolutionaries*, p. 219.

48 Ibid., pp. 218–19.

49 W. Coxe (ed.), *Private and Original Correspondence of Charles Talbot, Duke of Shrewsbury* (London, 1821), pp. 3–5.

50 Kenyon, *Robert Spencer*, p. 175.

51 Hoffman quoted in Haile, *Queen Mary of Modena*, p. 199. BL, Additional MS 32095, fo. 281.

52 Rizzini quoted in Haile, *Queen Mary of Modena*, p. 214. W. A. Speck, 'The Orangist conspiracy against James II', *Historical Journal*, XXX (1987), 453–62.

53 Geiter and Speck (eds), *Memoirs of Sir John Reresby*, p. 539. H. Y. Yallop, 'Col. Ambrose Norton's account of the defection of Lord Cornbury – 1688', *Journal of the Society for Army Historical Research*, LXX (1992), 231–8.

54 R. A. Beddard, *A Kingdom without a King: The Journal of the Provisional Government in the Revolution of 1688* (Oxford, 1988), pp. 25–9.

55 Ibid., pp. 29–31.

7

The reign of William III

Background to the 1690s

In the numerous officially approved portraits of the post-Revolution era the image of King William III is consistent. William is projected as the Protestant hero, a leader of strength, vision and ambition, and a master of the fields of war and politics. Yet very few of his contemporaries were ready to shed tears at the death of the Stadholder-King in 1702. As one of the Verney family noted: 'I am assured of one thing, that no King can be less lamented then this has been, even by those that was his greatest admirers in his life time'.[1] In comparison to the court politics of the reigns of Charles II and James II, the politics of William's reign from 1690 to 1702 appear to belong to a different world, and remain relatively little travelled by historians. The historical division of 1688 left the reign caught between the historians of the old Restoration world and those of the new world of eighteenth-century politics.[2] Perhaps this is not surprising, for William's reign cannot be simply characterised. It was a transitional period of conflict at home and abroad. The issues that emerged in the high politics of the reign seem to foreshadow the party squabbles of that of Queen Anne, as well as illuminate the problems of the previous decades. It is also clear that the nature of politics itself had begun to change in this period as they moved from an age of court faction into the age of political parties and the beginnings of the modern age.

From 1689 to 1702 William III's reign was dominated by a search for political stability that would allow the resources of England to be used in a major continental war against the power of Louis XIV's France. This basic fact of life created a new foreign policy, a different style of government, a plethora of offices, financial experimentation and indeed a 'revolution' in domestic politics. As far as they can be discerned, the King's main political aims of these years were three-fold: first, to settle English domestic politics into a balanced or 'trimming' ministry in which English politicians of both Whig and Tory persuasion could play a major role; secondly, to retain his prerogative powers relatively untouched; and thirdly, to contain French expansion on the continent. Unfortunately for William these aims were to be consistently fractured by the domestic political discord that emerged from the Revolution and in the reign itself.

This friction was to result from the nature of the European war, the problems of the new monarchy itself, and the conflict of party. The latter was in turn fuelled by personal rivalries, the struggle for office and government, and frequent elections, particularly after December 1694 and the passing of the Triennial Act. It was soon discovered that William himself was not willing to sell the crown to the control of any party, for he regarded all forms of party as obnoxious and damaging to his prerogative. But in spite of the new King's views, party struggle for office, the royal closet, cabinet and even the Privy Council grew apace. Created by the war, an 'administrative revolution' also produced an expansion in government and large numbers of offices that proved tempting to many a politician for the power, prerequisites and emoluments they brought with them. For some, office was an end in itself, for it conveyed power and status. But for others it became a necessity in order to gain party advantage and to pay off followers. Given the problems in forming a coherent government from the disparate parties involved, logic eventually dictated that a homogeneous party administration should be the solution to the regime's many maladies, especially given the rise of the court 'managers' who were often clearer in their views in this respect than William was himself.[3]

After the collapse of the Convention Parliament from 1690 to 1693 there was a shift in the regime from the Whigs towards the Tories. William initially used Carmarthen, the former earl of Danby, as one of his most significant parliamentary managers. This ministry soon floundered, mainly under the weight of the issues of war and finance and because William never trusted any English politician sufficiently enough to allow them to control the sources of patronage. From 1693 to 1697 there was a new phenomenon in the creation of the Whig Junto/Sunderland administration. This 'ministry' appeared to give William what he wanted, albeit briefly: cohesion in government, as well as support for royal policies and the war effort. However, the King entered into this scheme only reluctantly and the volatile mixture of ministers, and the power 'behind the curtain' in the person of the earl of Sunderland, could not survive the peace process of 1697. Whig disarray after the peace of Ryswick also meant that for the rest of his reign up to 1701 William returned to the 'patching' ministries of his earlier years. William governed with a loose amalgam of mostly Tory ministers from 1700 to 1701. But with the coming of a new European conflict it seemed likely that the King would once more have turned to the Junto to carry on his government. Unfortunately William's death in March 1702 cleared the way for the party conflicts in the reign of Queen Anne.[4]

William III

What sort of man and monarch was William? It is clear that unlike his predecessors the new King faced a number of problems on his accession to the English throne in 1689 which were to pursue him throughout his reign. How far he surmounted them is a debatable matter. Certainly by the time of his death in March 1702 William had apparently succeeded in holding together a largely conservative revolution and had successfully led a sometimes reluctant nation into prosecuting a major European war. In doing so he created the tools that his successors were to use well into the eighteenth century. This included financial stability, an expanded administration, and an army and navy, blooded in Europe's wars. More importantly, and in spite of the humiliations that Parliament heaped upon him in the Act of Settlement of 1701, he had managed to hold on to some of the now circumscribed, but not entirely defeated prerogative power of the monarchy. For if in many ways the theme of William's reign was that of change, this change tested the entire nation's institutions and resources and none more so than the monarchy and the court. Indeed there was a perceptible movement away from factional politics centred in the court to the age of political party, ministerial responsibility and parliamentary authority, which would in the end lead from 'court government' to 'constitutional monarchy'.[5]

Amongst the more significant problems facing William in 1689 was the fact that he was the first non-English monarch to sit on the English throne since James VI and I. He was Dutch by birth, upbringing and nature, and, it was soon clear, a natural autocrat. He was not given, as one contemporary pointed out, to being contradicted, having a 'great jealousy of being thought to be governed'.[6] William's title to the throne itself remained ever unsure. Although in the line of succession, both his wife Mary and his sister-in-law Anne had better claims to the throne than he, and James II's son, James Edward, had the best claim of all.[7] Unfortunately the war with France ensured that William had neither time, energy, nor for that matter inclination to concentrate much upon creating the image of a monarch to which his predecessors had devoted so much time and effort, and which the political nation had grown so accustomed to expect. Put simply, the English found William III a dose of cold water after the heat of King Charles's golden days – all straight lines, martial vigour and frigidity. Despite this, William, a taciturn man of action, was also a driven man. His intense will was focused on defeating his great enemy Louis XIV at all costs, and like so many of his predecessors he did set much of the tone for the complex political struggles of the 1690s both at home and abroad

Continued ill-health had formed William's character in his early manhood. Life in the difficult political world of the Dutch republic had done the rest. Starved of affection as a child, he had grown up trusting very few of those around him. The nature of the Dutch political system also meant that in spite of appearances he was a latecomer to royalty. By 1688 he had also apparently lost most of whatever social graces or social sense he had possessed. William's naturally brusque personality, as well as a life of hard campaigning and a preference for the company of men, can explain many of his most socially maladroit actions in his new role. To his courtiers, however, the King proved a difficult, abrupt man, harsh in his manner and continually suppressing his feelings to reason of state. He was also contemptuous of the trappings of monarchy. He was, as Burnet noted, apt to be 'peevish' in the face of such matters and disliked the 'whipped cream' of eloquence and flattery, the common currency of the political world of his day.[8] He also disliked 'time-serving' politicians, who seemed to surround him at every opportunity. He certainly disliked the ceremonies of monarchy, complaining not only of the coronation, but the thousand other things the office seemed to be heir to. Moreover, having once succeeded to the throne he did not temper his opinion and openly expressed this dislike and resentment. In turn English politicians believed that they, having brought William into power, at least deserved some attention. But they were continually repelled by his 'disgustingly dry' manner, his wracking cough and, more significantly, his frequent absences from the scene.

William's main policies in the course of the reign were governed above all by the need to ensure that the strength of England came into Europe's wars on the side of the alliance against France. By so doing he could protect his beloved Netherlands and restrain his great rival Louis XIV. Consequently he drove himself to extremes. The physical limitations of his body – he was in continual poor health for much of his life – were overcome by an intense belief in Calvinist predestination which gave him a righteousness as God's chosen instrument and a recklessness on the battlefield.[9] Eager to do everything himself, he became the most business-like Stuart monarch the country had yet possessed. When not on campaign he sat in his private rooms working. When on campaign he casually risked his life on the battlefield.

It was soon apparent to the political nation at large in the 1690s that 'Dutch William', Protestant hero or not, left much to be desired as their monarch. True, he had saved the realm, and themselves, from the horrors of popery and arbitrary government, or a return to republican rule. But it often seemed to both parties in the course of the reign that the bargain struck in 1688 was a lamentable one for each of them. The involvement of the country in a major war, the financial burden it brought with it, William's general attitude and the place of the favoured Dutch in his affections made many a prominent English politician's thoughts turn towards a pseudo-Jacobitism, or in some cases the real thing.

William disliked and distrusted most of the English politicians he came across. Early in the reign the Savoy ambassador had noted William's distrust of the 'fidelity or the capacity of his ministers'.[10] In retrospect this was natural enough, for William had of course known most of these men since his first dealings with them in the 1670s and found them largely self-seeking. The events of 1688 had only confirmed his prejudiced view of the English polity. He saw his English courtiers as fickle and untrustworthy. Indeed he rightly thought that if they could betray James II so easily then they would almost certainly betray their new master should the circumstances require it. As he cynically put it to one Dutch adviser: 'Now it is Hosannah here, but soon perhaps it will be crucify him'.[11] Daniel Defoe, a Williamite supporter, put it in more poetic, but no less forceful terms:

> We blame the K[ing] that he relies too much
> On strangers, Germans, Huguenots, and Dutch;
> And seldom does his great Affairs of State,
> To English counsellors communicate.
> The fact might very well be answered thus:
> He has so often been betrayed by us
> He must have been a Madman to rely
> On English G[entlemen]s Fidelity.[12]

Given this attitude and William's initially false view of the balance of power in English domestic politics, he proved to be uncertain in the first days of his rule. William also craved to have men around him who would produce a 'ministry of all the talents' for the struggle in Europe. English politicians, however, were more interested in domestic power. Their attitudes were commonly riven by factionalism and personal hatred, and in spite of the frequent urgency of European affairs they fought desperately to seize control of the domestic arena and bring down their opponents as they had always done.[13]

The series of acts by which William and Mary were hoisted on to the throne of James II have been well rehearsed by most historians, but needless to say both sides struggled hard to achieve what they believed were guarantees against a return to the waywardness of the House of Stuart.[14] An initial struggle over who was to occupy the throne once James was safely in exile resulted in the re-emergence of the political fissures that had preoccupied the nation in the 1660s and 1670s. While some were for making terms with James, others were for seeing William as regent, and many favoured Mary's outright succession; only a few men even considered the claims of James's rightful heir, his son James Edward. In the end a somewhat tangled solution emerged in that William and Mary were to reign jointly, but that William was to have the 'sole and full exercise of regal power'.

The acceptance of the Declaration of Rights led to a number of attempts to resolve the problems of *de facto* versus *de jure* kingship, the succession question, and the parameters for the exercise of royal power. There is little doubt that in reality the monarchy had changed with the removal of James. William may well have entered as a new conqueror, but he had to be swiftly legitimised in his new rule by an ever-anxious Parliament. This fact of life, if it did nothing else, changed the rules of monarchy. The eventual Act of Settlement in 1701 even managed the succession to the political nation's benefit – the old-style divine right monarchy thus finally disappeared into a welter of clauses and sub-clauses of parliamentary law. Not that this occurred overnight and William at least struggled manfully against the process. He was reluctant to oversee any further decay of the crown's prerogative powers, but the tide was against him. Parliament, with its annual session post-1689, had now become a wary partner in government, whether it, or the monarchy, liked it or not. Conversely our image of William as struggling in the coils of parliamentary hostility must be tempered by contemporary views of his regime. For many, William's regime had apparently ousted the principle of hereditary right. It was also militaristic, building huge armies and navies; it used the patronage at its disposal for dubious ends, set up innumerable new committees and used innovative methods of government. Moreover, it consisted of many an old politician who had been mightily dubious in their methods under previous monarchs and were unlikely to change their tactics because of the Revolution.[15]

Of course William still retained the right to choose or dismiss his ministers at pleasure and he also shaped policy as chief executive. Both he and the Parliament officially had little desire to have it otherwise. But the royal demands for increased supply meant that the regime could no longer ignore the central question of management of the Parliament. Moreover, the Triennial Act of 1694 was to lead to more frequent elections, increased political agitation and more fractious Parliaments.

Furthermore Parliament was no longer solely to be milked for finance. There were those who saw in it new opportunities for gaining power in an era in which progress at court was to become increasingly limited. With domesticity and respectability the order of the day at a socially declining, but numerically expanding court, the heated atmosphere of Parliament's activities provided the key to controlling new power bases and opportunities for those who knew where to look. The august bodies of Commons and Lords increasingly began to expand their interests into other areas of policy, especially in the face of what came to be believed as court corruption.

'Fatal experience', noted one author of 1698, 'has now more than convinced us that Courts have been the same in all ages, and that few persons have been found of such approved constancy and resolution as to withstand the powerful allurements and temptations which from thence have been constantly dispensed for the corrupting of men's minds, and debauching their honest principles.'[16] 'Honest principles', one of the catch phrases of 1690s political literature, was always contrasted with the view that even after 1688 and the cleansing of the Jacobite stable, the court was still prone to a natural corruption. This was given more weight by recurrent scandals in high places throughout the period. A poetic squib, directed at the earl of Dorset, William's Lord Chamberlain, illustrates the mood of the day most forcefully:

If Papist, Jew or Infidel
Would buy a place at Court:
Here Dorset lives, the Chamberlain,
To whom you may resort.
Then come away, make no delay,
Bring coin to plead your cases;
He'll turn the King's friends out of doors,
And put you in their places.[17]

In fact within the royal household further expansion was inevitable, but the occupants were not always the old retainers they had been. Many of the former servants of James II were turned out of office.[18] It was widely believed that William surrounded himself with Dutchmen, but although some of his Dutch servants were placed in strategic positions, the bulk of court offices went as they had always done to Englishmen. That these were mainly Whigs in the first instance was unfortunate. The Whig attitude to the court was generally unsympathetic. It had been born in the atmosphere of hostility of the

1680s and if the court was now seen as a place of opportunity, it was only given a reluctant loyalty. Court office and prestige, not to mention the other more substantial prerequisites that went with it, were mere pawns in the greater game of national politics. Moreover, 'Whig disaplin', as Sir Stephen Fox called it, also brought with it corruption, sometimes on a grand scale.[19] So in an attempt to stifle criticism and distance the court from its predecessors, as well as its alleged current corruption, a policy of court reformation was put into place. This was part of a general reformation of manners, with the virtuous Queen Mary placed at the forefront. Unfortunately, while the projection of a domesticity and sobriety in a virtuous court was attempted, the critics remained. Indeed the resurrection of a court–country axis in politics was in part based upon a hostile attitude amongst the country gentlemen to court corruption and parliamentary management. This attitude was never eradicated and these beliefs were added to the melting pot that was the House of Commons. And it was here in the Commons that the core of the reign's problems lay. The immense difficulties of actually managing this unwieldy body of men soon became of vital importance to the success of William's reign.

When he was actually in the country and not off on campaign William had little, if any, of the charm of Charles II. Indeed he soon abandoned the usual haunts of English monarchy at Whitehall and moved both himself and Mary further out from the London smog to Kensington Palace and Hampton Court. There were tactical as well as personal reasons for this move. In doing so he could not only distance himself from the squabbling of English politicians, but also inhabit a smaller and more intimate court, and spend much of the time in his private rooms. His courtiers undoubtedly resented this move, for William still ruled as well as reigned and necessary points of access to him were still vital for success. Mary did little without consulting her husband and so the average courtier who was familiar with using the court as a channel for money, office, rank and power now saw the most important point of access for winning royal favour diminished.[20] Although in fact the bulk of court offices went to Englishmen, the traditional social routes for any enterprising politician soon began to disappear. As Burnet pointed out, the face of the court as a rendezvous for the rich, powerful and ambitious was broken, which gave an 'early and general disgust [especially as] the gaiety and diversions of the court disappeared'.[21] William did occasionally appear at receptions, but seems to have regarded all such social gatherings with some distaste. There had of course been 'distant' monarchs in the past, and no man could stand more upon his dignity than had James II, but 'distant' monarchs also knew that they had to show themselves occasionally to their people. Semi-invisible monarchy was not what most courtiers thought the institution should be about, and a monarch who had few friends, most of whom were his fellow Dutchmen, and who appeared to have even fewer interests beyond hunting, war and politics, was disappointing to say the least.

Of course William's distance has sometimes been exaggerated. He could occasionally relax, even with his English courtiers, and he was willing to use the court to project an image of his monarchy.[22] But in the end his character meant a decline in the old court values was inevitable. As we have seen, this change in sensibility at court had been taking place for some time. John Evelyn had noticed the alterations in the public face of the court between the death of Charles II and the accession of his brother James. At least superficially the moral climate of James II's court had been much higher and had sought to discard the unacceptable elements of court life. William and Mary kept up this trend. The Society for the Reformation of Manners was founded in 1690 and William himself took an interest in this subject, hoping as one of the benefits of the peace in 1697 to devote his new-found leisure to 'rectify such corruptions and abuses as may have crept into any part of the administration during the war, and effectively discourage profaness and immorality'.[23]

In the pursuit of real power the offices of the royal household themselves began to be seen as financial perks rather than as seats of power. Of more significance were those government offices with departments attached to them. Departmental office under William saw an extraordinary expansion during the course of the war. Aspiring politicians greedily eyed the power, patronage and prerequisites the offices could bring. As William cynically observed, 'Everybody had a mind to get into the Treasury. They looked upon the best side of it [and were] Charmed with the name of the place where money groweth, forgetting the drudgery and the danger of it.'[24] Additionally, given the monarch's absences in the summer it seemed that under William's rule ministers could now have an even more vital influence on the day-to-day business of government. A real divorce thus began to emerge between the more weighty ministries and those offices left behind in the court. Of all William's ministers only Sunderland and Carmarthen tried to play the game in the old-fashioned way. But Carmarthen, as Lord President of the Council, was an ineffective presence after 1692, and Sunderland, because of his background, had to abstain from all office until 1697, being content to work behind the scenes until William mistakenly forced office upon him. Power shifted irrevocably to the departmental offices, increasingly separated from their court origins and subject to the processes of government and parliamentary inspection.[25]

The politics of the 1690s demanded much of William's attention and also much of his time was spent working to hold on to his throne, running a wartime administration, fighting battles and maintaining a European-wide alliance against Louis XIV. The pattern of the reign was soon set: William, with little time for the pleasures of court, or for the stupidities of English politicians who refused to see the wider picture, carried on his one-man crusade, and the old-fashioned aimless courtiers drifted away to new pleasures in the theatre, coffee-houses, City or salon.[26] Nevertheless the court's internal and external politics still continued, albeit with different frames of reference. While William struggled manfully with the unfamiliar problems of a recalcitrant Parliament, recalcitrant institutions of state, and various shady politicians using the activities of party politics and their own positions to profit themselves and make his life difficult, the life of court and nation rumbled on around him.

William and the politicians

William considered himself an active soldier first and foremost and thus almost every summer of his rule was spent trudging around the fields of Flanders or Ireland alongside his troops in yet another disappointing campaign. He was frequently absent from England as a consequence. The development of an alternative system of control in government was thus now essential. It must be recalled that William's predecessors had rarely been out of sight of their ministers at court and thus they could have a vital influence on day-to-day business. William's removal from the scene, as well as the rapid expansion of administration, finance and government, led to a growth in actual government processes. With increasingly more to do than his immediate predecessors, William found himself caught between his wish to retain control over as much of his power as possible and his inability to be everywhere at once. Correspondence could do some of the work, as could an effective secretariat. However, William's belief in the general untrustworthiness of the English polity and his lack of familiarity with English government meant that he was prone to errors and many of his selections for office lacked the basic skills for good government.

It has already been noted that William was reluctant to share his power with any 'prime' minister, distressing though this was to some, although he did come round to employing political managers, such as Carmarthen, Shrewsbury and Sunderland, who often appear to have performed a similar function. Of all the men around William only Sunderland came close to the position of first minister. William gave his limited trust to some of the other great independent magnates of the day such as Halifax, Nottingham or Somers, but he never trusted any of them completely. So hated was the Dutchman William Bentinck, earl of Portland, that although his was a position of intimacy with the King (he was Groom of the Stole, very much a court office), he wisely demurred from taking up any more prominent political station.[27] Portland had risen to become William's intimate and confidential man of business in the Netherlands and his rewards in 1689 followed his lengthy services, but the jealous and often xenophobic English courtiers resented the presence of this indispensable Dutchman so near to the King. Portland proved to be a useful contact point, a 'remembrancer' as contemporaries had it, particularly for officials in Scotland and Ireland who otherwise had small chance of getting their business to William, and he was still the most trusted man of affairs the King had about him. He often acted as a confidential servant on diplomatic missions and as William's liaison with the powerful elements in the Dutch republic. He also helped to screen William from those who sought his favour. They were usually fobbed off onto the earl and it was this more than his exaggerated greed that made Portland into a figure of hate for the English at court. He represented a basic fact of William's court life: that the Dutch-born King could very rarely, if ever, trust any of his English advisers as much as he trusted his old Dutch acquaintances. In turn William was exacting in his friendship with Portland and this demanding nature eventually led to their broken friendship. Matters came to a head over the rise at court of another Dutchman, William's favourite the young and personable Arnold Joost van Keppel, the earl of Albermarle, whom Portland grew to hate. Eventually Portland's dislike of his rival led to a petulant break from William's intimacy and the Groom of the Stole's voluntary retirement in 1699.[28] Revealingly, such behaviour, in another age, could have had serious consequences as the court would have split over which man to follow: the old favourite or the new. Under William's rule the events passed by, if not unnoticed, at least without creating the same reverberations as would once have occurred. This if anything shows the diminishment of court politics in the era.

Beyond Portland the constant theme of William's kingship in the era was his vain attempt to balance his regime between Whig and Tory grandees. William told Halifax that he at least openly relished the name of 'trimmer' and as such Halifax himself seemed the ideal candidate for high office in the new reign. He was made Lord Privy Seal, but while William may have trusted Halifax, the minister was unfortunately not cut out for the robust politics of his day. Carrying an inordinate amount of political baggage from the early 1680s, he was almost inevitably forced out of the regime in 1690.[29]

William denied the role of chief minister to the most obvious choice amongst politicians in the era in terms of service, experience and skill: Danby, soon made marquis of Carmarthen as a sop to his vanity. In part the denial to Carmarthen of a return to the Treasury was due to his dubious antecedents under Charles II, where the reputation of the 'thin ill-natured ghost ... impeached and pardoned', as one verse satire described him, lingered on well into the 1690s with good cause.[30] Placed in charge of bringing in the votes in the Commons, Carmarthen soon returned to his tried and trusted methods of manipulation and bribery, giving fresh ammunition to his opponents. William personally thought Carmarthen rather hectoring in his tone. He revealingly told Halifax that Carmarthen 'did never speak of anything but to recommend men ... [and] did not ask things as favours but as of his right' – an attitude guaranteed to alienate the rather touchy William at the best of times. Moreover, a tribe of relatives always surrounded Carmarthen, mostly drawn from the numerous Bertie clan whom William actively disliked even more than the marquis himself. As William noted, 'All [Carmarthen's] kindred and dependence voted against ... [me, and I] could not live with a man at that rate'.[31] Despite his previous obligations to Carmarthen – he had been one of the 'immortal seven' signatories and had helpfully arranged William's own marriage to Mary in 1677 – it is significant that William left the powerful office of Lord Treasurer, by far the most important of the offices of state, in commission. On to the Treasury Board went a mix of Tories and Whigs to argue and complain of one another: Sidney Godolphin, Lord Mordaunt, who became earl of Monmouth, Lord Delamare, Sir Henry Capel and Richard Hampden. Lacking the financial clout and patronage of this office, Carmarthen was in reality a less dominating figure than the bogeyman he represented to country politicians in myth.[32]

William made equally important decisions with his Secretaries of State and other prime officials. The Admiralty went into commission, as for a while did the position of Lord Chancellor. The nervous Shrewsbury, with his penchant for illness, was given a secretaryship. According to Gilbert Burnet, Shrewsbury had the 'greatest share of the King's confidence', but having never held office before he took it up only reluctantly. He was troubled in mind, in body and in his relations with other ministers, displaying a nervous energy that broke his health, or so he claimed. Shrewsbury was seemingly ever eager to try and loose himself from the burdens of state and nurture his health. In spite of this the 'King of Hearts', as Shrewsbury was called, remained an important figure in the period, especially when the Junto came to power. He was gifted, young, personable, modest and a link between the crown and the Whigs. However, he was also swiftly disillusioned about office.[33]

The other Secretary of State was more able: Daniel Finch, earl of Nottingham. The Tory balance to Shrewsbury's Whig, Nottingham had previously been at the Admiralty and thus had administrative experience, but he was only a reluctant convert to the regime. Nottingham tended to split opinions. He gave satisfaction to some and provoked hostility in others who believed he would infect the new monarch with 'prerogative notions' and damn the Whigs with his Tory ideas.[34] In fact Nottingham proved efficient enough, though prone to an air of superiority over his colleagues. While both of the Secretaries of State were politically balanced, in the early days of the reign they also proved inexperienced. Although William could compensate for this by supervising foreign policy himself, it was the management of Parliament, an area that had traditionally fallen to the secretaries, that proved one of the most acute areas of failure for the regime.

The management of the Commons in later-seventeenth-century England required the charm of a Charles II to achieve anything very much and even Charles II had failed to master Parliament in the end, being forced to live without a Parliament after 1681. An ability to smile amiably, give generously and lie between one's teeth certainly came more naturally to his uncle Charles than it did ever did to William. William's personal skills were undistinguished and his hopes of appointing reliable English politicians to perform this task for him soon foundered in dissent and personal rivalry. He was at a loss until the re-emergence of Sunderland. And after 1688 the 'old Whigs' became increasingly irritated by their inability to subdue everything in sight and dominate the King's government despite their belief that, as Lord Wharton put it almost to William's face, 'we … made you King'.[35] They grumbled about the tone and style of the King's early government, and they disliked the presence of Carmarthen, Halifax and Nottingham in it. Carmarthen was damned because of his reputation under Charles II, Halifax because of his defence of James in the 1680s and Nottingham simply because he was a Tory. In general the Tory position proved equally problematic. They were caught on the *de facto* question of William's kingship. While they were loyal to the idea of monarchy, and had at the time viewed the Revolution as a 'cruel necessity', William sought to use them, but as one of William's ministers archly pointed out he was not their monarch.[36] Their political philosophy (non-resistance, hereditary succession and loyalty to the crown) had also been considerably disrupted by James II's activities, and the actual change of monarch, which itself had only been reluctantly acceded to, had created still more problems, so that they were now splitting under the weight of their own contradictions. As a result, William was soon forced to rely more and more on the Whigs, who were at least generally pro-war, and additionally upon those moderate intermediaries who stood between himself and the parties as both cushions and brokers.

These 'court managers', undoubtedly the most important figures of the day, sought to promote stability in government so that its business could be carried through. The main business of the reign on the domestic front lay in financing the war in Europe. The war in Europe dominated the politics of William's reign and created a financial strain on the country. It also meant difficulties in the management of Parliament and the execution of the policies of the war. Achieving a degree of co-operation between the Parliament and the court was the aim of most of the governments of the era. In this the court had some advantages, as it still possessed extensive patronage, as well as the power of dissolution and, more covertly, methods of electoral interference. But getting a good Parliament was only the beginning of the government's problems, for it then had to ensure that these men toed the line in the House of Commons, a notoriously truculent beast at the best of times. Within the Commons William's regime could expect to control a small group of MPs who made up the court party: close friends or personal dependants of the managers and non-party placemen or 'civil servants'. In all other respects William's governments proved to be hard-fought coalitions managed by party bosses, who in turn dealt with the court managers, who dealt with the King.

The wealth of partisan literature of the 1690s does not disguise the fluidity of the era in terms of party. Individual party positions were subject to external pressures and circumstances. These could alter any individual's perception of his position in respect to this axis.[37] The loyalty of peers and placemen to the court on issues which had a non-party basis, as well as the traditional court–country divide, still make the idea of a fully stable party system a misnomer in the era. As Angus McInnes has pointed out, even the term Whig was something of a 'portmanteau word' post-1689 and the Whigs themselves suffered from as many internal divisions as the Tories.[38]

The nature of political parties in the era produced a series of important historical arguments in the 1950s and 1960s. While some historians followed the traditional model of their earlier Whig brethren, others took up the new Namierite line of a multi-party politics visible in the reign of George III. Much of the debate centred upon voting lists and how individuals perceived themselves in a variety of overlapping structures that created their position.[39] As a consequence of this debate, the view has emerged that the party groupings of William's reign were neither straightforward nor at the same time as erratic as many had thought. It was also clear that the basic ascendancy of Whig and Tory founded in the early 1680s continued to exist alongside periodic variations of court and country. In other words in the manner of a grand symphony the parliamentary politics of the day had both its main theme and its subsidiary themes merging, blending and occasionally standing out alongside it. If this produced discordant music then it was a reflection of the complexities of the day. It is clear that on the ground level the music of politics in the 1690s could at once be both simple and more complex than it appeared. Indeed many a staunch country gentlemen who thought of himself as a Whig and a holder of 'revolution principles' would also look askance at what he saw as court vice, bureaucratic abuses, or improprieties in the executive, military and electoral process and take a country stance as a result, opposing the court schemes in the Commons. At the same time the court Whigs led by the Junto of Thomas Wharton, Edward Russell, Charles Montague and John Somers were part of a new breed of professional politicians, whose eagerness for office sometimes left their more country brethren far behind and increasingly disaffected. There is no doubt, however, as Geoffrey Holmes has argued, that on the major issues of the age the Whig–Tory axis reveals the divides of the day. In other respects issues which could lead to the reformation of a court–country axis often blurred the boundaries between them. Such issues led, for example, to the emergence of the 'New Country' persuasion. These were men determined, as Robert Harley put it, to be the 'physicians of the state', and as such they were a 'protracted coalition of Country Tories and a minority of Country Whigs [who came] ... together to further a programme of (mainly) anti-prerogative reform, but without losing their primary identities'.[40] It was the parliamentary session of 1701 that in the end proved the watershed in the politics of the Williamite era that was to create the era to come. In that session of Parliament the attempted impeachment of the Whig Junto lords created a 'hurricane of humours from the mob to the highest [and made a] feud that ... will not die'. And so the confusion of William's reign merged into the age of party in Anne's era.[41]

The issues that divided the political nation in the 1690s were in many respects largely familiar ones, which accounts for much of the continued Whig–Tory dichotomy. In retrospect the issues of the era found their roots in many of the nation's problems since 1660: finance, religion, foreign policy, and the succession. Two new additions were 'revolution principles' and the war in Europe. The issue of dissent that had continually dogged English life rumbled on after 1690. While the Tories were convinced that any form of toleration would encourage heresy and that the Test and Corporation Acts were the last bulwark of defence for a state Church that was increasingly in 'danger', the Whigs favoured some form of toleration, to varying degrees, but did not wish for the removal of the Test Act because they were anti-Catholic. In the case of the succession not all Tories proved to be Jacobites, nor all Jacobites Tory, and most eventually accommodated themselves, in a pragmatic English way, to the change of regime by force of circumstance. They also proved willing to wait out William's reign, which remained something of an aberration in their mind, with the prospect of Anne and, until 1700, her son to come. This would mean the re-establishment of the principle of hereditary succession. But in the end they also proved equally as concerned as the Whigs to protect a Protestant succession and the Act of 1701 drew in support from all sides.[42] More problematic was the notion of 'revolution principles' in which both Whig and Tory had invested so much, the latter in notions of providence, as an excuse for supporting the current regime. Some social contract theory existed in Whig thought, as did a belief that parliamentary rather than divine right to the throne was the far more significant of the two. After the death of Mary in 1694, the passing of the Triennial Act, the establishment of the Bank of England and the breakthrough of the Junto, party loyalties tended to polarise over the war. It was not until 1701 that the Whigs really fused together more effectively. This was, as has already been noted, a result of Tory attacks on the Junto lords, as well as the crisis of the Spanish succession and the unwillingness of Tories to recognise the threat from France. Party divides thereafter swamped most of the court and country links.[43]

The matter of the war was more troublesome. It led to a rapidly expanded administration and massive expansion of government and finance. William's commitment to a major continental war to restore the balance of power in Europe and to protect his native Netherlands meant a continental commitment, unheard of in previous reigns. Only Parliament could guarantee this scheme and this meant winning the members over to the regime's views. The Tories were critical of the war and were generally supporters of a 'blue water' strategy. They would have relied on the Royal Navy to fight a war of blockade and commerce-raiding, while paying for mercenary allies to fight the European land war. In practice their views often proved to be isolationist with distinctive tinges of the innate xenophobia of most Englishmen. The Whigs, Junto, moderate or country, were willing to go along with William's plans and a continental commitment, again to varying degrees. They became identified with the war, although enough ground was left between them and within the parties to create difficulties for the King. Of course the war also proved expensive, leading to high taxation, and a heavy strain on a state which had never really experienced such strains before. In a booming economy the prospects for speculation and corruption added a further element to the mix. With a mass expansion of government office the opportunities for more civil servants and officers of the crown grew and this meant more opportunities for political patronage and rewards to followers. The flourishing of the moneyed interest and the increasing numbers of placemen in the Commons (by 1692–98 some 97–136 and in 1714 some 200) further increased tensions in the system.[44]

William and the political world, 1690–1702

William's honeymoon period in government, if such a thing had existed, was soon over. The political travails of 1690–95 created a period of uncertainty and instability. If the Convention Parliament of 1690 had been called in the hope of resolving a number of pressing problems, most particularly that of the succession, it rapidly fell into disarray through personal and party hatreds. It was full of 'jealousy and ill humour' and dominated by old Whig and Tory partisanship fighting old battles and seeking to open as many wounds as possible in one another.[45] It has been said that the Parliament's principal bulwark against a repeat of James II's reign was to refuse to vote William sufficient money to enable him to carry on the government and the result was a run of frequent Parliaments. It is doubtful whether this was so conscious a decision by the MPs. Parliament, however, certainly stood up for what it now perceived as its rights, as well as the rule of law, and certain MPs were also intent on limitations to the monarchy's prerogative powers. On the other hand William was also keen to work by the law of the land, but he had no more peace from his Parliaments than any other Stuart monarch. In part the unlucky nature of his regime in its early days increased his difficulties. There were ministerial conflicts to deal with, mainly as a result of the monarch's attempt at a balanced ministry, and extremists on both sides of the political divide fought one another largely uncontrolled. The 1690 election deposed the old Whigs, but the poor handling of the war itself brought no real relief to the mass of the political nation, who began to dislike both it and their Dutch leader with equal intensity. There was little to add to the credit of the regime abroad. The problems in Ireland, only partly resolved in 1690, were matched by losses at sea and on the continent. An ever-expanding and more expensive administration as well as increases in the army and navy also appeared to be riddled with corruption. The King's reliance on Dutch advisers and alleged Jacobites also distressed many of his supporters, who were equally greedy for office. Whether the regime could survive was a moot point and while it looked for victory in war the Williamite regime was found wanting on all fronts.[46]

The main uncertainties at home lay in the nature of the men to whom William had access and to whom he was forced to trust the highest levels of government. In an era fraught with personal jealousies, which inevitably clashed with party ambitions, a small core of professional politicians appeared to struggle over a monopoly of office while the majority of the political nation swayed this way and that in an effort to keep up with them. Of these men Carmarthen proved to be too greedy and rather too much of a spent force to give a genuine lead in the government. By now a tired man, he too often turned to the old ways of management he himself had launched under Charles II. His reputation also hampered his position. Carmarthen's notable enemy Halifax, although favoured by William, was never cut out for the robust politics of the era and soon retired from the heights of government office to lurk in opposition until his death in 1695. The government spokesmen in the Commons were Sir John Lowther and Sir Henry Goodricke. They proved to be poor managers of the House of Commons. Daniel Finch, earl of Nottingham, a principled high church Tory whom William brought in as Secretary of State, was thought suspect in his loyalty. In reality Nottingham proved as loyal to the regime as the next man, if not more so, but was willing to engage in endless squabbles about the navy with his Whig opponents.

Hope, if hope there was, existed in the lesser posts of government where an able and talented group of 'court Whigs' had begun to emerge. They were soon dissatisfied with their position. John Somers, Sir John Trenchard, Thomas Wharton, Charles Montague, Admiral Edward Russell and General Thomas Talmash soon began to walk the edge between government and opposition much as the duke of Buckingham once had. By occasionally joining in the agitation against corruption in high places they were also able to garner support amongst the country gentlemen in Parliament. In the meantime Sidney Godolphin, one of the few independent politicians whom William thought an asset on the Treasury bench because of his 'calm and cold way', in the end proved too uncommitted and too surrounded by Whigs, who resented him, to do that much good.[47]

On the other hand high-handed Tory politicians such as Bath and Rochester remained cool towards William's regime. Indeed James II's old servant Clarendon refused to take the oaths and was thus excluded from power. One of the potentially brightest stars of the reign, John Churchill, earl of Marlborough, quickly became resentful of Dutch influence in the court and in the army. He had in any case thrown in his lot with Princess Anne, but fell from grace in 1692, mostly for his attacks on Dutchmen in government and the army, but also due to his treasonable links with the exiled Jacobite court. This also caused a crisis between Queen Mary and her sister Anne whose wounds were never really healed. After his disgrace Marlborough was more of a presence behind the scenes until William's distrust lessened towards the end of his reign. Shrewsbury petulantly left the government in 1690 and proved hard to bring back into the fold. An important link with the court Whigs, he eventually staked the price of his support upon the passage of a Triennial bill.[48] In any case the Whigs in Parliament and in the government did not behave themselves over much in either area and grumbled at the Tory presence in William's affairs, increasingly seeking to overthrow Tories wherever they found them in order to control all the executive.

In part William's difficulties arose from his genuine reluctance to lead a 'party' government of one side or the other. We can perhaps see that his attempt to occupy a rapidly diminishing middle ground was doomed to failure. But at the time it was an attempt to act in such a way as his predecessors had done. The problem was that the context had changed. It must also be noted that at first the King had little interest in the travails of the English constitution or its feuding factions. As far as he was concerned they were all part of a venal mob intent on money, office and restraining his prerogative powers. In the early days of the regime at least the weight of the ministry had fallen upon the earl of Danby and Halifax in particular, both of who still bore resentments from Charles II's reign. Their political Punch and Judy show soon set the tone. Danby's desire was to be Lord Treasurer again, but William, unsure of himself and disliking Danby's method of aggressive posturing and constant demands for his clients, placed the office in commission and packed it with both Whigs and Tories. Danby regarded this as a blow to his prestige, and more significantly his lack of control over the minor offices of state dealt a hammer blow to his possible management of the Parliament. In general Danby's main aims in the period had now become part of a search for the long-coveted promotion in the peerage once promised by Charles II, and now more than ever desired for his services rendered, and the 'rights of his relatives'.[49] Other than this in political terms he wanted to regain his position of prominence and he could not see why William persisted in his reliance on a trimming ministry. Danby was fortunate that the Whigs hated Halifax even more than they hated him. Halifax was harassed out of office in 1690 and William lost yet another able adviser. Nor did the Whig attack stop there. Other 'delinquents' were soon sought out and William's balanced ministry of moderate men, aware of the threat from France, was soon swamped by infighting. As a result, the King grew tired of the political squabbles around him and his failure to satisfy both Whigs and Tories meant that they in turn grew tired of him. The breakdown of the early ministry was mainly due to infighting, but also to William's lack of tact, charm and knowledge of the English scene.

With Halifax out of office the first of a series of revolutions on the domestic front began. The ministry began to take on a broadly Tory feel to it, with Danby leading the way. His promotion to marquis of Carmarthen appeared to confirm his status. Nevertheless in reality Carmarthen could never dominate William or the men around him as he had under Charles II. The latter were players in their own right and Carmarthen lacked a department to sustain any push for power. Indeed at times he was more akin to a minister without portfolio and this was a block to his pre-eminence. Carmarthen had also lost none of the characteristics that had made him so hated in the 1670s and he was soon an obvious target for attack. Both Whigs and Tories sought backbench support to eliminate the minister from the scene. Carmarthen was fortunate in being able to use the abortive Preston Plot in 1694 temporarily to break their alliance. As a sop, however, William was forced to bring into the regime members of the 'opposition' to the Lord President, such as Seymour, Rochester and the two Whigs Somers and Montague, which curbed his power still further.[50]

In the long run William's shrewdest move was to allow the return to politics of the former Jacobite, Robert Spencer, earl of Sunderland, now suitably chastened by the Revolution of 1688.[51] Undeniably a realist of the first order, especially where his own interests were concerned, since his return from exile in May 1690 Sunderland had gradually gravitated towards the court. At first he was not willing to expose himself in politics. But he was willing to act as a clandestine adviser to William from the spring of 1692. For Sunderland, unlike some others, there was no point in making overtures to the exiled monarch at St Germain for he had betrayed James in a way that the exiled King would never forgive by reneging on his religious conversion to Roman Catholicism. As such Sunderland saw William as an opportunity and owed him much for his chance to live again politically. He soon began to focus his advice upon the management of the Commons. Some of his old assistants and clients had already returned to office. Henry Guy had become Secretary to the Treasury in June 1691, while William Bridgeman had returned to the secretariat in December 1690. The earl was soon advising William 'behind the curtain' to shed both Lowther and Goodricke and replace them with allies of his own: Sir John Trenchard and Henry Guy. He also informed William that only the Whigs could deliver what the King really wanted – a pro-Williamite regime and support for the war against France. The government, said Sunderland, must be put into a 'Method' and William must fill it with Whigs for 'Whenever the Government has leaned to the Whigs, it has been strong; whenever the other has prevailed, it has been despised'.[52] To Sunderland the Tories were, if loyal, not enthusiastic enough for his or the King's designs. Moreover, he perceived that a small knot of Whig politicians had also arisen who could do business for William and more importantly gain him the necessary supply so vital to the continuance of the war.

The formative 'Junto', as they became known, proved to be a mixture of personalities. Thomas Wharton, a rake and duellist in his private life, had embarked on his political career in the crisis over exclusion. He had joined William at Exeter during the invasion of 1688 and taken a prominent part in the Convention Parliament. He was made a Privy Councillor and Comptroller of the Household, but his bumptious arrogance meant that William personally disliked him. He was, however, a party man, electoral wizard and possibly the most dangerous of the Whigs. Edward Russell was the cousin of the Whig martyr Lord William Russell and as one of the 'immortal seven' expected some reward. His interest in naval affairs brought him high command in the Royal Navy, innumerable feuds with Nottingham, and eventually promotion as earl of Orford. Charles Montague became clerk to the Privy Council in 1689 and remained the Junto's financial expert. He was the younger son of a great Whig family and thus forced to make his way in the world, but he was to be responsible for the establishment of the Bank of England and became Chancellor of the Exchequer, First Lord of the Treasury and eventually earl of Halifax. John Somers was the legal workhorse of the Junto, able, reserved, and capable of great industry, and because of this he remained in William's confidence.[53]

But as yet William was reluctant to throw in his entire lot with such men. Russell and Thomas Wharton he disliked personally, and although William had been forced to turn to the Whigs in order to sustain the war, he never wanted them to have the complete monopoly of office they so desired. So he clung on to Nottingham and the other Tories. The Junto Whigs came to hate these men. The regime's increasing unpopularity, as well as constant squabbling over ministerial places and attempts to limit the number of office-holders in the House of Commons, brought piecemeal changes in the government. Lord Somers was brought further into government as Lord Keeper, while Sir John Trenchard was made Secretary of State. It was also thought that Nottingham would soon be dismissed, but as both he and Carmarthen made a fuss about the new appointments William retreated from any further moves, much to Sunderland's chagrin. Sunderland's view was clear enough: the administration must be further reformed and not 'by Patching' but by a 'good management' and this meant more Whigs in the government.[54]

Having succeeded so far, the Junto Whigs were left to their own devices and immediately took care to undermine the position of Nottingham in order to shift him out of office. Further attacks followed which used the conduct of the war as their excuse. These so undermined Nottingham's position that William finally forestalled his censure by dismissing him in November 1693. He also brought back Edward Russell as Admiral of the Fleet. Russell had previously been removed in 1692 for his errors at sea.[55] William's business now began to prosper as the Whig opposition split over the defection of Russell and Wharton and the Tories were divided over Nottingham's dismissal. Sunderland's management also began to pay off and the earl now took up the post of undertaker: a broker at court for those who would in turn undertake to manage the Commons. Sunderland and his associates were to control the reins of royal patronage and receive the orders of William and in turn they would govern those party parliamentary managers further down the political tree that could deliver the votes in the Commons. A meeting at Althrop, Sunderland's country residence, under his auspices in August 1693 brought further benefits to the regime. In return for Russell's appointment to the government, Montague and Wharton agreed to manage the Commons as court Whigs. Shrewsbury was also finally persuaded to re-enter the government in return for a Triennial bill in March 1694 and by May 1694 the King had been voted some £5,000,000 in supply.[56]

However, the emergence of the 'New Country' platform, led by Robert Harley and Paul Foley, meant that the war in the Commons at least was not concluded. They soon sponsored a place bill determined to remove office-holders and corruption from the Commons. William vetoed it in December 1693, and there was another split in the Whig position. Shrewsbury had been persuaded to fill the office of Secretary of State in March 1694, while Montague was made Chancellor. Seymour was dismissed and the courtiers such as Godolphin and Marlborough lost ground. Sunderland went along with plans to sweep out the last remaining Tories in summer 1694, but such volatile men as Montague and Wharton were not content to live under his patronage for long. They too wanted their place in the sun of the court and the rewards that went with it. The court managers were thus finally replaced with the Whig managers but instability in government and Parliament remained a problem. Queen Mary, William's most unfailing supporter, died from smallpox in December 1694 and left the King personally devastated and his position as sole reigning monarch even more dubious than it had been. Of the Junto Thomas Talmash was killed in action in 1694, while Trenchard was dying of tuberculosis. Greedy for power, Montague and Wharton increased the pressure on the court managers by joining in the attacks on the courtiers and official corruption. As a result Henry Guy, Secretary of the Treasury and a Sunderland client, was soon dismissed and committed to the Tower for bribery, while the Speaker of the House of Commons Trevor was expelled for the same crime. The Whigs even tried to impeach the duke of Leeds, as Carmarthen now was, for bribery in April 1695. Leeds protested his innocence and still managed to cling on to office, but he was an entirely broken force. At this point the scent of victory appears to have gone to the head of the court Whigs and in July 1695 they tried to ditch Sunderland himself. This was a move too far even for William and with his support the attack was beaten off. The Commons also became turbulent again, rejected the court Whig nominee as the Speaker and re-asserted its independence by appointing the country politician Paul Foley to control its business; a rapprochement however, led by Shrewsbury and Somers, meant that a form of peace broke out.[57]

William, with Sunderland, Shrewsbury and Somers now backing him, finally dissolved Parliament in the autumn 1695. However, the result satisfied very few of the parties concerned. The election of October–November 1695 gave both Foley and Harley more power. So much so that Sunderland swiftly opened negotiations with them to manage the Commons rather than the Junto Whigs. Two events destroyed the new scheme in 1696: the assassination plot and the failure of the Land Bank. The discovery of a new plot to murder William in February 1696 gave the Junto Whigs a chance to draw up an association that split the country Whigs and the Tories. The Land Bank was a country idea created to free William from Whig moneyed interest and their sources of City supply. It failed to gain support and both William and Sunderland were consequently thrown back on court Whigs. They now insisted on the removal of Godolphin from the Treasury as the price for this support in order to take some of the pressure from Shrewsbury and Russell, who had been accused of links with the Jacobites. In a typically devious move Sunderland persuaded Godolphin to offer his resignation, claiming that William would obviously refuse it and thus show his confidence in him. However, he secretly advised William to accept the resignation.[58] Charles Montague thus became First Lord of the Treasury while Wharton was made Secretary of the Admiralty and places were also found for Somers and Russell. But William never gave his full confidence to the Junto and as a consequence Sunderland was soon caught in the crossfire.

By 1697 the protean Sunderland's power once more began to slip away. As a reward for his services William pressed an official office on Sunderland and made him Lord Chamberlain and a Privy Councillor. By finally bringing Sunderland into the light from 'behind the curtain' he exposed the earl to attack in Parliament. For a while Sunderland, alongside Shrewsbury, managed the Junto's ability to deliver votes in the Commons and secure loans from the City, and he respected their enthusiasm for the war and loyalty to the principles of 1688, but his political demise was ever in their minds. It came about as the country element in the Commons once again attacked his unique and by now hated position. Sunderland had also managed to offend his court Whig accomplices. Still intent upon achieving a government staffed by the King's friends, in November 1697 he persuaded William to appoint James Vernon, a client of his, to the post of Secretary of State in preference to the Junto's Thomas Wharton. Wharton was furious at this slight over an office he had coveted. He naturally turned to his Junto colleagues for support against their erstwhile mentor Sunderland. The Tories also hated Sunderland and the earl once again found himself under serious attack. While the Junto Whigs stood and watched, the New Country platform led by Harley and Musgrave turned their guns against Sunderland. The political ground beneath Sunderland soon gave way and he was forced out of office in December 1697.[59]

In general the country party's views were solidly against the Bank, against the national debt and fearful of a corrupt government and standing army, but they were also xenophobic and some of them at least were ambitious for office. Sunderland was to prove their first victim, but they were not content to end the struggle there and others were soon marked down for removal. To gain power, however, they would now have to oust the Junto lords themselves and a relentless opposition to Junto policies and attacks on ministers soon began. If the country persuasion could prove to William that they were indispensable as managers then they in turn could succeed the Junto. They thus began to use Shaftesbury's old tactics of managing Parliament in such a way as not to be ignored by the court.

Attacks were launched against Charles Montague, a necessary player in the management of the Commons. Montague was condemned for unlawfully procuring grants from William. Although innocent in this case heated arguments against his position failed to carry the day and the attack petered out. Unfortunately, while the Junto was able to defend its own members they could not guarantee William his demands. Moves to restrain cuts in the standing army and defeat further triennial and place bills were thrown over in their haste to protect their own position. Such matters relied mainly on the independent standing and prejudice of the backbenchers, and the Junto refused to antagonise such men. With the fall of Sunderland others also foresaw the eventual collapse of the Junto. Shrewsbury sought to resign again and finally did so in the autumn of 1698.

Montague began to prepare a safe office as auditor of the Exchequer and made little effort to manage the Commons. In June 1699 he was able to resign as Chancellor of the Exchequer and by November he had left the Treasury altogether. With royal policies becoming ever more unpopular and a new Parliament hostile to the court, the country persuasion returned to savaging ministers at will. Russell, now Lord Orford, was attacked during an investigation into the state of the navy. Another rupture came over the standing army question. William, seeing the peace of 1697 with Louis as a mere interlude, wished to retain his army, but the Junto ministers stood aside in the House and to his fury Parliament reduced the army to the dangerously low number of 7,000 men. In May 1699 Orford resigned rather than face another barrage in Parliament. Somers was the next to suffer. Although his virtuous time in office made him a difficult target, a number of attacks on his position soon left him feeling isolated. With Harley refusing to sit in the same government as Somers, William was forced to dismiss him in April 1700.[60]

Having driven the Junto out of office, the country persuasion did not succeed in seizing control of the government. A re-organised regime brought in the moderate earls of Jersey, Bridgewater and Tankerville. The Great Seal went to Sir Nathan Wright, a Tory, while Leeds finally resigned as Lord President. His office went to Lord Pembroke, another moderate Tory, while Pembroke's old office as Privy Seal went to Lord Lonsdale. Sidney Godolphin was appointed First Commissioner of the Treasury and Lawrence Hyde, earl of Rochester, became Lord Lieutenant of Ireland. William was now openly siding with the Tories, but naturally the Tories demanded their pound of flesh in exchange. An example of the King's relations with his new ministers can be found in the vignette of Lord Jersey, who told Gilbert Burnet that Rochester was once with William and himself in the King's closet where Rochester 'took the liberty to tell the King, that princes must not only hear good advice, but must take it. After he was gone, the King stamped about the room, and [angrily] repeated the word "must", several times; at last turning to Lord Jersey, said, "If I had ordered him to be thrown out of the window, he must have gone".'[61] Tory preferment at court and in the new Parliament as well as the calling of Convocation still meant that William would only go so far. He agreed to remove Montague to the Lords as Baron Halifax and to support Robert Harley as Speaker and even dissolve Parliament, but in return the Tories were to bring in a bill of succession. This was now necessary, for the young duke of Gloucester had died. Another part of this deal was that Parliament would not revive quarrels in the Commons and would arrange for supply in order that William could continue to confute French designs on

Spain. Despite this the Tories were keen to destroy all chances of a Junto return to power and revelations about the partition treaties enabled them to do so.

The war with France had itself ended with the peace of Ryswick in 1697. Both sides were near exhaustion and reluctant to renew conflict even over the emerging problem of the Spanish succession. In Spain the unhealthy Carlos II waited for death, but it was not clear who would succeed him on the Spanish throne. Both William and Louis engaged in long and anxious negotiations in which progress was slow. Eventually the first Treaty of Partition was signed in September 1698. William governed the foreign policy of the country without any real reference to his English ministers and this treaty proved no different. The ministers knew very little of the negotiations until the treaty was virtually an accomplished fact. In turn, although they murmured some dissent when faced with its clauses, it was still signed and sealed. In this agreement the Spanish throne was to go to Joseph, electoral prince of Bavaria, while France was to gain control over Naples and Sicily by the election of the duke of Anjou to its throne, and some territories in northern Spain were to go to France. Duke Charles, the son of the Holy Roman Emperor, was to gain the Milanese territory. Unfortunately in February 1699 Prince Joseph died in Brussels. The agreement thus lapsed and a second negotiation to resolve the Spanish problem opened in 1700. Of the two claimants now remaining, England and Holland supported Archduke Charles but further negotiations resulted in a second Partition Treaty. In this Charles was to take the Spanish throne, while Philip of Anjou was to have the kingdoms of Naples and Sicily. The northern Spanish territories were to go to France alongside Milanese, which was to be exchanged for Lorraine.[62]

The Tories saw that once the treaties had been revealed there was a chance to destroy the Junto lords who had signed them. The partition treaties had in reality been signed without consultation of Parliament, although it had been in session at the time. When this became known in June 1700 voices were raised against the treaties and those who were seen as responsible for them. Ironically the impeachment of Somers, Orford and Halifax which followed raised the political pressure to such a height that it re-united the Whigs and gave the Junto lords a new standing amongst their fellow Whigs. These attacks and domestic conflicts, in a difficult European situation for the King, also split many country Whigs from their Tory colleagues.

In all of this it is clear that by 1701 party conflict had settled into a more regular mould. The two elections of 1701 had raised the tension and the issues of settlement of the crown, the impeachment of the Junto lords and the growing crisis in Europe began to renew the

The age of faction

ideological barriers between the political parties. In the dying light of William's reign it was clear that a new world was being born in which the court would play a lesser part. As one contemporary noted, 'This poor nation has been in a hurricane of humours from the mob to the highest. This matter [of impeachment] hath made a feud that I fear will not die', and so it proved as the age of faction became the age of party politics under Queen Anne.[63]

Notes

1   M. M. Lady Verney (ed.), *Verney Letters of the Eighteenth Century from the MSS at Claydon House* (2 vols, London, 1930), I, p. 107.

2   Standard works on the reign include S. B. Baxter, *William III* (London, 1966). G. Holmes, *British Politics in the Age of Anne* (revised edn, London, 1987). G. Holmes (ed.), *Britain after the Glorious Revolution* (London, 1969). D. Ogg, *England in the Reigns of James II and William III* (Oxford, 1984). H. Horwitz, *Parliament, Policy and Politics in the Reign of William III* (Manchester, 1977). D. Rubini, *Court and Country, 1688–1702* (London, 1967). T. Claydon, *William III and the Godly Revolution* (Cambridge, 1996). L. Pinkham, *William III and the Respectable Revolution: The Part Played by William of Orange in the Revolution of 1688* (Harvard, 1954). J. R. Jones (ed.), *Liberty Secured: Britain before and after 1688* (Stanford, 1992) G. H. Jones, *Convergent Forces: Immediate Causes of the Revolution of 1688 in England* (Ames IA, 1990). P. Hoftijzer and C. C. Barfoot (eds), *Fabrics and Fabrication: The Myth and Making of William and Mary* (Amsterdam, 1990). D. Hoak and M. Feingold (eds), *The World of William and Mary: Anglo-Dutch Perspectives of the Revolution of 1688–1689* (Stanford, 1996). J. J. Carafano, 'William III and the negative voice', *Albion*, XIX (1987), 509–25. H. Horwitz, 'The 1690s revisited: recent work on politics and political ideas in the reign of William III', *Parliamentary History*, XV (1996), 361–77. The classic narrative of William's reign remains T. B. Macaulay, *The History of England from the Accession of James II* (4 vols, London, 1953). See also L. von Ranke, *A History of England Principally in the Seventeenth Century* (6 vols, Oxford, 1875).

3   For an introduction to the court managers see Holmes, *British Politics in the Age of Anne*, pp. 185–9.

4   E. L. Ellis, 'William III and the politicians', in Holmes (ed.), *Britain after the Glorious Revolution*, pp. 115–34. Ogg, *England in the Reigns of James II and William III*. Horwitz, *Parliament, Policy and Politics*.

5   Ellis, 'William III and the politicians'.

6   Halifax, 'The Spencer House journals', in H. C. Foxcroft, *The Life and Letters of Sir George Savile, Bart., First Marquis of Halifax* (2 vols, London, 1898), p. 203.

7   Baxter, *William III*, pp. 223–5.

8   G. Burnet, *A History of My Own Time* (6 vols, 2nd edn, Oxford, 1833), IV, p. 2. B. D. Henning (ed.), *The History of Parliament: The House of Commons, 1660–1690* (3 vols, London, 1983), III, p. 739. *The character of*

William the third (1688). A. Boyer, *The History of King William the Third* (3 vols, London, 1702), II, pp. 405, 517–18. J. Dunton, *The Royal Diary or King William's Interiour Portraicture* (London, 1702), p. 45

9 Baxter, *William III*, pp. 59, 69, 130–1, 149, 154, 186, 227, 322, 352.

10 Hoffman quoted in M. E. Grew, *William Bentinck and William III: The Life of Bentinck, Earl of Portland, from the Welbeck Correspondence* (London, 1924), p. 154.

11 William III quoted in Grew, *William Bentinck and William III*, p. 149.

12 D. Defoe, 'The true-born Englishman', in *Poems on affairs of state from the reign of K. James the first to the present year 1703 written by the greatest wits of the age* (2 vols, 1703), II, p. 41.

13 Horwitz, *Parliament, Policy and Politics*, pp. 94–100.

14 Ibid., pp. 85–8.

15 See J. P. Kenyon, *Stuart England* (2nd edn, Harmondsworth, 1985), p. 290 for this argument.

16 'The danger of mercury parliaments' (1698), in G. Holmes and W. A. Speck, *The Divided Society: Party Conflict in England, 1694–1716* (London, 1970), p. 146.

17 'A new ballad as it was fixed on the lord Dorset's door at the Cockpit' (1689), in W. J. Cameron (ed.), *Poems on Affairs of State: Augustan Satirical Verse, 1660–1714* (7 vols, New Haven, 1963–75), V, 1688–97, pp. 100–1.

18 J. C. Sainty and R. O. Bucholz, *Officials of the Royal Household, 1660–1837, Part 1: Department of the Lord Chamberlain and Associated Offices* (London, 1997), p. lxi.

19 Sir Stephen Fox quoted in ibid., p. lxi.

20 Burnet, *History of My Own Time*, IV, pp. 2–3, 87–8, 152. Boyer, *The History of King William the Third*, II, p. 405.

21 Burnet, *History of My Own Time*, IV, p. 3.

22 See document 31.

23 William III quoted in Claydon, *William III and the Godly Revolution*, p. 225.

24 Halifax, 'The Spencer House journals', II, p. 205

25 Baxter, *William III*, pp. 272–3. Horwitz, *Parliament, Policy and Politics*, pp. 88–94.

26 See P. Grimblot (ed.), *Letters of William III and Louis XIV, 1697–1700* (2 vols, London, 1848), I, pp. 468–9. J. Brewer, *The Pleasures of the Imagination: English Culture in the Eighteenth Century* (London, 1997), pp. 10–13. M. Ede, *Arts and Society under William and Mary* (London, 1979), pp. 19–22, 25–8.

27 Grew, *William Bentinck and William III*, pp. 153–4. N. Japikse (ed.), *Correspondentie van Willem III en van Hans Willem Bentinck, eersten graf van Portland, eerste gedeelte het archief van Welbeck Abbey* (2 vols, The Hague, 1927–28), II, pp. 38–40.

28 Grimblot (ed.), *Letters of William III and Louis XIV*, I, pp. 468–9. Grew, *William Bentinck and William III*, pp. 269, 277–9.

29 Halifax, 'The Spencer House Journals', II, pp. 248–9. H. C.

Foxcroft (ed.), *Supplement to Burnet's History of My Own Time* (Oxford, 1902), pp. 313, 407. Horwitz, *Parliament, Policy and Politics*, p. 50. A. Browning, *Thomas Osborne, Earl of Danby and Duke of Leeds, 1632–1712* (3 vols, Glasgow, 1951), I, pp. 456–7.

30 'A satyr written when the K[ing] went to Flanders and left nine lords justices', in *Poems on affairs of state from the reign of K. James the first to the present year 1703 written by the greatest wits of the age*, II, pp. 211–13.

31 Halifax, 'The Spencer House journals', II, p. 206.

32 Browning, *Thomas Osborne*, I, pp. 437–62.

33 Burnet, *History of My Own Time*, IV, p. 3. T. C Nicholson and A. S. Turberville, *Charles Talbot, Duke of Shrewsbury* (Cambridge, 1930), pp. 25, 35, 39, 41–2.

34 See H. Horwitz, *Revolution Politicks: The Career of Daniel Finch, Second Earl of Nottingham, 1647–1730* (Cambridge, 1968) for an account of his career.

35 Wharton quoted in G. Holmes, *The Making of a Great Power: Late Stuart and Early Georgian Britain, 1660–1702* (London, 1993), p. 347.

36 Sunderland in J. P. Kenyon, *Robert Spencer, Earl of Sunderland, 1641–1702* (London, 1958), p. 251.

37 D. Hayton, 'Sir Richard Cocks: the political anatomy of a country Whig', *Albion* XX (1988), 221–46. Holmes, *Making of a Great Power*, chapter 21. H. Horwitz, 'The structure of parliamentary politics', in Holmes (ed.), *Britain after the Glorious Revolution*, pp. 96–114. T. Harris, *Politics under the Later Stuarts: Party Conflict in a Divided Society, 1660–1715* (London, 1993), chapters 6 and 7. D. Rubini, 'Party and the Augustan constitution, 1694–1716: politics and the power of the executive', *Albion*, X (1978), 193–208. C. Brooks, 'The Country persuasion and political responsibility in England during the 1690s', *Parliaments, Estates and Representation*, IV (1984), 135–46.

38 A. McInnes, *Robert Harley, Puritan Politician* (London, 1970), pp. 28–9. A useful contemporary view of the pattern of earlier 'Whig' thought can be found outlined in *Vox populi: or the peoples claim to their parliaments sitting* (1681). See also 'A dialogue betwixt Whig and Tory alias Williamite and Jacobite', *A collection of state tracts published during the reign of King William III* (3 vols, 1706), II, pp. 371–92.

39 Horwitz, 'The structure of parliamentary politics', 96–114. Holmes, *Making of a Great Power*, chapter 21. Horwitz, *Parliament, Policy and Politics*, pp. 94–100. Rubini, *Court and Country*, pp. 15–38.

40 Holmes, *Making of a Great Power*, p. 337.

41 British Library (hereafter BL), Additional MSS 22851, fo. 131. Holmes, *Making of a Great Power*, p. 338.

42 Holmes, *Making of a Great Power*, chapter 21. Horwitz, 'The structure of parliamentary politics', 96–114. Harris, *Politics under the Later Stuarts*, chapters 6 and 7.

43 Holmes, *Making of a Great Power*, chapter 21. Horwitz, 'The structure of parliamentary politics', 96–114.

44 Holmes, *Making of a Great Power*, chapter 21. Horwitz, 'The structure of parliamentary politics', 96–114.

45 Burnet, *History of My Own Time*, IV, p. 60. C. Roberts, 'The constitutional significance of the financial settlement of 1690', *Historical Journal*, XX (1977), 59–76.

46 For the war and its impact see the essays in Holmes, *Britain after the Glorious Revolution*. For the war in Flanders see J. Childs, *The Nine Years War and the British Army, 1688–97: The Operations in the Low Countries* (Manchester, 1991) and Holmes, *Making of a Great Power*, chapters 14–17. J. Brewer, *The Sinews of Power: War, Money and the English State, 1688–1783* (London, 1989). R. Doherty, *The Williamite War in Ireland, 1688–1691* (Dublin, 1998).

47 See E. L. Ellis, 'William III and the politicians', in Holmes (ed.), *Britain after the Glorious Revolution*, pp. 115–35. Horwitz, *Parliament, Policy and Politics*, chapters 2–5.

48 Holmes and Speck, *Divided Society*, p. 10.

49 Browning, *Thomas Osborne*, I, pp. 441–2.

50 Horwitz, *Parliament, Policy and Politics*, chapters 6 and 7.

51 See Kenyon, *Robert Spencer*, for Sunderland's later career.

52 Sunderland in Kenyon, *Robert Spencer*, pp. 251, 266.

53 For the Junto see Horwitz, *Parliament, Policy and Politics*, chapters 6–9. K. Feiling, *A History of the Tory Party 1640–1714* (Oxford, 1959), pp. 275–329. W. L. Sachse, *Lord Somers: A Political Portrait* (Manchester, 1975), pp. 113–45. Kenyon, *Robert Spencer*, pp. 256–300. J. P. Kenyon, 'The earl of Sunderland and the King's administration, 1693–5', *English Historical Review*, LXXI (1956), 576–602. Rubini, *Court and Country*, pp. 20–3.

54 Sunderland in Kenyon, 'The earl of Sunderland and the King's administration', 587.

55 Ibid., 588.

56 Ibid., 588.

57 Horwitz, *Parliament, Policy and Politics*, chapters 6–9. Feiling, *History of the Tory Party*, pp. 275–329. Sachse, *Lord Somers*, pp. 113–45. Kenyon, *Robert Spencer*, pp. 256–300.

58 Kenyon, *Robert Spencer*, p. 285

59 Ibid, pp. 289–300.

60 Sachse, *Lord Somers*, pp. 146–67. Feiling, *History of the Tory Party*, pp. 349–50. Von Ranke, *History of England*, V, pp. 200–4.

61 Burnet, *History of My Own Time*, IV, p. 518.

62 Von Ranke, *History of England*, V, pp. 154–96 details these treaties and the conflict which followed.

63 BL Additional MSS, 22851, fo. 131. For Anne's reign see Holmes, *British Politics in the Age of Anne*.

Selected documents

The spelling and punctuation in these documents has been modernised where necessary to clarify the text. Contractions have generally been expanded.

Document 1

A yearly annotated list of offices at the later Stuart court can be found in the publications by Edward Chamberlayne. His books went through a number of editions and provide a 'Who's Who', as well as a general statistical and information guide for interested parties. They also give some idea of what was expected from the major officers of the court. These extracts are drawn from the volume for 1673–74.

Edward Chamberlayne, *The Present State of England* (1673–74), pp. 165–9, 179.

> For the civil government of the Kings-court, the chief officer is the Lord Steward … The state of the Kings House is committed to him, to be ruled and guided by his discretion; and all his commands in court to be obeyed and served. And as his power is great so is his dignity, state and honour … he hath authority over all officers and servants of the Kings House, except those of his Majesty's Chapel, Chamber and Stable &c … The Lord Steward is a White Staff-Officer … This White Staff is taken for a Commission; at the death of the King, over the hearse made for the King's body, he breaketh this staff, and thereby dischargeth all the officers, whom the succeeding King, out of his mere grace, doth re-establish each one in his former office. This eminent employment is now enjoyed by James Duke of Ormond, whose fee is 100 *l* yearly, and sixteen dishes daily each meal, with wine, beer &c … The next officer is the Lord Chamber-

184

lain, who hath the over-sight of all officers belonging to the King's chamber except the precincts of the King's Bed-Chamber, which is wholly under the Groom of the Stole; and all above stairs ... The third great office of the King's Court, is the Master of the Horse ... This great officer hath now the ordering and disposal of all the King's stables ... This great honour is now enjoyed by George, Duke of Buckingham. His yearly fee is 666 *l* 16s 4d. and a table of sixteen dishes each meal ... [Then there are the] Gentlemen of the Bedchamber, whereof the first is called Groom of the Stole ... He having the honour to present and put on his Majesty's first garment or shirt every morning, and to order the things of the Bedchamber. The Gentlemen of the Bedchamber consist usually of the prime Nobility of England. Their office in general, is one in his turn, to wait a week in every quarter in the King's Bed-Chamber, there to lie by the King on a pallet-bed all night, and in the absence of the Groom of the Stole to supply his place. Moreover they wait upon the King when he eats in private, for then the Cup-Bearers, Carvers, and Sewers [*sic*] do not wait. The yearly fee to each is 1000 *l*.

Document 2

The following schematic diagram (not to scale) illustrates the typical arrangement in the later seventeenth century of the monarch's public and privy chambers. It is based upon the suite of rooms built for King William III at Hampton Court. The rooms in the palace were the so-called 'axis of honour'. The further the courtier could penetrate into these rooms, the more significant he or she would be at court. Attendance on the monarch in the private apartments was the pinnacle of this system.

KEY
A: State Bedchamber F: Court
B: King's Dressing Room G: Ante-Room
C: King's Closet H: Private Rooms
D: Backstairs I: Private Rooms
E: Queen's Closet

King's Staircase										Queen's Gallery
	F	G	King's Gallery or Great Council Chamber		H		Court			
King's Guard Chamber	Presence Chamber		Second Presence Chamber	Audience Chamber	Drawing Room			I	D	E
						A	B	C		

Document 3

Day-to-day life at the later Stuart court was often motivated as much by petty jealousies and personal rivalries as actual policy. Here, in a letter from 1678, George Villers, second duke of Buckingham, is shown in yet another attempt to regain the favour of the monarch. The words in brackets were originally in a cipher code.

The earl of Arran to the duke of Ormonde, 9 February 1678, Historical Manuscripts Commission, Ormonde MSS, IV (1906), pp. 105–6.

> On Thursday night [the duke of Buckingham] was at [Court] attending [the King] at his supper. He assures his friends that he is as well with [the King] as ever, knowing (though [the King] be [change]able) better than any man when he speaks his heart and when not. That he has told [the King] how all his affairs were out of order, so that he would not meddle with them or with other men's works. And being desired by [the King] to make friends with [the Lord Treasurer Danby] he said he could not [do so] with one whom he [despised] not only as an [ungrateful] but an [ignorant] [man]. I gave him (said he) to [the King] as one who could tell that 2 and 2 made 4 and 2 more 6. But I did not think you would put him [to rule kingdoms]. He uses [the duchess of Portsmouth] not much better. [Arlington] passed on him in the House of [Lords] some compliment on his return to [Court], to which he answered that if [the Lord Treasurer] saw them speak, it would at least give him a motion. [The duke of Monmouth] is sorely afflicted at this progress. And all this is from [the duke of Buckingham] his own words to one I dare credit.
>
> Yesterday [the Bishop of London] told me with heavy heart to the effect aforesaid, saying that he looked on [the Lord Treasurer] as a lost man. That all this has been brewing since those entertainments at [Nelly's], upon which and the scenes of abuse there passing on [the Lord Treasurer] it seems [the Lord Chancellor] did take upon him to remonstrate to [the King] the evil of those things. To which in substance this was the answer, that he would not deny himself an hour's divertissement for the sake of any man. That [the duke of York] has with all his power dissuaded and exhorted therein, but can avail nothing. About a month since [William Penn] foretold me much of this. [The duke of Buckingham] has used arts with him, and such as he, to transform himself into an angel of light. They allow, indeed, some personal failings and immoralities still remaining. But never had any man a truer notion of this government and of the things which must make an English nation happy.
>
> I have said enough at once for any use to frame consequences [for change in Court]. And where it will stop (in such a conjuncture as this) God only can tell. And God direct [the King] aright.

Document 4

In the court satires of the period many a minister's personal qualities
were satirised without mercy. Often these satires took the form of an
advice to a prospective portrait painter of the great man. This example is drawn from a Tory vision of the court of William III in the later
1690s and it attacks William himself (the usual accusations of homosexuality being thrown in for good measure), as well as his ministers
Portland and Sunderland.

'Advice to a painter' (1697), *Poems on affairs of state from the reign of K. James
the first to this present year 1703 written by the greatest wits of the age* (2 vols,
1703), II, pp. 428–30.

Here Painter, here employ thy utmost Skill;
With War and Slav'ry the large Canvas fill:
And that the Lines be easier understood,
Paint not with fading Colours, paint with Blood;
Blood of our bravest Youth in Battel slain,
At *Steenkirk* spilt, and at *Landen's* fatal Plain ...
First draw the Hero seated on the Throne,
Spite of all Law, himself observing none;
Let English rights all gasping round him lie,
And native Freedom thrown neglected by:
On either Hand the Priest and Lawyer set,
Two fit Supporters of the Monarch's Seat ...
Next cringing *B[entin]g* place, whose Earth-born Race
The Coronet and Garter does disgrace;
Of undescended Parentage, made great
By Chance, his Vertues not discover'd yet.
Patron o'th' Noblest Order, O be just
To thy Heroick Founder's injur'd Dust!
Let not his Breast thy Rays of Honour wear;
To black Designs and Lust let him remain
A servile Favorite, and Grants obtain ...
T'expose the Secrets of the Cabinet;
Or tell how they their looser Minutes spend;
That guilty Scene would all chast Eyes offend.
For should you pry into the close Alcove,
And draw the Exercise of Royal Love,
K[eppe]ll and He are *Ganymede* and *Jove*.
Avert the Omen, Heaven! O may I ne'er
Purchase a Title at a Rate so dear:
In some mean Cottage let me die unknown,
Rather than thus be Darling of a Throne.
Now Painter, even thy Art is at a stand,
For who can draw the *Proteus S[underlan]d*?
The deep Reserves of whose Apostate Mind,
No Skill can reach, no Principles can bind;

187

Whose working Brain does more Disguises bear
Than ever yet in Vision did appear.
A supple whispering Minister, ne'er just,
Considered still, still failing in his Trust,
And only constant to unnat'ral Lust.
For Witchery and prostituted faith made great
Yet this is he that must support the Weight,
And prop the Ruins of a sinking State.

Document 5

John Evelyn, an *habitué* of the court and a friend to both Henry
Bennet, earl of Arlington, and Joseph Williamson his client, gives us
some insight into their relationship and how it brought mutual benefit to both sides.

E. S. de Beer (ed.), *The Diary of John Evelyn* (6 vols, London, 1955), IV, 22 July
1674, pp. 38–9.

> I went to Windsor with my wife & son … to do my duty to his Maj-
> esty … I returned in the evening with Sir Jos[eph] Williamson now
> declared Secretary of State: Sir Jos[eph]: was son of a mean clergy-
> man some where in Cumberlandshire, brought up at Queens
> Coll[ege] Ox[ford] of which he came to be a fellow; [He] then trav-
> elled … & returning when the King was restored, was received as a
> Clerk under Mr. Secretary Nicholas: Sir Hen[ry] Bennet (now
> L[ord] Arlington) succeeding, Williamson is transferred to Sir
> Henry: who loving his ease more than business, (though suffi-
> ciently able had he applied himself to it) remitted all to his man
> Williamson, & in a short time let him so into the secret of affairs,
> that (as his Lordship himself told me) there was a kind of necessity
> to advance him; & so by his subtlety, dexterity & insinuation, he got
> now to be principal Secretary; absolutely my L[or]d: Arlington's
> Creature, and ungrateful enough; for so it has been the fate of this
> obliging favourite, to advance those who soon forgot their original:
> Sir Joseph was a Musician, [who] could play at *jëu de Goblets*, ex-
> ceeding formal; a severe master to his Servants; but so inward with
> my Lord O'Brian, that after a few months of that gent[leman's]:
> death, he married his widow.

Document 6

Sir William Temple, another client of Arlington, became reluctantly
involved in the scramble for court office and in this letter to his father
he reveals his mystification at the dealings and traffic in places at
court.

Sir William Temple to Sir John Temple, 27 March 1674, in *The Works of Sir William Temple* (2 vols, 1731), II, pp. 296–8.

London, March 27, 1674
Sir
Upon your expression of so much dislike to my journey into Spain; I acquainted the King with it; and gave that, for the only reason, of my excusing myself from it. I made his Majesty, at the same time, the greatest acknowledgements I could, for the honour he had done me, by the offer of it; and assured him, how glad I should be, to deserve so good an opinion, as he had pleased to express, in thinking me worthy of an employment, which, for my own part, I esteemed one of the best he had to give. The King was pleased to reply very graciously, that he thought so too, but yet he intended me a better … He was pleased to say no more, but walked away; and I seemed to take no notice of what he meant. But the day after, I told all that had pas'd to my Lord Arlington: he seemed a good deal surprised at my refusing the Spanish embassy, and said, he believed the King had few subjects that would not be glad of it … That for his own part, unless I was sure of his Secretary's place, he should not yet advise me to refuse the other.

This was said, with a face, and in a way, something graver than his had been of late towards me; and, I confess, surprized me more than he pretended, I had done him. I told him, that I did not at all know what he meant, by saying, 'If I were not sure of his Secretary's place': That it was a thing I never had once in my thoughts, but when he had put it there, a great while ago, upon the resolution of Sir John Trevor's coming into the other [place]: That my circumstances had been since much changed; and he knew I had thought of nothing but my garden and a private life, for these three or four years past, till the King sent for me upon this peace with Holland. That he knew what had passed since, and he knew all; for I was no man of mystery nor intrigue; that I went abroad, when the King called me, and I liked my errand: and when these did not happen, I stayed at home. But I was still desirous to know what gave him occasion of saying that to me … He told me, that he knew I was related to my Lord Treasurer [Sir Thomas Osborne, earl of Danby], and heard I was much in his favour; that he was now the Great Man, and could do what he pleased, and thought he might do this among other things; and could not imagine I would refuse the Spanish embassy, unless my Lord Treasurer and I had agreed upon the other [place]. I found where his matter pinch'd, and said, smiling, 'That he was never more mistaken in his life: That it was true my wife was related to my Lord Treasurer; and that we were great companions, when we were both together young travellers and tennis players in France; But that for near twenty years past, we had not at all fallen in one another's way, till upon what had passed since the late Councils, about a peace with Holland, in which our opinions seemed to agree: That since, we had met sometimes, but not often, nor in any confidences. That I knew he was a Great Man, but I could not tell yet, to what points of the compass he intended to steer: that I left him, as I did every body else, to take his own measures; and for mine, he knew very well how little I troubled my friends about them'.

Upon this he began with another countenance than in the beginning of this conversation, to tell me, that he easily believed all I told him; that he was so far from disliking my being well with my Lord Treasurer, how ill soever he was with him, that he advised me, as a friend, to be as well with him as I could. That he confess'd, he thought, I might have enter'd with him into a concert, of getting into his place, instead of Sir Joseph Williamson, which would have been no injury to him; for he knew I would not think of it, but upon the same terms as the other: That since we were fallen into this discourse, he would go father with me, and tell me, 'twas true he had a good while had in mind to leave the toil of his place, and, perhaps the envy; and so had agreed with Sir Joseph Williamson, to come in, and give him six thousand pounds, when my Lord St. Albans should be willing to part with the [Lord] Chamberlain's staff, for which he was to give him ten. That my Lord St. Albans had been of late very much unresolved in this matter, and he knew not when he would fix: That whenever he did, he was engaged in the other to Sir Joseph Williamson, by the King's consent, and would do nothing to break it. But if I had a mind, and could make interest enough in my Lord Treasurer to turn it another way, and bring my Lord St. Albans to a resolution, he would leave me wholly to play my own game; and for his own part, it should be all one to him, from whom he received the six thousand pounds: And he would not only be passive in it, but if the King should ask his opinion, as to the fitness or capacity of the persons, he would tell him freely, with all the preference to me that I deserv'd.

I gave his Lordship many thanks for the kindness and frankness of this discourse; but I told him, I believed it need go no farther. That, for my own part, I was both against his going out of the Secretary's place, and against my own, or any body's, coming into it for money; and I ended this conversation, with saying a great deal, to dissuade him from leaving his place. ... I have ever detested the custom grown amongst us of selling places, and much more those of so much importance to the Crown. I think it no great honour to be preferred before Sir Joseph Williamson, and yet I would not do him an injury neither, as this would seem to be. I have seen such changes at Court, that I know not yet what to make of this last; and still remember poor Monsieur de Witt's words of *Fluctuation perpetuele dans la conduite d' Angleterre*; which of all things in the world I am not made for, and had rather, once for all, break my head with going on, than be wrenching my self continually with sudden turns. I need say no more of this matter; it lies before you.

Document 7

Published pamphlets purporting to relate the ways of making a fortune at court were fairly commonplace. In this example drawn from 1675 the author is keen to stress the art of living at court and gaining status there.

The courtier's calling shewing the ways of making a fortune and the art of living at court according to the maxims of policy and morality (1675), pp. 8–9, 17, 23, 50–1, 53–4, 60, 61–2, 66, 167, 168–9, 175, 186.

The [Courtier's] great secret is to render himself agreeable, to use complaisance, and be diligent, and very expert in those exercises in which [the Prince] chiefly delights ... experience teaches us, that no money is so advantageously employ'd, as when they choose discreetly on whom to bestow it. This age has seen a grand minister admired by all, a most exact observer of this Maxim, which ever succeeded well to him ... I look upon a Courtier to be in a great perplexity, that reckons Priests and Women amongst his secret Friends: This last remedy is not convenient to him, and such a Gallantry of spirit is unseasonable. These are indeed a sort of flies, which although not of great force, are very importuning. Prince's Cabinets are filled with them; and I hold him a prudent and discreet man, who can win them to his party: in order to which, it is requisite to use complaisance, sweetness and some times liberality. If the Court be devout, he must beware of Men in Orders; the weakness of these people is not less to be feared, than the malice of others: They are commonly possessed with chimerical fancies; they think they have the authority to judge the whole world ... A Courtier becomes ridiculous, when he avoids the divertissement, of which the whole Court approves: 'tis a strange means of advancing his fortune, to go hear a Sermon, when the prince goes to a Play: And ... he makes his addresses very ill, to retire himself to his Chamber, when the Court is at a Ball, where his good ... and gentle behaviour might gain him both advantage and esteem ... It is a duty incumbent on him, either to conform himself to the manners of the Court, or not to come at it ... [For the] world is a comedy; the best Actors are those that represent their parts the most naturally; but the wisest do not always act Kings and Great lords, and are seldom the Hero's of the Play ... [indeed] those who walk in the Long gallery without being admitted into the Council-Chamber are like the Souls in Limbo, who cannot go to Paradise. The most difficult thing is to make their worth known ... [Thus] Our services ought to be sincere and faithful, but not perpetual ... [Some say that you should seek fortune in the retinue of a Prince or Minister of State thus little by little] from a page he should attempt to become a Gentleman-attendant, or Master of his Game ... [or his secretary, for in the latter case] never anyone missed a Fortune [and] an Ingenious person in this employ, must necessarily have an opportunity of raising his Fortune, without wounding his Honour, or offending his Virtue. 'Tis the most fair place in the whole House to acquire Friends, because the Favours and graces of Princes are distributed by his hands; he has a thousand occasions every day of observing persons of quality.

Document 8

The rise of Louise de Keroualle, duchess of Portsmouth, was a notable event at court. She became King Charles II's favourite and the target for many a politician's ambitions, for they saw in her a chance to influence the King. The French ambassador's interest in Louise grew accordingly and here he relates the latest news of her rise to power to Louvois, minister of Louis XIV.

Colbert to Louvois, 8 October 1671, in H. Forneron, *Louise de Keroualle, Duchess of Portsmouth, 1649–1734* (2nd edn, London, 1887), pp. 66–8.

It is certain that the King of England shows a warm passion for Mademoiselle Keroualle; and perhaps you may have heard ... what a finely furnished set of lodgings have been given to her at Whitehall. His Majesty goes to her rooms at nine o'clock every morning, never stays there for less than an hour, and often remains until eleven o'clock. He returns after dinner, and shares at her card-table in all her stakes and losses, never letting her want for anything. All the ministers therefore seek her friendship. Milord Arlington said to me quite recently, that he was much pleased at this new attachment of the king; and that although his Majesty never communicated state affairs to ladies, still, as they could whenever they pleased, render ill-services to statesmen, and defeat their plans, it was well for the King's good servants that his majesty should have a fancy for Mademoiselle Keroualle, who was not of an evil disposition, and was a lady. It was better to have dealings with her than with lewd and bouncing orange girls and actresses, of whom no man of quality could take the measure. She was no termagant or scold, and when the King was with her, persons of breeding could, without loss of dignity, go to her rooms and pay him and her their court. Milord Arlington told me to advise Mademoiselle Keroualle to cultivate the King's good graces, and to so manage, that he should only find at her lodgings enjoyment, peace, and quietness. He added that, if Lady Arlington took his advice, she would urge the new favourite either to yield unreservedly to the King, or to retire to a French convent. In his opinion, I should also advise her, in this sense. I answered jocularly, that I was not such a fool, or so ungrateful to the King, as to tell her to prefer religion to his good graces, that I was persuaded she did not await my advice, but that nevertheless, I should not spare it upon her, to show how both I and Milord appreciated her influence, and in what esteem he held her. I believe I can assure you that she has so got round King Charles as to be the greatest service to our sovereign and master, if she only does her duty.

Document 9

William Chiffinch proved an exemplary servant to both Charles II and James II and was a notable figure upon the court scene. Here Roger North illuminates this most private servant's character and some of his alleged activities on behalf of his monarch.

R. North, *Lives of the Norths* (3 vols, London, 1890), I, pp. 273–4.

[Chiffinch was] a true secretary as well as page; for he had a lodging at the back-stairs, which might have been properly termed the spy-office; where the King spoke with particular persons about intrigues of all kinds: and all little informers, projectors &c were carried to Chiffinch's lodging. He was a most impetuous drinker and, in that capacity, an admirable spy; for he let none part from him sober, if it were possible to get them drunk; and by his great artifice was pushing idolatrous health's of his good master, and being always in haste, 'for the King is coming'; which was his word. Nor, to make sure work would he scruple to put his master's salutiferous drops (which he called the King's, of the nature of Goddards) into the glasses; and being an Hercules well-breathed at the sport himself, he commonly had the better; and so fished out many secrets and discontented men's characters, which the King could never obtained the knowledge of by any other means.

Document 10

One of Arlington's clients, Ralph Montagu, ambassador to France, took great care to reveal to the secretary one of the more usual problems which could undermine any minister of Charles II, and in which the French court all too obviously took an interest.

Ralph Montagu to the earl of Arlington, 19 October 1669, Paris, Historical Manuscripts Commission, Buccleuch and Queensberry MSS (1899), pp. 442–3.

Mr. de St. Agrian, that comes lately out of England, tells this not only to the King and Ministers here, but spoke it publicly before all the Court ... He said it is a custom in England that when the King is angry with anybody, that he makes them be acted, and that my lord Buckingham and Bab May had acted you to the King and endeavoured to turn you to *en ridicule* ... Secretaries of State are otherwise used in this country, though there be as good *railleurs* and mimics as in other places. Pray God in heaven keep you from the Court's falling on you in jest and the parliament in earnest, when the King does not take your part.

Document 11

Louis XIV's attempts to influence events in England continued throughout his long reign. One means of doing so was to bribe English politicians, many of whom readily accepted his gifts. Here Louis advises his ambassador to attempt to foster the rivalry between Buckingham and Arlington; interestingly, although Sir Robert Leyton took the French King's money, Joseph Williamson refused and remained, in the ambassador's words, 'incorruptible'.

Louis XIV to Colbert, ambassador to England, 7 November 1668, in H. Forneron, *Louise de Keroualle, Duchess of Portsmouth, 1649–1734* (2nd edn, London, 1887), pp. 32–4.

Arlington does not act towards me in a way to make me desire the continuance of his influence. You are to make both one and the other [Buckingham] think the recall of the ... Chancellor possible, and even probable, if I support him. If they engage to effect the union between me and their king, you can give all the sureties they ask ... But I see very well that I shall make no real progress as long as I have not gained the Duke and Arlington by forwarding their separate interests. If each has a strong motive for helping me, they will both, however they may detest each other, plot for the common object. Hints may be held out to [Buckingham's man, Sir Robert] Leyton and [to Joseph] Williamson, that they are to receive some gifts from me. I prefer that it should be in money. When they have received payment of this kind, I shall in a degree have the advantage of them; and it seems to me, that when they are thus in my power, you can without danger use plain speech with them. Let me know what sums should be offered to the two agents, as well as to the Duke and to Lord Arlington.

Document 12

Popular images of the archetypal courtier can be found in the pamphlet literature and drama of the day. On the whole they were not complementary, as this example illustrates.

The character of a town-gallant exposing the extravagant fopperies of some vain self-conceited pretenders to gentility and good breeding (1675), pp. 2–3, 7–8.

A Town-gallant is a bundle of vanity, composed of ignorance, and pride, folly and debauchery, a silly huffing thing, three parts fop and the rest Hector. A kind of walking mercer's shop, that shows one stuff today, and another tomorrow, and is valuable just according to the price of his suit, and the merits of his tailor ... His first care is his dress, and next his body ... His trade is trade is making of love, yet he knows no difference between that and lust ... But for the most delicious recreation of whoring, he protests a gentleman cannot live without it ... his mind is hung with Arentine's pictures, and the contemplation of them is all his devotion: Everything with him is an incentive to lust, and every women devil enough to tempt him ... and plays with women as he does at cards, not caring what suit he turns up trump ... [He also] stayed at University just long enough ... [to] understand the humours of the Town. 'Tis but wearing fashionable clothes, talking loud, and laughing at all one does not understand and the business is done ... Thus the Iliad's of our Gallants accomplishments ... His three cardinal virtues being only swearing, wenching and drinking, and if other men's lives may be compared to a play, his is certainly but a farce, which is acted only on three scenes. The Ordinary, the Play-House and the Tavern. His religion ... is ... Hobbesian. And he swears the Leviathan may supply all the lost leaves of Solomon, yet he never saw it in his life, and for ought he knows it may be a treatise about catching of sprats, or new regulating the Greenland fishing trade. However, the rattle of it at Coffee houses, has taught him to laugh at spirits, and maintain that there are no angels, but those in petticoats ... And by these arts does a man now a days come to be counted a person well-bred, and fit for a generous conversation [but] of himself he is a painted butterfly, a baboon, usurping human shape.

Document 13

The Venetian ambassador's report on the Caroline government of 1671 reveals an outsider's view of some of the major players at the Stuart court and in the government. Although sometimes dubious in factual terms, this report does go some way to reveal the character of the nation's leaders in the early 1670s.

An account of England by Pietro Mocenigo, 9 June 1671, in *Calendar of State Papers Venice, 1671–72* (London, 1939), pp. 61–8.

King Charles II has attained the age of 41 years and has learned from his well-known misfortunes not to fear the aspect of either good or bad fortune. He is of a generous and intrepid spirit, with a quick and ready intelligence full of good qualities and of scientific knowledge, which, joined with a natural affability win him at once affection and respect. He possesses many tongues, but the one he uses most is French ... His own pleasures do not distract his attention from attending to the serious affairs of government. He is assiduous at the councils and over important matters, consulting only those who enjoy his most intimate confidence ... Divine Providence has preserved the duke of York, the foundation of the royal

House, a prince as good as he is prudent. Arrived at the age of thirty-seven his most kindly bearing displays the great qualities of his spirit. The King shows the affection and esteem that he professes for his Highness by a generous assignment of appendages, decorating him with influential titles and admitting him to the confidences of important transactions … With the fall of the chancellor the government changed its aspect … Upon the ruins of this person the duke of Buckingham, his declared enemy, and Lord Arlington, secretary of state, built the advantage of their own influence with the king, the first of a lofty spirit and the other endowed with a mature judgement … the ability of the duke of Buckingham was made to shine forth and he had an opportunity to re-establish himself in his Majesty's favour … As he goes in search of popular applause, he appears independent of religion, for not having any, he tries, with the name, to render himself benevolent to all. He cultivates the leaders of the parties in parliament, who, united with his favourites, form a large party for him. To win universal popularity he is lavish in expenditure. He neglects the management of his private affairs and for the ruin of his fortune he has reports spread of his great generosity. Most attentive to all the internal affairs of the kingdom, he is anxious to make himself appear important to the people. For the rest he likes to please himself. He does not hold tight the reins of government which Fortune offers him, to direct all the affairs of the crown … Arlington, the secretary of state is the most polite and obliging minister the English Court has. He does not need to call witnesses to prove his loyalty to the king as he carries on his own face the glorious and indelible mark of it, received in battle in the civil wars. He followed the king constantly in his exile, employed his talent at the Court of Spain, where he resided a long time … At present he enjoys titles and fortune in reward for his services, recognised by the king's goodness. As a consequence of his office his attention to all the internal and external affairs of the realm has established him strongly and deservedly in the kings' regard, so much so that after the chancellor's fall he had the satisfaction of seeing all the interests of the crown pass though his hands.

As he is a man who is circumspect in affairs, so, with his fine prudence knowing the inconstancy of the country, he proceeds very deliberately in dealing with serious matters and contingencies, and so while ripe in consultation he is correspondingly slow in execution, proceeding with hesitating steps in all matters of the negotiations at that Court. He has no enemies except those who are moved by envy and as he is the one with whom the foreign ministers deal, he gives them complete satisfaction in negotiating, fulfilling all his duties with courtesy, skill and candour.

Document 14

Sir John Reresby was already close to the earl of Danby as a fellow Yorkshireman. Here he is won over to the Danby method by a large amount of personal attention. The document also illuminates King Charles II's opinion on the conflicts of party in the 1670s.

M. K. Geiter and W. A. Speck (eds), *Memoirs of Sir John Reresby* (2nd edn, London, 1991), February 1676, pp. 110–13.

I no sooner arrived at London but my Lord Treasurer [Danby] sent to speak to me. I went to his lordship, and found [him] very free in his discourse upon several subjects, but most lamenting that his countrymen would not give him opportunity to serve them near the King; [he] made several protestations that all the jealousies of such as called themselves of the country party were groundless; that the King to his knowledge had no design but to preserve the religion and government as established by law; and wished that neither himself nor prosperity might prosper if he did not speak his belief; that if there was any danger to the government, it was from those that pretended to be zealous for it, who, under that colour, were straining matters to so high a pitch on that side (by pinching the Crown in supplies and in the prerogative) as to create discontents betwixt the King and his people, that confusion might be the issue ... I replied that I hoped I was not one to suffer myself to be misled ... [Later having performed well in Parliament] My Lord Treasurer took this so well, that ... he would needs carry me to kiss his Majesty's hand ... He presented me to him in the lobby of the House of Lords, next to the prince his lodgings, there being nobody present but the King, his lordship, and myself. My Lord told the King a great many things of me more than I deserved, but last that as my family had been loyal he knew my disposition was to follow the steps of it, and the best way to be confirmed in that was to understand how little truth there was in the pretences now set on foot to withdraw gentlemen from their duty in that particular.

The King said he had known me long, and hoped I knew him so well that I should not believe those reports of him. I know, says he, it is said that I intend the subversion of the religion and government, that I intend to govern by an army and by arbitrary power, to lay aside parliaments, and to raise money by other ways. But every man, nay those that say it the most, know it is false. There is no subject that lives under me whose safety and well doing I desire less than my own, and should be as sorry to invade his property and liberty as that another should invade mine. Those members of Parliament, said the King, that pretend this great zeal for the public good, are of two kinds, either such as would subvert the government themselves and bring it to a commonwealth again, or such as seem to join with that party and talk loud against the Court hoping to have their mouths stopped by places or preferments. Indeed my

Lord Treasurer had named some of the heads of that party to me, that had desired such and such things of the King, and would have com'd over upon those terms. I replied that it was true that the pretences were many and plausible (I believed to some) ... but it had gained little upon me ... and had been so lately confirmed in my belief by those assurances received from my Lord Treasurer ... The King told me that he was very well pleased that he had seen me [and] commanded me to wait upon him sometimes and said I should have access to him when and wherever I desired it.

This condescension in the King to give so mean a person this satisfaction did much convince me of the reality of what he said, joined with the temper and constitution ... of the prince, who was not stirring nor ambitious, but easy, loved pleasures, and seemed chiefly to desire quiet and security for his own time.

Document 15

The earl of Lindsey gave his assessment of Danby's position at court in the autumn of 1675. His opinion on the government, and the monarch Danby was attempting to lead, may well reflect the earl's own views.

The earl of Lindsey to the earl of Danby, 25 August 1675, Historical Manuscript Commission, Lindsey MSS (1895), p. 377.

I always thought the Court of no good complexion towards your Lordship, and that if such small things as Bab May, Chiffinch, Godolphin, and others had had influence enough with their master to have removed you, it had been long since effected, by the allusion your Lordship makes of a schoolboy's returning to school after Christmas. I cannot but observe what a strange creature man is, who is seldom or never pleased with his present condition. And at the same time I admire God's providence who makes all conditions supportable. Those who want power and the gilded troublesome pageantry that attends it, have the greater leisure to follow their own private affairs, are not to provide to secure themselves from the malicious design of their enemies at Court, are not in pain what the people think of them, not affecting popularity out of any intention to promote themselves to places of preferment, or to enrich themselves as Sir Thomas of my country does by the sake of a penned speech pronounced in Parliament. Possibly your Lordship might think this good advice to my Lord Shaftesbury, who at St. Giles enjoys the pleasures of a great and ample fortune, and who hath been so successful in his knavery as to save both his head and estate; and yet your Lordship observes the restlessness of that man's conditions and how easily he would be induced to abandon all these rural satisfactions for a Court trifle. But for yourself I would not have you weary of your load, though I confess it almost insupportable, and what I protest I think I should have ten thousand times quitted if I had been in your Lordship's case; and that which makes it the more so to you in the intentions you have of acting like a man of honour. The aim you have to settle the Church and State; to defend the one against schismatics, and papists, and the other against Commonwealthsmen and rebels. These are indeed things that would make a man's head ache and his heart too especially when one in the world that your Lordship knows will be so wanting to himself as not to be concurring in this design to his own advantage. The greater the difficulty the more glorious the conquest, and I do really believe God hath raised you to this eminency of condition to save a tottering monarchy, which if your counsel is not followed I am confident will be quickly changed into an anarchy of confusion. The gentleman I mention is certainly apoplectic, you must bleed him, purge him, fright him, and the Great God of heaven bless your endeavours.

Document 16

Sir Edmund Berry Godfrey's Ghost (1679) is an example of one of the many topical satirical poems published in 1679. Godfrey died mysteriously in 1678 and was thereafter portrayed as a Protestant martyr in the Popish Plot scandal that followed his death and the revelations of Titus Oates. Here he is used as a figure of warning and attacks are made upon the King, Portsmouth, James, duke of York, and Danby to show to what depths the court had shrunk in popular imagination.

Anon., *Sir Edmund Berry Godfrey's Ghost* (1679).

It happen'd in the twilight of the day,
As England's monarch in his closet lay,
And Chiffinch stepp'd to fetch the female prey:
The bloody shape of Godfrey did appear,
And in sad vocal sounds these things declare …
Shake off your brandy slumbers, for my words
More truth than all your close cabal affords.
A Court you have with luxury o'ergrown,
And all the vices e'er in nature known,
Where pimps and panders on their crutches ride
And in lampoons and songs your lusts deride;
Old bawds and slighted whores there tell with shame
The dull romance of your lascivious flame.
Players and scaramouches are your joy;
Priests and French apes do all the land annoy,
Still so profuse, you are insolvent grown,
A mighty bankrupt on a golden throne.
Your nauseous palate the worst food doth crave,
No wholesome viands can an entrance have;

Each night you lodge in that French siren's arms,
She straight betrays you with her wanton charms,
Works on your heart, soften'd with love and wine,
And then betrays you to some Philistine.
Imperial lust does o'er your scepter sway,
And, though a sov'reign, makes you obey,
She that from Lisbon came with such renown
And to enrich you with the Afric town ...
Next he who 'gainst the senate's vote did wed,
Took defil'd Hyde and Este to his bed;
Envy and paleness in his front are set,
His hag-like chin always with drivel's wet;
Fiend in his face, apostle in his name,
Contriv'd two wars to your eternal shame.
He ancient laws and properties defies,
On standing guards and new rais'd force relies;
The Teagues he courts, and does the French admire,
And fain he would be mounting one step higher.
All this by you must needs be plainly seen,
And yet he awes you with his daring spleen.
Th' unhappy kingdom suffer'd much of old,
When Spencer and loose Gaveston controll'd;
Yet they by just decree were timely sent
To suffer a perpetual banishment:
But your bold statesmen nothing can restrain,
Their most enormous courses you maintain:
They, like the headstrong horses of the sun
Guided by the unskillful Phaeton,
Your tott'ring chariot bear through uncouth ways
Till the next world's enflamed with your rays.
Witness that man who had for divers years
Paid the brib'd Commons pensions and arrears;
Though your Exchequer were at his command,
Durst not before his just accusers stand;
His crimes and treasons of so black a hue,
None dare to prove his advocate but you.
Whoe'er within your palace gate remains
Abhors your acts and serves you but for gains ...
Repent in time, and banish from your sight
The pimp, the whore, buffoon, Church parasite;
Let innocence deck your remaining days
That after ages may unfold your praise:
So may historians in new method write,
And draw a curtain 'twixt your black and white.
The ghost spake thus, groan'd thrice, and said no more:
Straight in comes Chiffinch hand in hand with whore.
The King, though much concern'd 'twixt joy and fear,
Starts from his couch and bids the dame draw near.

Document 17

Henry Bagshaw's letter of thanks to his patron the earl of Danby was written in July 1681. Despite Danby's incarceration in the Tower he still had some friends. The letter also illustrates some of the unctuous nature of client–patron relations.

British Library, Additional Manuscripts, 28053, fo. 269.

29th July 1681 from Durham
My Lord,
I know your goodness will excuse the trouble of this letter, since I could not look upon myself as completely settled in the place lately conferred on me, without rendering a particular acknowledgement to your Lordship, from whose noble patronage I gained this honour of that enjoyment. This is a gift I shall always owe to the power of your interest, and the advantages I have received by it I shall ever preserve, as I do those public ones wherein the whole nation had a share. But these have been ill regarded through [the] injustice of men; and such is the corruption of this age that they mind not the worth but the fortunes of the doer; and so judgement as well as memory comes to be spoiled under the wretchedness of that influence. My Lord I humbly crave leave to boast my freedom from that infection; who as I do gratefully remember your favours bestowed [up]on me; so I do also rightly estimate your other actings; nor can any prison darken before me the lustre of your innocence and the integrity of your power, which still maintains you in your true greatness. All the return I can make is my daily prayer that God would restore your lordship to all the liberty and happiness of state, and establish you fully with his blessings which is earnestly craved by my Noble Lord
Your lordship's most obliged most obedient servant
Henry Bagshaw

Document 18

Entertainment at the Restoration court could be quite varied. Here an official payment is made to James Davies for a particular form of entertainment given before the King and some visiting dignitaries.

British Library, Additional Manuscripts, 5750, fo. 207.

To Sir Edmund Griffin kn[igh]t.
Treasurer of His Majesties Chamber
These are to pray and require you to pay, or cause to be paid unto James Davies Esq. Master of his Majesty's Game of Bears, Bulls, and Dogs the sum of ten pounds for making ready the rooms at the Bear Garden and baiting the Bears before the Spanish Ambassador [on] the seventeenth of January last, 1675. And this shall be your

warrant.

Given under my hand this 28th day of March 1676 in the 28th year
of His Majesty's Reign

Arlington

Document 19

James, duke of York, exiled by his brother in the midst of the crisis
over his succession, proffers his advice on the crisis and foreshadows
the problems of his own government of 1685–88.

James, duke of York, to George Legge, 16 January 1680, Historical Manuscripts Commission, Dartmouth (1887), I, pp. 45–6.

> His Majesty must now take bold and resolute councils, and stick to
> them, and who dar[e]s advise him to them without I be with him,
> to help support them; and believe me other measures must be
> taken, and not departed from, and one would think the measures
> of the former ministers should not be followed. You know some of
> them did make good projects enough, but their hearts failed them,
> when it came to it, and I cannot help remembering one thing,
> which is, that the very same faults Lord Arlington committed, and
> the same fearful steps he trod, have been followed by all those who
> succeeded him, I mean lord Danby and lord Sunderland, tho' still
> at their first entrance they found fault with the other's timorous-
> ness and the wrong measures he had taken, which to some of them
> have proved as fatal to his Majesty, and methinks that they [who]
> come after them, whosoever they be, should not steer the same
> course, to be lost upon the same rocks but should steer another
> course, and look out for another passage, which no doubt may be
> found, to get on's port.

Document 20

John Evelyn's portrait of the last Sunday at court before the death of
Charles II is a brilliant summation of the decadent chaos that existed
at the royal court and makes an interesting contrast with the account
of the court of his successor William III given in document 31.

E. S. de Beer (ed.), *The Diary of John Evelyn* (6 vols, Oxford, 1955), IV, 6–8
February 1685, pp. 413–14.

> I am never to forget the unexpressable luxury, & prophaneses,
> gaming, & all dissolution, and as it were [the] total forgetfulness of
> God (it being a Sunday evening) which this day sennight, I was
> witness of; the King, sitting and toying with his Concubines Port-
> smouth, Cleveland, & Mazarine: &c: A French boy singing love
> songs, in that glorious Gallery, whilst about 20 of the great

Courtiers & other dissolute persons were at Basset round a large table, a bank of at least 2000 in Gold before them, upon which [the] two Gent[lemen]: that were with me made reflections with astonishment, it being a scene of utmost vanity; and surely as they thought would never have an End: six days after was all in the dust.

Document 21

Here, in the King's company, Evelyn paid a visit to the King's mistress Louise de Keroualle, duchess of Portsmouth, in October 1683, and incidentally gives a good impression of the luxury of some seventeenth-century palace lodgings.

E. S. de Beer (ed.), *The Diary of John Evelyn* (6 vols, Oxford, 1955), IV, 4 October 1683, pp. 343–4.

Following his Majesty this morning through the Gallery, I went (with the few who attended him) into the Duchess of Portsmouth's dressing room, within her bed-chamber, where she was in her morning loose garment, her maids Combing her, newly out of her bed: his Majesty & the Gallants standing about her: but that which ingag'd my curiosity, was the rich & splendid furniture of this woman's apartment, now twice or thrice, pul[le]d down, & rebuilt, to satisfy her prodigal & expensive pleasures, whilst her Majesty [Queen Catherine] does not exceed, some Gentlemen's Ladies furniture & accommodation: Here I saw the new fabric of *French Tapestry*, for design, tenderness of work, & incomparable imitation of the best paintings; beyond any thing, I had ever beheld: some pieces had Versailles, St. Germans & other Palaces of the French King with Huntings, figures & Landsc[apes], Exotic fowl & all to the life rarely don[e]; Then for Japon Cabinets, Screens, Pendule Clocks, huge Vasas of wrought plate, Tables, Stands, Chimney furniture, sconces, branches, Braseros &c they were all of massive silver, & without number, besides of his Majesties best paintings: Surfeiting of this, I din'd yet at Sir Steph[en]: Fox's, & went contentedly home to my poor, but quiet Villa. Lord, what contentment can there be in the riches & splendour of this world, purchas'd with [such] vice & dishonour.

Document 22

Thomas Shadwell's comedy *The Lancashire Witches* (1682) was given a Whiggish tinge in parts by its author and subsequently censored. Caricature or not, it typifies some of the main elements of the ideology of the country party. A contrast is made between Whig fears, many of which could be found any day at the court, and the foundations of 'old England', her gentry, and more traditional country views. In Shadwell's comic vein, which foreshadows Fielding's Squire Western, the words put into the mouth of Sir Edward Hartfort, 'a true English Gentleman, of good understanding and honest principles', clearly illustrate what many thought the crisis of the 1680s was really about. Here we find a romantic and sympathetic vision of old England under threat from foreigners, their ideas, popery and arbitrary government.

Thomas Shadwell, *The Lancashire Witches or Teague O'Dively, the Irish Priest* (1682), Act III, scene I, pp. 29–30.

Enter Sir Edward Hartfort, Belfort and Doubty.

Doubt.   You have extremely delighted us this morning, by your House, Gardens, your accommodation, and your way of living; you put me in mind of the renowned Sidney's admirable description of Kalandar.

Sir Edw.   Sir you complement me too much.

Bell.   Methinks you represent to us the golden days of Queen Elizabeth, such were our gentry then; now they are grown servile apes to foreign customs, they leave off hospitality, for which we were famous all over Europe, and turn Servants to board-wages.

Sir Edw.   For my part, I love to have my servants part of my family, the other were, to hire day labourers to wait upon me; I had rather my Friends, Kindred, Tenants and Servants should live well out of me, than Coach-makers, Tailors, Embroiderers, and Lacemen should: To be pointed at in the Streets, and have Fools stare at my equipage, is a vanity I have always scorn'd.

Doubt.   You speak like one descended from those Noble Ancestors that made France tremble, and all the rest of Europe honour 'em.

Sir Edw.   I reverence the memory of 'em; but our new-fashion'd Gentry love the French too well to fight against 'em; they are bred abroad without knowing any thing of our constitution, and come home tainted with foppery, slavish principles, and Popish Religion.

Bell.   They bring home arts of building from hot countries to serve for our cold one; and frugality from those places where they have little meat and small stomachs, to suffice us who have great plenty and lusty appetites.

Doubt.   They build houses with halls in 'em, not so big as former porches; beggars were better entertain'd by their ancestors, than their tenants by them.

Sir Edw.   For my part, I think 'twas never good days, but when great tables were kept in large halls; the buttery-hatch always open, black jacks, and a good smell of meat and

	March-Beer, with dogs turds and may-bones as ornaments in the hall: These were signs of good housekeeping, I hate to see Italian fine buildings with no meat or drink in 'em.
Bell.	I like not their little plates, methinks there's virtue in an English Sur-loyn.
Doubt.	Our Sparks bring nothing but foreign vices and follies home; 'tis ridiculous to be bred in one country to learn to live in another.
Sir Edw.	While we lived thus (to borrow a Coxcombly word) we made a better figure in the world.
Bell.	You have a mind that suits your fortune, and can make your own happiness.
Sir Edw.	The greatest is the enjoyment of my friends, and such worthy gentlemen as your selves, and when I cannot have enough of that, I have a library, good horses, and good music.
Doubt.	Princes may envy such an English gentleman.
Sir Edw.	You are too kind, I am a true English-man, I love the Prince's rights and Peoples liberties, and will defend them both with the last penny in my purse, and the last drop in my veins, and dare defy the witless plots of Papists.
Bell.	Spoken like a noble patriot.
Sir Edw.	Pardon me, you talk like Englishmen, and you have warm'd me; I hope to see the Prince and People flourish yet, old as I am, in spite of Jesuits; I am sure our constitution is the noblest in the world.
Doubt.	Would there were enough such English gentlemen.
Bell.	'Twere to be wisht; but our gentry are so much poisoned with foreign vanities, that methinks the Genius of England seems sunk into the Yeomanry.
Sir Edw.	We have indeed too many rotten members. You speak like gentlemen, worthy of such noble fathers as both you had[.]

Document 23

Roger North had become the Queen's solicitor in James II's reign, but his attendance at what was becoming the Catholic court of the King proved increasingly uncomfortable.

R. North, *Lives of the Norths* (3 vols, London, 1890), III, p. 179.

I went to Court as often as before, bur rarely in my habit to the Queen's court. The times began to grow sour, all favour leaned towards the Catholics and such as prostituted to that interest. We who were steady to the laws and the Church were worst looked upon, and I could perceive at the King's levee and at the Queen's Court I was looked upon with an evil discouraging eye, which made me forebear. I thought my person was no agreeable object, and it was better court to keep it away. If I had been pert and forward, as in truth I was perfectly otherwise, as being modest and diffident, I might have gone into the closet and told what opinion I had of the King's dispensing power, and have laid up a sure interest for preferment (if it had pleased) ... But that was not my character, however clear I had been in their interests, I could not put myself forward, which made me sensible of my incurable unfitness for a Court interest.

Document 24

Despite James II's determination to have it otherwise, factional struggles continued to break out at the court, where in 1686 the rivalry between Sunderland and Rochester grew apace.

Don Pedro Ronquillo to Sir William Trumbull, 12 June 1686, Historical Manuscripts Commission, Downshire MSS (1924), I, pt I, p. 182.

Sunderland aims at destroying [Lord Rochester, the Treasurer], and getting rid of the Catholics. It is he who instigated the Scotch to their evil resolutions, and he has joined the Chancellor, who is not so keen for the Catholics, and that being the King's chief motive, the breach in the King's mind is plain. But he is persuaded that the Treasurer is loyal and that he has no one to put in his place. Nevertheless the latter is in danger, because he will not modify his views ... all Three Ministers are firm, yet suspected. If the Treasurer would only tone down, he has the King's favour, and more so than Sunderland – otherwise he would have gone long ago, for the Queen is more for Sunderland ... [The King's] inner council ... consists of the said Three Ministers only. But there is a third party who tell the King not to dismiss any of these three, but to take in two others to counterbalance the intrigues of the three.

Document 25

Princess Anne gave her surprisingly shrewd view of Sunderland's activities in the reign of her father to her sister the Princess Mary of Orange.

Princess Anne to her sister the Princess Mary of Orange, 13 March 1687, B. C. Brown (ed.), *The Letters and Diplomatic Instructions of Queen Anne* (London, 1935), pp. 24–6.

Lord Sunderland ... the K[ing trusts] with everything ... I thought Lord Sunderland a very ill man, and I am more confirmed everyday in this opinion. Everybody knows how often this man turned backwards and forward in the late king's time; and now, to complete all his virtues, he is working with all his might to bring in Popery. He is perpetually with the priests and stirs up the K[ing] to do things further than I believe he would of himself. Things are come to that pass now, that, if they go on much longer, I believe in a little while no Protestant will be able to live here ... This worthy Lord does not go publicly to Mass, but hears it privately at a priest's chamber, and never lets anybody be there but a servant of his. So that there is nobody but a priest can say they have seen him at Mass, for to be sure his servant will turn at any time as he does. Thus he thinks he carries his matters swimming, and hope you will hear none of these things that he may always be as great as he is now.

Document 26

Lawrence Hyde, earl of Rochester, was soon in fear of losing his place if he did not convert to Roman Catholicism. In December 1686 he had a private meeting with the King in which his fears were realised and his fate was sealed.

'Minutes of a conference between the King and the Earl of Rochester on the subject of religion', in S. W. Singer (ed.), *The Correspondence of Henry Hyde, Earl of Clarendon and of his Brother Lawrence Hyde, Earl of Rochester, with the Diary of Lord Clarendon from 1687 to 1690* (2 vols, London, 1828), II, pp. 116–18.

Sunday Night December the 19th, 1686.
The King having appointed me to come to him after his supper, began with telling me, that he must declare to me, that he found it absolutely necessary for the good of his affairs that no man must be at the head of his affairs that was not of his own opinion; that I might have observed with what concern he had begun to recommend that affair to me, some time since; and that I might have seen the warmth with which he afterwards proceeded in it, was on some other account than even the persuading me to change my religion: to wit, to prevent his doing a thing which would have been uneasy to him, as putting me out of my employment, where he confessed I had behaved myself throughout to his satisfaction, in my integrity, in my honesty, and ability; and that if he should be forced to part with men, he was satisfied it was not fit to put so great a trust again into any one man's hand, neither would he ever have a Treasurer again. That he acknowledged his inclination to me; and he added, his obligation too was such, that there was nothing so uneasy to him as his coming to this extremity; that he exhorted me therefore to think again, and pressed me to it, and to read over again his brother's papers; and that he would give me some little time to consider of it, that if it were possible, I might yet prevent him, for

there was nothing that went more against him: but Kings were to look to the general good of their affairs, and were not to have the natural affections that other men might; they were to do any thing in order to their great designs, and not consider any body that could cross them; and that it was impossible to keep a man in so ... eminent a station, where there was so much dependence, that was of an interest so contrary to that which he must support and own and advance. But whatever I did he would be my friend ... He wept almost all the time he spoke to me; and said all this, and much more, without giving me time to put in one word. He put me in mind of two advices I had given him: the one at his first coming to the crown, not to make a public profession of his religion, by going to the public exercise of it; and the other after the Duke of Monmouth's rebellion was ended, not to take any more persons into my employment of the Catholic religion; in both which, he said, no man of sense could have been of my opinion but a Protestant; and setting that consideration aside, it could not have been possible that I should have been of that mind; and from hence, he argued and concluded, that in all his other business.

Document 27

Thomas, earl of Ailesbury, who was present at court at the end of James II's reign, was later able to give an insider's view of the last hours of James's court before the King's first flight from London in December 1688.

T. Bruce, earl of Ailesbury, *The Memoirs of Thomas Bruce, Earl of Ailesbury* (2 vols, London, 1890), I, pp. 193–7.

That Monday the King was most thoughtful, and all the day and evening, save for meals and those short ones, he gave audience to one and the other in a room by his bedchamber. I attended all the time, save to eat, and more to sustain nature than through appetite. In the afternoon Mr. Charles Bertie, brother to the old Earl of Lindsey, Lord Grand Chamberlain ... had a long conference with men in the bedchamber, the King being in his inward room. He was sent to me by several officers of the army that stuck to the King ... that they would have ready at twenty-four hours warning, between three and four thousand horse ready to march with him wherever he would command them ... The King (and his royal brother also) knew my custom, which was to be heard of last, and at leisure, and therefore by both I was always most courteously received, which maxim I learnt by seeing so many that would be heard out of time, when the Kings were in haste to go into their closet, and scarce minded what was said to them, and this rule of mine was so well approved of, that both Kings, if they were not at leisure, would smilingly tell me that they were in haste, and would after of themselves ask me if I had anything to say to them. I perfectly followed my maxim on this melancholy day and evening, and I may add night, for just as the clock struck twelve, Sir Stephen Fox ... came out from the King, who then took me into his private closet, with these words, 'I know you love to be heard at leisure, and 'twas for that reason I did not call for you into my ante-closet until all was over with others'; and then went up the steps into his closet, and ordered me to shut the door, and that he would hear me out. And what follows is as true as particular, and I will relate it in as few words as the nature of the thing can permit. I being well informed that the King was to go away after my separating from him, I fell on my knees with tears, humbly beseeching him not to think of going. He answered, 'That is a Coffee House report; and why can you imagine it?' I replied, 'For the love of God, Sir, why will you hide it from me, that knows that your horses are now actually at Lambeth, and that you ride on [the] bay Ailesbury, that Sir Edward Halles is there to attend you. Mr. Ralph Sheldon your Equerry, la Badie page of the backstairs, and Dick Smith your groom.' This I found startled him, and no doubt was the rise of what follows. After still persisting, and refusing me his hand at parting, as I knew he would, but he said 'no', but in a manner he begged the question, viz:- 'If I should go, who can wonder after the treatment I have found? My daughter hath deserted me, my army also, and him that I raised from nothing the same, on whom I heaped all favours; and if such betrays me, what can I expect from those I have done so little for? I knew not who to speak to or who to trust; some would have persuaded me that you was a confederate with them, but I could not believe it.' ... To return, I told him that I had in Commission from many of the chief officers and others of his army ... that [they] would stand by him to the last drop of their blood ... To finish this melancholy conference, I humbly besought the King to stay, at least until he had heard from his three Lords Commissioners that were sent by him to the Prince of Orange, whom they joined at Hungerford; and again humbly beseeching him to give me his hand to kiss. He told me he would speak to me in the morning, and so with tears I retired. In the Guard Chamber I met the Earl of Middleton, and I asked him what news from the Commissioners. If I remember well, his answer was neither good nor bad. No doubt he made his report to the King, but this I am sure, he was not long with him, for the footman I left at the bottom of the private stairs came to me in half an hour and told me that the King was gone. It is needless to insert what a melancholy night I passed.

Document 28

In exile after his flight of 1688 James II had ample time to muse on the problems of monarchs, ministers and the court.

James II, 'For my son the Prince of Wales, 1692', in J. S. Clarke (ed.), *The Life of James II, Collected out of Memoirs Writ of his own Hand* (2 vols, London, 1816), II, pp. 629–38.

Princes must be on their guard [more] then others, there being in all Courts men that are given that way themselves, who to cover their own Vices and to keep themselves in countenance, will use all their endeavours, all their skill, to engage Princes into such dangerous and unlawful courses; others in hopes to ingratiate themselves with their Princes, or masters, especially such as know themselves so well as to be sensible they want merit to advance their fortune by lawful ways, will make use of such mean and pitiful ones of raising themselves, not caring what the world thinks of them so they gain their point. Abhor such sad wretches and never trust them, for they have so little Christianity and have such mean souls, will for a little gain sell you and betray you; do not wonder if I enlarge so much on this Subject, having been but too much led away by it myself, having found by sad experience all what I have said on it to be true, and I cannot but remember and take notice of what one of our English Historians observes and remarks concerning Henry 2d, That he was punished for his sin of incontinancy, to which he was much addicted, by the rebellion of all his four sons, who in their several turns joined with the factions and took arms against him, tho at last returned to their duty ...

Be very careful in the choice of your chief Ministers, 'tis of the last concern to you, it being impossible for a Prince to do all himself, they must not only be men of good sense, and sound judgement, but of great probity and well founded as to Christianity, and that it appear by their way of living; for a loose liver, or one that by his actions or discourses shews himself profane, or Atheisticaly inclined, never trust or rely on, for how can you expect that those that fly in God Almighty's face every day, can be thoroughly true to their King ... I speak knowingly of this, and by my experience, and never knew but one of the late King my brother's ministers, namely the L[or]d Clifford, that served him through-out faithfully, and without reproach; Let them see you have entire trust and confidence in them, but let them not impose upon you, the favours and graces you do, let those on whom you bestow them, be sensible they owe them wholly to yourself, and not to others, or their own importunity; Let your ears be open to such as you know to be good men, that you may be truly informed of all truths, which others might not be willing you should be informed of.

Document 29

In the early days of the reign of William and Mary, Queen Mary jotted down some memoirs which give one of the few real insights to a monarch's reaction to her position in the court.

R. Doebner (ed.), *Memoirs of Mary Queen of England (1689–1693) together with her Letters and those of Kings James II and William III to the Electress Sophia of Hanover* (Leipzig, 1886), pp. 10, 11, 15, 19, 23, 29, 30, 36, 58.

1688
I found a great change in my life, from a strict retirement, where I led the life of a nun, I was come into a noisy world full of vanity ... [We were] both bewailing the loss of liberty we had left behind [in Holland] and were sensible we should never enjoy here; and in that moment we found a beginning of the constraint we were to endure hereafter, for we durst not let ourselves go on with those reflections ... The misfortune of the King's health which hindered him living at Whitehall, put people out of humour, being here naturally lazy ...
[The royal couple soon moved to Kensington Palace, then on the fringes of London, and Mary commented that the Palace was a place] where I hope to be more at leisure to serve my maker and to work out my own salvation ...

1690
My opinion having ever been that women should not meddle in government, I have never given myself to be inquisitive into those kind of matters. I have ever used myself not to trouble the King about business, since I was married to him; for I saw him so full of it that I thought, and he has told me so himself, that when he could get from it, he was glad to come to me and have his thoughts diverted by other discourse ...
[On William's going into Ireland to the wars there Mary was left in command and was given nine councillors to assist her. Her comments on these men are pithy and to the point:]
Lord President [Danby] was one to whom, I must ever own obligations, yet of a temper I can never like ... Lord Stewart [earl of Dorset] weak and obstinate made a mere tool by a party ... [Devonshire, the Lord Chamberlain, was] too lazy to give himself the trouble of business, so of little use ... [Lord Pembroke] is as mad as most of his family, tho' very good natured, and, a man of honour, but not very steady ... [Lord Nottingham] suspected by most as not true to the government. None would trust or have anything to do with him, tho' in [his] post ... he must do all ... [Lord Monmouth] is mad and his wife, who is madder, governs him ... [Lord Marlborough] can never deserve either trust nor esteem ... [Sir John Lowther] a very honest but weak man ... [Mr Russell] recommended to me for sincerity, yet he had his faults ...

1691
[I] was told the King and I were less loved, that we had many enemies but no friends, on the contrary all discontented, and each seeking only their own advantage

1693

I saw parties so much increase and a kind of affection to do all that was insolent to the King without fear of punishment, that he could not govern his own servants, nay that he durst not punish them, but was obliged to keep those in his service who least deserved it and who he might be pretty sure would not really serve him.

Document 30

Robert Spencer, earl of Sunderland, here outlines his plans to the earl of Portland on 20 June 1693 for keeping King William's allies sweet in the new world in which all at court found themselves.

The earl of Sunderland to the earl of Portland, 20 June 1693, in N. Japikse (ed.), *Correpondentie van Willem III en van Hans Willem Bentinck, eersten graf van Portland, esrte gedeelte het archief van Welbeck Abbey* (2 vols, The Hague, 1927–28), II, pp. 38–40.

[Mr.] Speaker, Mr Guy and myself have done a great deal in order to persuade men to serve the King, and I think with good success; they have acted with great industry, diligence and skill. Most of those we named to you being fixt, I have talked to many of the principal, and doubt not but they will do well. I need not tell you the particulars of what will suffice such as are to have money, but I can assure you it will come within compass. But I must be particular concerning such as are to have something besides money, as E(arls) of Mulgrave, Bath and Brandon. I hope you will not think, that because some are right set, others may be neglected, for two or three bad angry men will spoil what many others cannot mend, and be assured that there is sufficient matter ready and preparing to disorder the next sessions. I have spoke to E(arl) of Mulgrave and have let him know, that what has been proposed for him, is all agreed to, but only that he must not expect the title, till there is a promotion, which he takes just as if the whole were refused; he says, he valued it chiefly because he thought he should have it alone, for to be made a marquis when others are made dukes, he had rather be as he is, and so looks upon the whole business at an end. I desired him not to do so, for I would represent what he said. I write only the substance of what passed. At last with great difficulty he promised to engage in nothing till I had an answer to the letter I said I would write, but that that answer should determine him positively one way or other, and that he would look upon any delay or uncertainty as a denial, for he says, if such a thing as this in question comes so hard, it must be a very foolish thing of him to think of being a courtier. I hope the King will agree to the whole, and not put him of to a promotion, for if he does, he is lost, and you know it is then to no purpose to manage the House of Lords, for though a great deal more is necessary, all the rest will be insignificant without him, and I think, if he behaves himself well, it will be more to the K[ing's] advantage then to his to make him a marquis (!), and declare he does so because he is satisfied with him. As the K[ing's] affairs stand, nothing will give more credit to the Government after all the boldness or rather deadness of it, and the dissatisfaction which has been showed, then to ingage men of estates and understanding who are interested and cautious to appear publicly for it, and I will be bold to say, if it can be done to this man, and some more I shall name, when the K[ing] returns, it will give a new life to business, which must be given some way or other. If a title should be granted to E[arl] Mulgrave, nobody can except against it, but such as have the same sort of pretentions, who all depend upon the K[ing] and may very well stay, and will be the more desirous of such favours. Concerning E[arl] of Bath I do propose that the K[ing] will pass by Lord Lansdouns fault, make amends to J. Greenville for what was taken from him, and then tell E[arl] of Bath how he expects to be served by him and his family. I hope the K[ing] will promise My lord Brandon a regiment of horse at the end of these sessions, My lord of Oxford's when it falls, and to make him a major general. I could say a great deal in his behalf to show all this to be reasonable, and particularly the chief part, his being a major general, but I will say only this, that, without excepting any man, none can doe more good or hurt than he, and if the K[ing] tak's him into his service, he will be well served by him. E[arl] Stanford and other lords must have money. I would be glad more of that House might be gained, but the means are difficult, and therefore I will mention nothing of it till the K[ing] returns, though I have important things to offer. I desire you will lay this before the King, and I hope you will make all easy concerning Mulgrave, Bath and E[arl] Branden, for what is proposed for every one of them is necessary to gain them, and it is necessary to gain every one of them; to make the K[ing's] business go on, nothing must be neglected or thought superfluous. Pray, My lord, let me know the King's mind as soon as you can, perticularly in relation to the three lords. The Speaker and his friend are positively of my opinion. Mr Smith's nephew must not be forgot. Sir R. Howard is in very ill humour, he thinks himself extremely ill used, but may soon be set right, and I hope will be. Since I came hither, Sir William Trumball has been with me to excuse his not going to Ireland. The reasons are unfit for a letter, they relate to the ministers, and perticularly to Lord Rochester. After many complaints of them, he professed all the duty possible for the King, and before he left me, he desired me to write to Your Lordship to recommend him to the Bishop of Canterbury ... I told him I did not believe my credit could do a thing of that kind, but I thought his might, and therefore, if he would give me his request in writing, I would send it to you, which I now inclose. I believe he is the fittest man in England for the employment, and that he is entirely for this government. If you will recommend him, pray let me know it. I cannot end this letter without conjuring you to persuade the King not to stay a moment longer abroad than is necessary. If people write you truth, you will hear so much of the discontent or rather rage people are in concerning the fleets, the admirals and the ministers, that is to no purpose to mention anything of it. I have made use of my friends cyphers for letters and for names. It is so long since I have writ anything of this kind. I am afraid you will hardly read this letter. I am forever yours.

Document 31

William III, although not noted for his social graces, mellowed towards the end of his reign, and he could be charming when he wished to be so. Here the countess of Rutland writes to her husband of a Thursday evening in April 1701, which she spent in the King's company at Kensington Palace. The air of domesticity at William's court makes a direct contrast with the atmosphere at the court of Charles II, and in many ways foreshadows the domestic life of eighteenth-century British monarchy.

The countess of Rutland to the earl of Rutland, April 1701, Historical Manuscripts Commission, Rutland MSS (1899), pp. 166–7.

I was last night at Kensington, my dear Lord, altho[ugh] my cold yet is far from being gone, and I received so great an honour from his Majesty, who 'tis said, is observed to not talk much to ladies, that I cannot miss acquainting you with it, who was extremely concerned in both the conferences his Majesty and I had. As soon as he came out into the gallery from his own apartment, he found a crowd of company of both sexes, and the Duchess of Somerset, Ormond, Queensbrough and myself talking together just by the card table and his chair, so he made his legs to all the ladies, and everyone that played took their stools, which was the three Duchess I have named, Lady Arlington, Lady Barramore, Lord Feversham, Lord Rumney, Lord Albermarle, and Mr. Boucher that dealt, and the King called to me and told me he did not ask me now to play because I refused it before, but asked if I never played at that or no other game at card. I told him I had played at *Bassett* when the Queen was alive and commanded me, and it was a silver table, but [a] gold one was to[o] deep for the ill luck I generally had. Then he asked me how you had your ill health, and said he heard [you] had not enjoyed it extreme well, which he was sorry for. So I was forced to draw nearer his chair, and stand between the Duchess of Somerset['s] stool and it, and told the King that indeed you had been so often ill that you had never stirred from home these several years, which was the reason you could not pay your duty to him, as you would else have done. He said he thought Belvoir seemed to stand not only very finely but healthfully, and asked if you had no thoughts of coming to it again. So I said I heard you had, and thus the first conference ended, and after his playing a little at the gold table he ... [rose] and went to go to the other tables, as he always does, so I gave back to make the King's way, and pressed the ladies behind to do so to, which the King seeing said it was 'No matter, my lady Rutland, for I can come over the stool', so strode over it and when [he] came just by me stopped and told I looked might well, and that since he could not see you which he should have been very glad to have done, he was mightily pleased to see me, and asked how long I had been in Town, and told me I was so great a stranger he hoped I would not leave them, as he termed it quickly. I told the King I did not know whether I should have had or no that honour and good fortune I then had of speaking to him myself, but that ... I had your particular command to give him your humble duty, and assure him he had no subject whatsoever had more duty for him, was more devoted to his interest, and prayed more for his prosperity and long life, than your self, and that you had sent your two sons to do him all the service they could and testify the sincerity of yours and their loyalty, as I hoped they did so. Upon which he told me he was extremely satisfied with it, and took it very kindly all I had told him, and since I had done that, desired I would take the trouble upon me to give you back his thanks when I wrote, and return you his complements, which was his own words.

While all this passed between us, I could hear a world of the crowd, who knew me not, ask 'Who is she, what is she, that the King takes such notice of, and looks so pleased all the while he talks to?' and abundance that did know me asked what his Majesty and I could find to talk of so long. I told them it was fine speeches of civility, on both sides, and several speak also to Dolly of it, who went with me to Kensington, and was very fine, and to-day in a visit to Mrs. Cheetwine, she said it was observed by all that the King looked brisker and pleasanter when he was doing me that honour amongst so much company than had been seen to do of some time ... *Postscript*: - I desire to miss not a Kensington day if there be more then next.

Selected bibliography

Selected manuscript sources

Bodleian Library, Oxford
Carte MSS 31–9, 46, 69, 81
Rawlinson A 173–5, 183,185, 188.

British Library, London
Additional MS 4201
Additional MS 5750
Additional MS 15643
Additional MS 22919–20
Additional MS 27872
Additional MS 28054
Additional MS 28945
Additional MS 30015
Additional MS 41803–46
Egerton MS 2533–62
Harleian MS 3364
Stowe MS 203–17
Stowe MS 563

Public Records Office, London
SP 9   State Papers Miscellaneous: Sir Joseph Williamson
            Collection
SP 29   State Papers Charles II
SP 44   Entry Books
SP 78   State Papers France
PRO 30/24   Shaftesbury Papers
PRO 31/3   Transcripts of French Diplomatic Correspondence
LC 3   Lord Chamberlain's Papers, Registers
LC 5   Miscellanea

Printed primary sources

An account of the life and memorable actions of Father Petre the Jesuit (1689).

Airey, O. (ed.), *Essex Papers, 1672–1679* (London, 1890).

Ashbee, A. (ed.), *Records of English Court Music* (14 vols, Aldershot, 1986–96).

Beddard, R. A., *A Kingdom Without a King: The Journal of the Provisional Government in the Revolution of 1688* (Oxford, 1988).

Beer, E. S. de (ed.), *The Diary of John Evelyn* (6 vols, Oxford, 1955).

Blencowe, R. D. (ed.), *The Diary of the Times of Charles the Second by Henry Sidney* (2 vols, London, 1843).

Boyer, A., *The History of King William the Third* (3 vols, London, 1702).

Brown, B. C. (ed.), *The Letters and Diplomatic Instructions of Queen Anne* (London, 1935).

Bruce, T., earl of Ailesbury, *The Memoirs of Thomas Bruce, Earl of Ailesbury* (2 vols, London, 1890).

Burnet, G., *A History of My Own Time* (6 vols, 2nd edn, Oxford, 1833).

Burnet, G., *A History of My Own Time, Part I: The Reign of Charles II* (2 vols, Oxford, 1897).

Calendar of State Papers Domestic Series (London, 1860–).

Calendar of State Papers Venice, 1671–72 (London, 1931–47).

Calendar of Treasury Books (London, 1904–).

Castiglione, B., *The Book of the Courtier* (Harmondsworth, 1981).

Cavelli, E. Marquise Campana de, *Les Derniers Stuarts à Saint-Germain-en-laye: documents inédits et authentiques* (2 vols, Paris, 1871).

Chamberlayne, E., *The Present State of England* (London, 1673–74).

The character of a town-gallant exposing the extravagant fopperies of some vain self-conceited pretenders to gentility and good breeding (1675).

The character of William the third (1688).

Christie, W. D. (ed.), *Letters Addressed from London to Sir Joseph Williamson while Plenipotentiary at the Congress of Cologne in the Years 1673 and 1674* (2 vols, London, 1874).

Clarendon, E. Hyde, first earl of, *The Life of Edward, Earl of Clarendon, Lord High Chancellor of England* (2 vols, Oxford, 1857).

Clarendon, E. Hyde, first earl of, *State Papers Collected by Edward, Earl of Clarendon* (3 vols, Oxford, 1786).

Clarke, J. S. (ed.), *The Life of James II, Collected out of Memoirs Writ of his Own Hand* (2 vols, London, 1816).

A collection of state tracts published during the reign of King William III (3 vols, 1706).

The court in mourning, being the life and worthy actions of Ralph, first duke of Montague (1709).

The courtier's calling shewing the ways of making a fortune and the art of living at court according to the maxims of policy and morality (1675).

Coxe, W. (ed.), *Private and Original Correspondence of Charles Talbot, Duke of Shrewsbury* (London, 1821).

A deep sigh breathed through the lodgings at Whitehall deploring the absence of the court and the miseries of the palace (1642).

Doebner, R. (ed.), *Memoirs of Queen Mary of England (1689–93) Together with her Letters and those of Kings James II and William III to the Electress Sophia of Hanover* (Leipzig, 1886).

Dunton, J., *The Royal Diary: or King William's Interiour Portraicture* (London, 1702).

Ellis, F. S. (ed.), *John Wilmot, Earl of Rochester: The Complete Works* (Harmondsworth, 1994).

Ellis, G. A. E. (ed.), *The Ellis Correspondence* (2 vols, London, 1829).

Foxcroft, H. C., *Supplement to Burnet's History of My Own Time* (Oxford, 1902).

Geiter, M. K. and Speck, W. A. (eds), *Memoirs of Sir John Reresby* (2nd edn, London, 1991).

Gilbert, G. D. (ed.), *Marie Catherine d'Aulnoy, Memoirs of the Court of England in 1675* (London, 1913)

Grimblot, P. (ed.), *Letters of William III and Louis XIV, 1697–1700* (2 vols, London, 1848).

Historical Manuscripts Commission Reports.

Hobbes, T., *Leviathan* (1651) (Harmondsworth, 1985).

Japikse, N. (ed.), *Correspondentie van Willem III en van Hans Willem Bentinck, eersten graf van Portland, eerste gedeelte het archief van Welbeck Abbey* (2 vols, The Hague, 1927–28).

Kenyon, J. P. (ed.), *Halifax: The Complete Works* (Harmondsworth, 1969).

Latham, R. and Matthews, W. (eds), *The Diary of Samuel Pepys* (11 vols, London, 1970–83).

Le Neve, J., *Lives and Characters of the Most Illustrious Persons British and Foreign who Died in the Year 1712* (London, 1713).

Life, amours, and secret history of Francelia, late duchess of Portsmouth favourite mistress to King Charles II (1734).

Lord, G. F. de (general ed.), *Poems on Affairs of State: Augustan Satirical Verse, 1660–1714* (7 vols, London, 1963–75).

Lowther, J., Lord Viscount, *Memoirs of the Reign of James II* (York, 1808).

Manners-Sutton, H. (ed.), *The Lexington Papers* (London, 1851).

Moor Smith, G. C. (ed.), *The Letters of Dorothy Osborne to William Temple* (Oxford, 1928).

North, R., *Lives of the Norths* (3 vols, London, 1890).

Patrides, C. A. (ed.), *John Milton: Selected Prose* (Harmondsworth, 1979).

Pegge, S., *Curialia* (2 vols, London, 1791–1806).

Phipps, C. (ed.), *Buckingham, Public and Private Man: The Prose, Poems and Commonplace Book of George Villiers, Second Duke of Buckingham (1628–1687)* (New York, 1985).

Poems on affairs of state from the reign of K. James the first to this present year 1703 written by the greatest wits of the age (2 vols, 1703).

The Popish champion or the complete history of the life and military actions of Richard, earl of Tyrconnel, generallisimo of all the Irish forces now in arms (1689).

Reflections upon a paper intitled, some reflections upon the earl of Danby in relation to the murder of sir Edmund bury Godfrey in a letter to Edward Christian (1679).

Scott, W. (ed.), *Somers Tracts* (13 vols, 2nd edn, Edinburgh, 1809–15).

The sentiments, a poem to the earl of Danby in the Tower by a person of quality (1679).

Shadwell, T., *The Lancashire Witches or Teague O'Divelly, the Irish Priest* (1682).

Singer, S. W. (ed.), *Correspondence of Henry Hyde, Earl of Clarendon and of his Brother Lawrence Hyde, Earl of Rochester with the Diary of Lord Clarendon from 1687–1690* (2 vols, London, 1828).

Slaughter, T. P. (ed.), *Ideology and Politics on the Eve of the Restoration: Newcastle's Advice to Charles II* (Philadelphia, 1984).

Springarn, J. E. (ed.), *Critical Essays of the Seventeenth Century* (3 vols, Oxford, 1908).

Strachey, C. (ed.), *The Letters of the Earl of Chesterfield to his Son* (2 vols, 2nd edn, London, 1924).

Summers, M. (ed.), *The Complete Works of Thomas Shadwell* (5 vols, London, 1927).

Temple, W., *The Works of Sir William Temple* (2 vols, London, 1731).

Verney, M. M., Lady (ed.), *Verney Letters of the Eighteenth Century from the MSS at Claydon House* (2 vols, London, 1930).

Vox populi: or the people's claim to their parliaments sitting (1681).

Walker, K. (ed.), *John Dryden* (Oxford, 1987).

Walker, K. (ed.), *The Poems of John Wilmot, Earl of Rochester* (London, 1984).

Williams, N., *Imago saeculi: the image of the age represented in four characters viz: the ambitious statesman, instatiable miser, aetheistical gallant, factious schismatick* (Oxford, 1676).

Wilson, J. H., *Court Satires of the Restoration* (Columbus OH, 1975).

Wootton, D. (ed.), *Divine Right and Democracy: An Anthology of Political Writing in Stuart England* (Harmondsworth, 1988).

Yallop, H. Y., 'Colonel Ambrose Norton's account of the defection of Lord Cornbury – 1688', *Journal of the Society for Army Historical Research*, LXX (1992).

Secondary sources

Allen, D., 'Bridget Hyde and Lord Treasurer Danby's alliance with Lord Mayor Vyner', *Guildhall Studies in London History*, II, pt 1 (1975).

Allen, D., 'The political function of Charles II's Chiffinch', *Huntingdon Library Quarterly*, XXXIX (1975–76).

Asch, R. G. and Birke, A. M. (eds), *Princes, Patronage and Nobility: The Court at the Beginning of the Modern Age c.1450–1650* (Oxford, 1991).

Aylmer, G. E., 'From office holding to civil service: the genesis of modern bureaucracy', *Transactions of the Royal Historical Society*, 5th series, XXX (1980).

Aylmer, G. E., *The King's Servants: The Civil Service of Charles I, 1625–1642* (London, 1961).

Aylmer, G. E., *The State's Servants: The Civil Service under the English Republic, 1649–1660* (London, 1973).

Ballie, H. M., 'Etiquette and the planning of the state apartment in

Baroque palaces', *Archaelogia*, CI (1967).

Barbour, V., *Henry Bennet, Earl of Arlington, Secretary of State to Charles II* (Washington, 1914).

Barnes, A. S., 'Catholic chapels royal under the Stuart kings: IV the later years of Charles II and James II', *Downside Review*, XXI (1902).

Baxter, S. B., *The Development of the Treasury 1660–1702* (London, 1957).

Baxter, S. B., *William III* (London, 1966).

Beattie, J. M., *The English Court in the Reign of George I* (Cambridge, 1967).

Beckett, J. C., *The Cavalier Duke: A Life of James Butler, First Duke of Ormonde, 1610–1688* (Belfast, 1990).

Bell, H. E. and Ollard, R. L. (eds), *Historical Essays, 1600–1750, Presented to David Ogg* (London, 1964).

Bennet, A. and Royle, N., *An Introduction to Literature, Criticism and Theory: Key Critical Concepts* (London, 1995).

Benson, D. R., 'Halifax and the trimmers', *Huntingdon Library Quarterly*, XXVII (1963–64).

Berger, R. W., *A Royal Passion: Louis XIV as a Patron of Architecture* (Cambridge, 1994).

Birrell, T. A., 'Roger North and political morality in the late Stuart period', *Scrutiny*, XVII (1951).

Black, J. and Gregory, J. (eds), *Culture, Politics and Society in Britain, 1660–1800* (Manchester, 1991).

Bloch, M., *The Royal Touch: Sacred Monarchy and Scrofula in England and France* (London, 1973).

Boissevain, J., *Friends of Friends: Networks, Manipulators and Coalition* (Oxford, 1974).

Borgman, A. S., *Thomas Shadwell, his Life and Comedies* (New York, 1989).

Boyer, R. E., *English Declarations of Indulgence, 1687 and 1688* (The Hague, 1968).

Bredvold, G., *The Intellectual Milieu of John Dryden: Studies in Some Aspects of Seventeenth-Century Thought* (Ann Arbor, 1956).

Brewer, J., *The Sinews of Power: War, Money and the English State, 1688–1783* (London, 1989).

Brewer, J., *The Pleasures of the Imagination: English Culture in the Eighteenth Century* (London, 1997).

Brooks, C., 'The country persuasion and political responsibility in England during the 1690s', *Parliaments, Estates and Representation*, IV (1984).

Brown, H. C. (ed.), *Hobbes Studies* (Oxford, 1985).

Brown, J. and Elliott, J. H., *A Palace Fit for a King: The Buen Retiro and the Court of Philip IV* (New Haven, 1980).

Brown, M., 'Trimmers and moderates in the reign of Charles II', *Huntingdon Library Quarterly*, XXXVII (1973–74).

Browning, A., 'Parties and party organization in the reign of Charles II', *Transactions of the Royal Historical Society*, 4th series, XXX (1946).

Browning, A., 'The stop of the Exchequer', *History*, XIV (1930).

Browning, A., *Thomas Osborne, Earl of Danby and Duke of Leeds, 1632–1712* (3 vols, Glasgow, 1951).

Bucholz, R. O., *The Augustan Court: Queen Anne and the Decline of Court Culture* (Stanford CA, 1993).

Buck, A., Kaufman, G., Spahr, B. G. and Wiedemann, C. (eds), *Europäische Hofkultur im 16 und 17 Jahrhundret* (3 vols, Hamburg, 1981).

Burgess, G., *The Politics of the Ancient Constitution: An Introduction to English Political Thought, 1603–1642* (London, 1992).

Burke, P., *The Fabrication of Louis XIV* (New Haven, 1992).

Burns, E. (ed.), *Reading Rochester: English Texts and Sub-texts* (Liverpool, 1995).

Camden, C. (ed.), *Restoration and Eighteenth-Century Literature* (Chicago, 1983).

Cannadine, D. and Price, S. (eds), *Rituals of Royalty: Power and Ceremonial in Traditional Society* (Cambridge, 1987).

Cannon, J., *The Modern British Monarchy: A Study in Adaptation*, The Stenton Lecture 1986 (Reading, 1987).

Carafano, J. J., 'William III and the negative voice', *Albion*, XIX (1987).

Carpenter, E., *The Protestant Bishop, Being the Life of Henry Compton 1632–1713 Bishop of London* (London, 1956).

Carroll, 'The by–election at Aldborough, 1673', *Huntingdon Library Quarterly*, XXVIII (1964–65).

Carter, J., 'Cabinet records for the reign of William III', *English Historical Review* LXXVIII (1963).

Chanderman, C. D., *The English Public Revenue, 1660–1688* (Oxford, 1975).

Chapman, H. W., *Mary II, Queen of England* (London, 1953).

Chernaik, W. L., *Sexual Freedom in Restoration Literature* (Cambridge, 1995).

Churchill, W. S., *Marlborough, his Life and Times* (2 vols, London, 1966).

Clarke, J. C. D., 'A general theory of party, opposition and government, 1688–1832', *Historical Journal*, XXIII (1980).

Clay, C., *Public Finance and Private Wealth: The Career of Sir Stephen Fox, 1627–1716* (Oxford, 1978).

Claydon, T., *William III and the Godly Revolution* (Cambridge, 1996).

Colvin, H. M., *The History of the King's Works* (7 vols, London, 1976).

Corp, E., *James II and Toleration: The Years in Exile at Saint-Germain-en-laye* (Huntingdon, 1997).

Craik, H., *The Life of Edward, Earl of Clarendon* (2 vols, London, 1911).

Crawford, R., *The Last Days of Charles II* (Oxford, 1909).

Cregan, D. F., 'An Irish cavalier: Daniel O'Neill in exile and restoration 1651–1664', *Studia Hibernica*, LI (1965).

Dickens, A. G. (ed.), *The Courts of Europe: Politics, Patronage and Royalty, 1400–1800* (London, 1977).

Dickinson, H. T., *Walpole and the Whig Supremacy* (London, 1973).

Dolan, Dom G., 'James II and the Benedictines in London', *Downside Review*, XVIII (1899).

Dugdale, G. S., *Whitehall Through the Centuries* (London, 1950).

Ede, M., *Arts and Society under William and Mary* (London, 1979).

Edie, C. A., 'The public face of royal ritual: sermons, medals and civil ceremony in late stuart coronations, *Huntingdon Library Quarterly*, LIII (1990).

Edwards, H. J. and Edwards, E. A., *A Short Life of Marlborough* (London, 1926).

Elias, N., *The Civilising Process* (2 vols, Oxford, 1982).

Elias, N., *The Court Society* (Oxford, 1983).

Elton, G. R., 'Tudor government: the points of contact: III the court', *Transactions of the Royal Historical Society*, 5th series, XXVI (1976).

Evans, A. M., 'The imprisonment of Lord Danby in the Tower, 1679–1684', *Transactions of the Royal Historical Society*, 4th series, XII (1929).

Feiling, K., *A History of the Tory Party, 1640–1714* (Oxford, 1959).

Figgis, J. N., *The Theory of the Divine Right of Kings* (Cambridge, 1896).

Forneron, H., *Louise de Keroualle, Duchess of Portsmouth, 1649–1734* (2nd edn, London, 1887).

Foxcroft, H. C., *The Character of a Trimmer, Being a Short Life of the First Marquis of Halifax* (Cambridge, 1946).

Foxcroft, H. C., *The Life and Letters of Sir George Savile, Bart., First Marquis of Halifax* (2 vols, London, 1898).

Foxon, D., *Libertine Literature in England, 1660–1745* (New York, 1965).

Fraser, A., *King Charles II* (London, 1980).

Fraser, A., *The Weaker Vessel: Women's Lot in Seventeenth-Century England* (London, 1987).

George, R. H., 'The financial relations of Louis XIV and James II', *Journal of Modern History*, III (1931).

Genet-Rouffiac, N., 'Le Jacobites à Paris et Saint-Germain-en-laye', *Reve de la Bibliotheque Nationale* , XLVI (1992).

Girouard, M., *Life in the English Country House: A Social and Architectural History* (New Haven, 1978).

Gregg, E., *Queen Anne* (London, 1984).

Grew, M. E., *William Bentinck and William III: The Life of Bentinck, Earl of Portland, from the Welbeck Correspondence* (London, 1924).

Grose, C. L., 'Louis XIV's financial relations with Charles II and the English parliament', *Journal of Modern History*, I (1929).

Guy, J. (ed.), *The Tudor Monarchy* (London, 1997).

Haile, M., *Queen Mary of Modena, her Life and Letters* (London, 1905).

Haley, K. H. D., *The First Earl of Shaftesbury* (Oxford, 1968).

Halfpenny, E., 'Musicians at James II's coronation', *Music and Letters*, XXXII (1951).

Harris, B. J., 'Women in politics in early Tudor England', *Historical Journal*, XXXIII (1990).

Harris, T, 'From rage of party to the age of oligarchy? Re-thinking the late Stuart and early Hanoverian period', *Journal of Modern History*, LXIV (1992).

Harris, T, *Politics under the Later Stuarts: Party Conflict in a Divided Society, 1660–1715* (London, 1993).

Hartmann, C. H., *The King's Friend: A Life of Charles Berkeley, Viscount Fitzhardinge of Falmouth, 1630–1665* (London, 1951).

Hatton, R. (ed.), *Louis XIV and Absolutism* (London, 1976).

Hayden, J., *Symbol and Privilege: The Ritual Context of British Monarchy* (Tucson, 1987).

Hayton, D., 'Sir Richard Cocks: the political anatomy of a country Whig', *Albion*, XX (1988).

Henning, B. D. (ed.), *The History of Parliament: The Commons, 1660–1690* (3 vols, London, 1983).

Henshall, N., *The Myth of Absolutism: Change and Continuity in Early Modern Monarchy* (London, 1992).

Hibbert, C., *The Court at Windsor: A Domestic History* (Harmondsworth, 1964).

Hibbert, C., *George IV* (Harmondsworth, 1976).

Hill, J. W. F., *Tudor and Stuart Lincoln* (Cambridge, 1956).

Hoak, D. and Feingold, M. (eds), *The World of William and Mary: Anglo-Dutch Perspectives of the Revolution of 1688–1689* (Stanford, 1996).

Hobsbawn, E. and Ranger, T. (eds), *The Invention of Tradition* (Cambridge 1983).

Hoftijzer, P. and Barfoot, C. C. (eds), *Fabrics and Fabrification: The Myth and Making of William and Mary* (Amsterdam, 1990).

Holman, P., *Four and Twenty Fiddlers: The Violin at the English Court 1540–1690* (Oxford, 1993).

Holmes, G., *British Politics in the Age of Anne* (revised edn, London, 1987).

Holmes, G., *The Making of a Great Power: Late Stuart and Early Georgian Britain, 1660–1722* (London, 1993).

Holmes, G. (ed.), *Britain after the Glorious Revolution* (London, 1969).

Holmes, G. and Speck, W. A., *The Divided Society: Party Conflict in England, 1694–1716* (London, 1970).

Hook, J., *The Baroque Age in England* (London, 1976).

Horwitz, H., *Parliament, Policy and Politics in the Reign of William III* (Manchester, 1977).

Horwitz, H., *Revolution Politicks: The Career of Daniel Finch, Second Earl of Nottingham, 1647–1730* (Cambridge, 1968).

Horwitz, H., 'The 1690s revisited: recent work on politics and political ideas in the reign of William III', *Parliamentary History*, XV (1996).

Howarth, D., *Images of Rule: Art and Politics in the English Renaissance 1485–1649* (London, 1997).

Hume, R. D., *The Development of English Drama in the Late Seventeenth Century* (Oxford, 1976).

Hutton, R., *Charles II, King of England, Scotland and Ireland* (Oxford, 1989).

Hutton, R., *The Restoration: A Political and Religious History of England and Wales, 1658–1667* (Oxford, 1985).

Israel, J. (ed.), *The Anglo-Dutch Moment: Essays in the Glorious Revolution and its World Impact* (Cambridge, 1991).

Jones, G. H., *Convergent Forces: Immediate Causes of the Revolution of 1688 in England* (Ames IA, 1990).

Jones, J. R., 'The building works and court style of William and Mary', *Journal of Garden History*, VIII (1988).

Jones, J. R., *Charles II, Royal Politician* (London, 1987).

Jones, J. R., 'Court dependants in 1664', *Bulletin of the Institute of Historical Research*, XXXIV (1961).

Jones, J. R., *The First Whigs: The Politics of the Exclusion Crisis, 1678–1683* (Oxford, 1961).

Jones, J. R. (ed.), *Liberty Secured: Britain before and after 1688* (Stanford, 1992).

Jones, J. R., *Marlborough* (Cambridge, 1993).

Jones, J. R., *The Revolution of 1688 in England* (London, 1984).

Jusserand, J. J., *A French Ambassador at the Court of Charles the Second* (London, 1892).

Kanner, B. (ed.), *The Women of England from the Anglo-Saxon Times to the Present: Interpretative Bibliographical Essays* (London, 1980).

Kelsey, S., *Inventing a Republic: The Political Culture of the English Commonwealth, 1649–1653* (Manchester, 1997).

Kenyon, J. P., 'The earl of Sunderland and the King's administration, 1693–5', *English Historical Review*, LXXI (1956).

Kenyon, J. P., *The Popish Plot* (Harmondsworth, 1974).

Kenyon, J. P., *Robert Spencer, Earl of Sunderland, 1641–1702* (London, 1958).

Kenyon, J. P., *Stuart England* (2nd edn, Harmondsworth, 1985).

Kenyon, J. P., *The Stuarts: A Study in English Kingship* (London, 1979).

Kernan, A., *The Cankered Muse: Satire of the English Renaissance* (Hamden CT, 1976).

Kettering, S., *Patrons, Brokers and Clients in Seventeenth-Century France* (Oxford, 1986).

Khun, W. M., *Democratic Royalism: The Transformation of the British Monarchy 1861–1914* (London, 1996).

King, R., *Henry Purcell* (London, 1994).

Kleinman, R., 'Social dynamics at the French court: the household of Anne of Austria', *French Historical Studies*, XVI (1990).

Knights, M., *Politics and Opinion in Crisis, 1678–81* (Cambridge, 1994).

Korshin, P. J. (ed.), *Studies in Change and Revolution: Aspects of English Intellectual History, 1640–1800* (Menston, 1972).

Lee, M., 'The earl of Arlington and the treaty of Dover', *Journal of British Studies*, I (1961).

Lee, M., *The Cabal* (Urbana, 1965).

Lewis, I. (ed.), *Symbols and Sentiment: Cross-cultural Studies in Symbolism* (London, 1977).

Lister, T. H., *The Life and Administration of Edward, First Earl of Clarendon* (3 vols, London, 1838).

Macaulay, T. B., *The History of England from the Accession of James II* (4 vols, London, 1953).

MacCormick, C. (ed.), *The Secret History of the Court and Reign of Charles the Second by a Member of his Privy Council* (2 vols, London, 1792).

Maccubbin, R. P. and Hamilton-Philips, M. (eds), *The Age of William III and Mary II: Power, Politics and Patronage* (Williamsburg VA, 1989).

McInnes, A., *Robert Harley, Puritan Politician* (London, 1970).

Mair, L., *Primitive Government* (Harmondsworth, 1972).

Marshall, A., *Intelligence and Espionage in the Reign of Charles II, 1660–1685*

(Cambridge, 1994).

Marshall, A., 'Sir Joseph Williamson and the conduct of administration in Restoration England', *Historical Research*, LXIX, (1996).

Marshall, W. G., *The Restoration Mind* (Newark, 1997).

Mejer, A. de, 'James Willemart OSA at the court of James II, the fourth attempt to re-establish the English Augustinian province', *Analecta Augustina*, XLI (1978).

Metzger, E. C., *Ralph, First Duke of Montagu, 1638–1709* (New York, 1987).

Milburn, D. J., *The Age of Wit, 1650–1750* (New York, 1966).

Miller, G. E., *Edward Hyde, Earl of Clarendon* (Boston, 1983).

Miller, J., *Bourbon and Stuart: Kings and Kingship in France and England in the Seventeenth Century* (London, 1987).

Miller, J., *Charles II* (London, 1991).

Miller, J., *James II: A Study in Kingship* (London, 1989).

Miller, J. (ed.), *Absolutism in Seventeenth-Century Europe* (London, 1990).

Milton, P., 'Hobbes, heresy and Lord Arlington', *History of Political Thought*, XIV (1993).

Molesworth, H. D., *The Princes* (London, 1969).

Morrill, J., Slack, P. and Woolf, D. (eds), *Public Duty and Private Conscience in Seventeenth-Century England: Essays Presented to G. E. Aylmer* (Oxford, 1993).

Murdoch, W. G. B., 'Charles the second: his connection with art and letters', *Scottish Historical Review*, III (1905).

Nicholson, T. C. and Turberville, A. S., *Charles Talbot, Duke of Shrewsbury* (Cambridge, 1930).

Nussbaum, F. A., *The Brink of All We Hate: English Satires on Women, 1660–1750* (Lexington, 1984).

O'Dowd, M. and Wickett, S., 'Chattle, servant or citizen: women's status in church, state and society', *Historical Studies*, XIX (1995).

O'Neill, J. H., *George Villiers, Second Duke of Buckingham* (Boston, 1984).

Ogg, D., *England in the Reigns of James II and William III* (Oxford, 1984).

Owen, S. J., *Restoration Theatre and Crisis* (Oxford, 1996).

Peck, L. L., *Court Patronage and Corruption in Early Stuart England* (London, 1990).

Petherick, M., *Restoration Rogues* (London, 1951).

Pinkham, L., *William III and the Respectable Revolution: The Part Played by William of Orange in the Revolution of 1688* (Harvard, 1954).

Pinto, V. de Sola, *Enthusiast in Wit: A Portrait of John Wilmot, Earl of Rochester, 1647–1680* (London, 1962).

Pinto, V. de Sola, *Restoration Carnival: Five Courtier Poets: Rochester, Dorset, Sedley, Etheredge and Sheffield* (London, 1954).

Plumb, J. H., *The First Four Georges* (London, 1956).

Plumb, J. H., *The Growth of Political Stability in England, 1675–1725* (London, 1991).

Powell, J., *Restoration Theatre Production* (London, 1984).

Ralph, J., *The History of England during the Reigns of King William and Queen Anne and King George I with Introductory Review of the Reigns of the Royal Brothers Charles and James* (2 vols, London, 1744–46).

Ranke, L. von, *A History of England Principally in the Seventeenth Century* (6 vols, Oxford, 1875).

Robb, N., *William of Orange: A Personal Portrait* (2 vols, London, 1966).

Roberts, C., 'The constitutional significance of the financial settlement of 1690', *Historical Journal*, XX (1977).

Roberts, C., 'The growth of political stability reconsidered', *Albion*, XXV (1993).

Roberts, C., 'The impeachment of the earl of Clarendon', *Historical Journal*, XIII (1957).

Rubini, D., *Court and Country, 1688–1702* (London, 1967).

Rubini, D., 'Party and the Augustan constitution, 1694–1716: politics and the power of the executive', *Albion*, X (1978).

Runciman, W. G. and Matthews, E., *Max Weber: Selections in Translation* (Cambridge, 1978).

Sachse, W., *Lord Somers: A Political Portrait* (Manchester, 1975).

Sainty J. C. and Bucholz, R. O., *Officials of the Royal Household 1660–1837. Part I: Department of the Lord Chamberlain and Associated Offices* (London, 1997).

Scattergood, V. J. and Sherborne, J. W. (eds), *English Court Culture in the Late Middle Ages* (London, 1983).

Scholei, P. A., 'The Chapel Royal', *Musical Times*, XLII (1902).

Schwoerer, L. G., 'Women and the Glorious Revolution', *Albion*, XVIII (1986).

Schwoerer, L. G. (ed.), *The Revolution of 1688–1689: Changing Perspectives* (Cambridge, 1992).

Scott, J., *Algernon Sidney and the Restoration Crisis* (Cambridge, 1991).

Scott, Dom G., *The Sacredness of Majesty: The English Benedictines and the Cult of James II* (Huntingdon, 1984).

Sharpe, K., *The Personal Rule of Charles I* (New Haven, 1992).

Shepherd, R., 'Court factions in early modern England', *Journal of Modern History*, LXIV (1992).

Sherwood, R., *The Court of Oliver Cromwell* (Cambridge, 1977).

Sherwood, R., *Oliver Cromwell, King in All but Name, 1653–1658* (Stroud, 1997).

Smuts, R. M. (ed.), *Court Culture and the Origins of Royalist Tradition in Early Stuart England* (Philadelphia, 1987).

Speck, W. A., 'The Orangist conspiracy against James II', *Historical Journal*, XXX (1987).

Speck, W. A., *Reluctant Revolutionaries: Englishmen and the Revolution of 1688* (Oxford, 1988).

Springarn, J. E. (ed.), *Critical Essays of the Seventeenth Century* (3 vols, Oxford, 1908).

Spurr, J. *The Restoration Church of England 1646–1689* (London, 1991).

Starkey, D. (ed.), *The English Court from the Wars of the Roses to the Civil War* (London, 1987).

Stone, L., *The Crisis of the Aristocracy, 1558–1641* (abridged edn, Oxford, 1967).

Stone, L., *An Imperial State at War: Britain from 1689–1815* (London, 1994).

Strange, E. F., 'The furnishing of Hampton Court in 1699', *The Connoisseur*, XIV (1906).

Sutch, V. D., *Gilbert Sheldon, Architect of Anglican Survival 1640–1675* (The Hague, 1973).

Sutherland, J., *Restoration Literature 1660–1700: Dryden, Bunyan and Pepys* (Oxford, 1990).

Teeler, L., 'The dramatic use of Hobbes's political ideas', *English Literary History*, III (1936).

Thormählen, M., *Rochester: The Poems in Context* (Cambridge, 1995).

Thurley, S., *The Whitehall Palace Plan of 1670* (London, 1998).

Treglowen, J., *Spirit of Wit: Reconsiderations of Rochester* (Oxford, 1982).

Turner, F. C., *James II* (London, 1948).

Watkins, D., *The Royal Interiors of Regency England from Watercolours Published by W.H. Pyne in 1817–1820* (London, 1984).

Webb, S. S., 'Brave men and servants to his royal highness the household of James Stuart in the evolution of English imperialism', *Perspectives in American History*, VIII (1974).

Weber, H., *The Restoration Rake-hero: Transformations in Sexual Understanding in Seventeenth-Century England* (Madison WI, 1986).

Wilson, J. H., *The Court Wits of the Restoration: An Introduction* (London, 1967).

Whinney, M. and Millar, O., *English Art, 1625–1714* (Oxford, 1957).

Whitaker-Wilson, C., *Whitehall Palace* (London, 1934).

Wildeblood, J., *The Polite World: A Guide to English Manners and Deportment from the Thirteenth to the Nineteenth Century* (Oxford, 1965).

Yardley, B., 'George Villiers, second duke of Buckingham and the politics of toleration', *Huntingdon Library Quarterly*, LV (1992).

Zimmermann, F. B., *Henry Purcell 1659–1695, his Life and Times* (2nd edn, London, 1983).

Index